69-17196

D1613549

5-24.71

*First published in 1969
by Routledge & Kegan Paul Ltd
Broadway House, 68–74 Carter Lane
London, E.C.4*

*Printed in Great Britain
by C. Tinling & Co. Ltd
Liverpool, London and Prescot*

© *Geoffrey K. Nelson Ph.D. 1969*

SBN 7100 6252 4

CONTENTS

ACKNOWLEDGMENTS

This book is based on two theses accepted by the University of London. The first part is based on a Master's thesis entitled 'The Origins of Modern Spiritualism in America' and the second and third parts on a Doctoral thesis entitled 'The Organization and Development of the Spiritualist Movement in Britain'.

I should like to acknowledge the advice I received from Professor Ronald Fletcher of the University of York and Dr David Martin of the London School of Economics. I should also like to acknowledge the help received from the librarians at the University of London Library and to the many members of the Spiritualist movement who have made me welcome in their groups.

INTRODUCTION

My initial interest in Spiritualism took the form of a study of psychic phenomena, and out of this developed an interest in the origins of Spiritualism as a religious movement. The results of this study are reported in the first part of this book where I examine the social and religious factors in the rise of modern Spiritualism in America. The apparent contrast between the early and rapid success of the movement in America and the slow but perhaps steadier progress in Britain led to a study of the movement in this country.

In order to carry out this study I had to compile a history of the movement, since no such history existed. Some histories of Spiritualism had indeed been published, but these all concentrated on a study of the personalities and the activities of great mediums, and on the evolution of psychic phenomena, and no account had been written of the development of organization within the movement.

The second part of this book therefore consists of an account of the development and growth of the Spiritualist movement. This is based on contemporary journals and other publications. It is followed by an account of the structure of the movement and of its beliefs and practices in the nineteen-sixties, based on the published records and statements of the existing organizations, a study of the magazines and publications of the movement, and on information obtained through interviews and by the technique of participant observation. My observation has extended over a period of about fifteen years, mainly in London, the South and the Midlands.

In the third part of this book the Spiritualist movement is analyzed in terms of sociological theory.

The major problem that emerged from an examination of the historical evidence was the problem of explaining the continuance of a minimal form of organization in the movement. Spiritualists have indeed become more organized. At first only small groups meeting spontaneously and having no structure existed. These have developed into local churches, and local churches have come together into regional and national bodies, but in the Spiritualist movement the bodies above the level of the local church tend to have little power or authority. Further, the growth of institutionalization has not reduced the importance of the small group lacking organization and meeting in private houses. This form of grouping known as the Home Circle among spiritualists still forms the basis of Spiritualism. In brief, the problem sociologically is to explain why Spiritualism has remained a movement and not become an organization.

Could this be explained in terms of any existing sociological theory of religious organization? An examination of the Church-Sect typology in all its various forms reveals that Spiritualism does not fit into this typology. I have therefore suggested that the Spiritualist movement can only fit into such a typology if we extend and refine the definition of a Cult. The variation of organization and belief in the movement leads me to suggest that the cult itself may take several forms.

The analysis along a Church-Sect-Cult continuum is in fact simply classificatory. We are simply classifying the religious unit in terms of a structural scheme, which in fact we have had to extend and modify in order to accommodate it. Classification in terms of Church-Sect or Cult in fact explains nothing.

We therefore go on to a more fundamental analysis. It appears that there is a fear of institutionalization and a resistance to the growth of organization amongst spiritualists, and continuing groups seem to be democratically based and structured. It is postulated that fear of institutionalization arises because the movement is based on the charismatic powers of mediums, and that routinization and institutionalization are seen as restrictive of the spontaneous expression of the charisma of mediums. This belief may clearly lead to the autocratic dominance of the medium, but this has not happened in the majority sectors of the movement because spiritualists believe that all individuals are potentially mediums. In consequence of this belief it becomes necessary to treat all members as equal, and this can only be expressed in a democratic and voluntary form of organization.

This leads us to conclude that the form of organization is determined by the belief system, and in the case of Spiritualism this is derived from the experience of psychic phenomena. The analysis of the social conditions in which Spiritualism arises leads us to suggest that a testable hypothesis can be produced which takes the form of suggesting that whenever religious and social conditions take a certain form, then modern Spiritualism will arise to satisfy the religious needs of certain groups of people. The study of Spiritualism also reveals certain facts about the nature of religion and gives rise to an hypothesis about the nature and origin of religion.

Spiritualism appears in the nineteenth century as a religion based almost entirely on what its proponents claim are empirical facts, the facts of psychic phenomena. These facts have indeed been disputed, but the weight of evidence seems to indicate that, at least occasionally, psychic phenomena are genuine. In some fields closely related to the phenomena of Spiritualism (namely the field of the study of extra-sensory-perception) the existence of certain human mental facilities such as telepathy and psycho-kinesis have been established if not explained.

These facts give rise to the hypothesis that the origin of religion is to be found in the experience of genuine psychic phenomena, and that this experience is moulded and shaped by geographical and social forces. The superstructure of religious belief and practice is firmly based on psychic experience, but its form is determined by the influences of the physical and social environment and by the development of autonomous religious institutions.

Part One

THE ORIGINS OF
MODERN SPIRITUALISM

Chapter One

BEGINNINGS IN AMERICA

The Fox Family

The origin of modern Spiritualism can be dated, with great accuracy, to the year 1848. Before that year there was no Spiritualism in the modern sense of that term. There were indeed many instances of the occurrence of the phenomena that later became distinctive of Spiritualism before 1848, for such phenomena, as we shall show, are a universal element in all human societies, and many groups and individuals throughout history have claimed the ability to communicate with the 'dead' or other spirits as part of their religious practices, but there had been no movement in civilized societies entirely based on a belief in, and the practise of, regular communication with the dead.

In 1848 the many trends which led to the origin of modern Spiritualism became focused in the episode of the Fox family.

In December 1847 John Fox, a farmer, his wife and two daughters moved into a house in Hydesville, a village within the township of Arcadia, Wayne Co., New York State, U.S.A. In addition to the two daughters, Margaretta, aged fifteen, and Kate, aged twelve, the family included a married son, David, who lived some two miles away, and a married daughter Leah Fish who lived in Rochester, N.Y. (She later remarried twice, becoming in turn Mrs Brown and Mrs Underhill.)

During the first three months of their residence, the Fox family were disturbed by mysterious noises in the house. These occurred only at night, and broke their rest night after night. The disturbances usually took the form of bangs and raps, and the Foxes were unable to discover the cause.

On the night of Friday, 31st March, 1848, the family had gone to bed early, in an attempt to catch up on their rest, and the children had been strictly told 'to be still' when the rapping broke out more loudly than usual. The children seem not to have

3

been frightened by this, and Kate is said to have snapped her fingers and called out to the invisible rapper, 'Here Mr Splitfoot do as I do', whereupon the raps imitated her. Later she held up her fingers and a number of raps was given equal to the number of fingers she held up. She called out 'Only look mother, look it can see as well as hear'. Mrs Fox and her daughter continued to ask questions, which were answered with the correct number of knocks.

The neighbours were called in, and a system of communication by raps was built up. Mrs Fox and the children left to obtain some rest in a neighbour's house and the raps continued in the presence of Mr Fox and between seventy and eighty of his neighbours.

The entity responsible for the raps declared that it was the spirit of a pedlar who had been murdered in the house some four or five years earlier; and that he had been buried in the cellar and he said that his name was Charles B. Roena.[1] The Foxes are said to have made an attempt to prove these statements by digging in the cellar in April, but this attempt was unsuccessful and had to be discontinued, when their excavation filled with water. They resumed digging again in the summer of 1848 and claimed to have found human hair and bones.[2] Sir Arthur Conan Doyle states that their claims were finally established in 1904 when further digging on the site disclosed a human skeleton.[3]

Many further phenomena are claimed to have occurred in the house during the Foxes' residence and the Foxes were plagued with a continual stream of curious inquirers, until eventually Mrs Fox took both her daughters to reside in Rochester with their married sister. In Rochester the phenomena continued to manifest itself in the presence of the Foxes and also of their sister Leah Fish. In the early stages of the story, the Foxes seem to have suffered rather than gained by their association with this strange phenomena. They were censured by the Methodist Church to which they belonged, and Mrs Fish, who was a music teacher in Rochester, seems to have suffered in her professional career, and for a time they tried all the methods they could think to obtain relief from the presence of the 'spirits'. For a while it seems the

---

[1] E. W. Capron, *Modern Spiritualism*, Boston, 1855; E. Hardinge, *Modern American Spiritualism: A Twenty Years Record*, Pub. by Author, New York, 1870.
[2] Mrs Underhill, *The Missing Link in Modern Spiritualism*, p. 18, New York, 1885.
[3] A. Conan-Doyle, *The History of Spiritualism*, 1926.

phenomena stopped, but after about a fortnight it broke out again. A number of clergymen attempted to exorcize the spirits, but they were all unsuccessful. Other clergymen condemned it as the work of the devil or as an imposture.

A few clergymen and others were genuinely interested in the investigation of the phenomena; these included the Rev. A. H. Jervis, a Methodist minister, George Willetts, a member of the Society of Friends and E. W. Capron, who later became a well known supporter of the Spiritualist movement.

The circle of friends that grew up around the Foxes in Rochester became the first Spiritualist Circle, but news of these events spread and circles developed in many places.

In 1849 the first public investigation of Spiritualism took place. On 14th November of that year a public demonstration was given in the Corinthian Hall, the largest public hall in Rochester. A Committee of responsible persons investigated the proceedings and reported to a second public meeting that they had been unable to detect any fraud. The audience was dissatisfied with this report and a second committee of investigation was set up. This also reported in favour of the Foxes, much to the disgust of the sceptics in the town. A third committee, composed of those most vocal in their opposition to the Foxes, was set up. After a vigorous investigation this committee was also forced to admit that it could discover no imposture. The final public meeting broke up in riot and disorder, started by the enemies of the Foxes.

These meetings at Rochester gave the new movement great publicity. Many newspapers reported the events in Rochester, and while these were mainly unsympathetic they made the phenomena widely known throughout the country.

Emma Hardinge, an early historian of the movement, suggests that phenomena arose spontaneously, 'in sections of the country where echoes of the Rochester vibrations could never even have reached'. She goes on to say, 'Spiritualism did not radiate from a definite centre, but sprang with a spontaneous and irresistible life of its own, independent of human propagandism, the contagious force of public sentiment or the psychological effect of common report'.[4]

Mediums certainly seemed to appear rapidly in many places, and a number of circles were established in 1849 without any *direct contact* with the Fox family.

[4] E. Hardinge, p. 55.

This may however be explained without postulating, as Mrs Hardinge did the intervention of the spirits. For as Joseph McCabe says, 'In the course of 1849 the piquant narrative of the fight over the "Rochester rappings" spread from journal to journal in the United States and people began to experiment in many towns'.[5]

Later in his book McCabe says that if spirits were at work 'They ought simultaneously to have manifested in a score or a hundred centres,————. Instead of this we find the movement slowly spreading in waves from Hydesville ————. It takes a year to reach New York, four years to reach London or San Francisco, five years to Cuba, six years to South America, seven years to Turkey and so on.'[6]

This statement by McCabe however ignores the fact that phenomena similar to the Spiritualist manifestations had long been familiar in many parts of the world, and that it was only the interpretation put upon such phenomena that was new in the Spiritualist movement and that the interpretation can be said to have spread outwards from Hydesville.

It is certain that the travels of the Fox family helped greatly in the spread of the movement and many circles were the direct result of their visits.[7] One circle which definitely arose as the result of a visit from Catharine Fox was the famous Auburn Circle. An outbreak of mediumship followed the visit of Catharine Fox to the home of Mr E. W. Capron in Auburn.[8]

The Foxes were often challenged but it was some time before anyone was able to suggest a physical explanation for the raps. In December 1850 the Fox sisters visited Buffalo, New York; here they were investigated by three professors from Buffalo University, Drs Flint, Lee and Coventry. In letters to the Buffalo newspaper, *Commercial Advertiser* on 17th and 21st February 1851 they stated that in their opinion the rappings could be explained as the result of movements of the knee-joints.

On 17th April a relation of the Foxes, Mrs N. Culver, made a statement that Catherine Fox had confessed to her that the raps were produced by the knees and toes. This statement was published in the *New York Herald*.[9]

[5] Joseph McCabe, *Spiritualism. A Popular History from 1847*, p. 47, London, 1920.
[6] Joseph McCabe, op. cit., p. 98.
[7] Capron and Barron, *Explanation and History of the Mysterious Communion with the Spirits*, New York, 1850.
[8] E. W. Capron, *Modern Spiritualism*, 10s. cit.
[9] F. Podmore, *Modern Spiritualism*, pp. 185–6.

6

These exposures seem to have had little influence on the spread of the movement. The Buffalo professors had failed to prove that the raps were in fact produced by physical movements, and had only succeeded in proving that they could have been so produced. Many spiritualists claimed that the raps were often heard to come from objects at a distance from the mediums.[10] The major difficulty of a physical explanation was that, even assuming the physical production of the raps, this did not explain how the medium could correctly answer questions the answers to which were only known to the questioner, and further, could answer correctly mental questions.

Much later on, in 1888, the two Fox sisters, Margaretta (then Mrs Kane) and Catherine (Mrs Jencken) confessed that the raps had been fraudulently produced,[11] though Mrs Jencken later recanted her confession.

Progress in the East

Emma Hardinge records that in 1850 circles were started in 'Philadelphia, Penn; Providence, Rhode Island; Binghampton, Westfield, Albany, Troy, Waterford and numerous other places in New York State; in Cincinnati; in Memphis, Tennessee; St Louis, Missouri; California, Oregon, Texas, South America, Maine, Vermont and New Hampshire'.[12]

The spread of the movement was extremely rapid throughout the eastern states of the U.S.A. and seems to have aroused great public interest wherever its advocates penetrated. In the early stages the movement was completely unorganized, in that no 'churches' or permanent societies were set up. Interest centred in private circles and irregular public meetings, lectures and demonstrations.

In New York City the phenomena were first reported to have appeared in December 1848, when a lady who was a magnetic clairvoyant approached Dr Hallock, a magnetist, with a request that he should 'magnetize' her in order that she might investigate at first hand the 'Hydesville rappings', which had recently been reported in the *New York Tribune*. Dr Hallock became a Spiritualist,

10 Mrs de. Morgan, *From Matter to Spirit*, 1863.
11 R. B. Davenport, *The Death-blow to Spiritualism*, New York, 1888.
12 E. Hardinge, op. cit., p. 60.

and the movement was active in the city before the first visit of the Foxes in the spring of 1850.[13]

The visit of the Fox family further stimulated interest in the movement. They succeeded in converting the Hon. Horace Greeley, editor of the *New York Tribune*, the most influential newspaperman in the country, who proved a most valuable ally of the cause.

Early in 1851 Judge J. W. Edmonds, a former Justice of the Supreme Court and at that time a Judge of the Court of Appeals, and Charles Partridge, a wealthy merchant, were also converted.

The New York Circle which was formed in 1851 was as Mrs Hardinge said, 'The first organic society'. It included among its members Judge Edmonds, Professor Burt and the Rev. J. B. Britten. This circle, in November 1851, brought together all those who were sympathetic to Spiritualism and organized the New York conference. Under the auspices of the conference regular weekly meetings were organized. After two years these became public Sunday meetings.

By 1851, it was estimated, there were fifty circles in Brooklyn and 100 in Williamsburg and a committee of the conference had been set up to assist in the establishment of new circles.

Spiritualist papers and magazines sprang up in many places; there were six or seven by 1851, including the *Spiritual Messenger* of Springfield, Mass; which had been established in 1849; *The Spiritual and Moral Instructor* of Auburn; *Heat and Light* published in Boston; and the *Spirit World* also of Boston which had been first published as *Spiritual Philosopher* in 1850.

Other papers rapidly grew up, but in most cases were published for only a few issues. In 1852 *Shekinah* first saw publication and *The Spiritual Telegraph* was also first published in that year. It continued publication for eight years. *New Era* of Boston, and *Light from the Spirit World* of St Louis both appeared at this time. Many books and pamphlets helped to spread knowledge of the movement.

The secular press also widely reported the sensational events that occurred within spiritualist circles. While the press was often hostile, its reports gave great publicity to the movement, and the existence of a cheap and popular press throughout America at the

[13] E. Hardinge, op. cit., p. 62.

time must be counted as one of the factors favouring the rapid spread of the movement.[14]

The movement however did not progress without opposition. This was strong and came both from the churches and the press. Many spiritualists suffered persecution, some even lost their jobs and in a few cases the opposition resorted to violence. In 1850 Margaret Fox was attacked by a gang of Irish Catholics while on a visit to Troy.

At this time an attempt was made by the Rev. Chauncey Burr to expose the tricks of the spiritualists and for a time he gave a series of demonstrations in which he produced 'rappings' by cracking his toe joints. His performances however were very amateurish, and he was finally discredited when Mrs Fish (Leah Fox) sued him for slander. Another person who attempted to discredit Spiritualism at this time was Leo Miller, whose meetings attracted large crowds. Unfortunately for the opponents of Spiritualism, Miller fell into a trance in the middle of one of his meetings and delivered a lecture affirming the truth of Spiritualism, much to the disgust of his former supporters. After his sudden conversion Miller became a staunch supporter of the movement.[15]

Another similar event is also reported by Mrs Hardinge.[16] In September 1857, the Rev. C. H. Harvey, a Methodist episcopal minister, attempted to give a lecture denouncing Spiritualism. Soon after commencing his lecture he collapsed, and a doctor pronounced him to be dead. A Spiritualist in the audience however succeeded in rousing him, and when he had recovered he tried to carry on with his lecture, but he was struck dumb, and after a further unsuccessful attempt to speak he was forced to abandon the attempt. Harvey himself thought that he was being attacked by evil spirit forces. It seems that at one time he had been sympathetically interested in Spiritualism and that he had given it up because of the conflict with orthodox Christian teachings. His collapse while denouncing Spiritualism was probably only the result of the stress put upon him by conflicting beliefs. Nevertheless it undoubtedly impressed many people at the time.

In 1851 Judge Edmonds was violently attacked by the press for his support of the movement. Governor Tallmadge, an

[14] E. W. Capron, *Modern Spiritualism.*
[15] E. Hardinge, op. cit., pp. 94–5.
[16] E. Hardinge, op. cit., pp. 144–5.

ex-Governor of the State of Wisconsin, came to the defence of Edmonds, and as a result of his investigations became converted himself in 1853.

Tallmadge's conversion led to the press becoming more sympathetic to Spiritualism. Previously the press had largely been antagonistic. In the same year Dr Robert Hare, a professor at Pennsylvania University, investigated Spiritualism and became converted.

N. P. Willis, the editor of *Home Journal*, estimated that in 1853 there were 40,000 Spiritualists in New York and that in that city there were some 300 circles. In Brooklyn and Williamsburg he thought there were twice that number of circles. He said that at least twenty public test mediums and 100 clairvoyant and medical mediums were practising at that time.

As early as the beginning of the eighteen fifties phenomena such as speaking in foreign languages, healings, spirit paintings and levitations were becoming well known.

In 1854 the Spiritualists became so confident of the truth of their cause that they petitioned Congress to set up a Commission to investigate their claims. This 'Spiritualists Memorial' was signed by 15,000 people. Congress however did not take the Memorial seriously and resolved that it should be 'laid on the table'.

The Society For The Diffusion of Spiritual Knowledge was formed in New York in 1854 and continued to exist until 1857. It published a magazine, *The Christian Spiritualist*, and engaged Kate Fox to give free seances daily. A library and a printing office were also established.

From 1853 a number of regular Sunday meetings were held in New York. The first of these was held at the Stuyvesant Institute; from there it moved to Hope Chapel and later to Dodworth Hall. Others were held at Lamartine Hall in 6th Avenue, in Brooklyn, the Bowery, Williamsburg and Morrisonia.

Boston was the home of a vigorous Spiritualist movement, and several papers were published there. *The Spiritual Philosopher* edited by Mr Sunderland appeared in 1850. In 1853 A. E. Newton edited *New England Spiritualist*, and later produced *Spiritual Age*. Bela Marsh opened a publishing office where the *Banner of Light* was produced and also seances and meetings were held.

An interesting sidelight on the way in which Spiritualism was spread is to be found in the story of Dr Gardner of Boston. In 1849 Gardner, went on a voyage to California. On the way a Chinese sailor was taken ill; Gardner was able to cure this man by spiritual healing. The sailor was converted and became a medium. He later landed at Hong Kong where he spread the knowledge of Spiritualism, from where, we are told, it spread rapidly into China. This however is not all; on arrival in San Francisco, Gardner was accosted in the street by a stranger who asked him if he knew anything about the spirit rapping which was so popular in the eastern states. In this way Gardner contacted interested persons in San Francisco and was instrumental in getting circles established there. On his return to Boston, Gardner became a leader of the movement there and instigated regular Sunday meetings at the Melodeon Hall.

The early history of the movement in Philadelphia is well documented – a 'History of Spiritualism in Philadelphia' by Dr H. Child was published in *The Religio-Philosophical Journal* in 1866; it was later reprinted in Mrs Hardinge's book. It records that interest in the subject first developed in 1848–49 when the Psychological Society studied A. J. Davis' book *Nature's Divine Revelations*. Interest increased after the arrival of news of the Rochester phenomena and a circle was formed on 9th October 1850. In spite of regular meetings (seances) no manifestations occurred until 10th February 1851. The success of this circle led to the formation of others. In April 1852 members of six of these circles formed the Harmonial Benevolent Society. This organization held regular weekly meetings. In 1864 The First Association of Spiritualists was formed. It absorbed the earlier organization, and it started groups for children, called Progressive Lyceums. That year a society called the Penetralium was also formed for the scientific study of Spiritualism. It was probably the first society of that nature in the world. It was at Brookfield, Tioga County, Pennsylvania that certain remarkable manifestations of a spiritualist nature occurred in 1855. Some ten years before the Rochester 'rappings' this part of the country had been greatly affected by the religious revival. The tremendous religious fervour aroused by this revival culminated in the occurrence of pentecostal phenomena, which were so prevalent in certain areas of the country, that these areas were known as 'burnt districts' as a result of their having been swept by pentecostal fires.

The Rev. John Crapsey, a High Church minister, of Brookfield, was holding a meeting at Roulette, Potter County, Penn. When, just as he was quoting the words of Jesus on the cross *Eli, Eli, lama sabachthani*, 'a mighty invisible power seemed suddenly to possess him, and a luminous appearance scintillated upon and around his hand, shining with brilliant effulgence in the eyes of all beholders'. 'Under an impulse which I could not resist, I sprang,' says Mr Crapsey, 'from the desk out upon the middle of the floor into the midst of the congregation; great signs and wonders then ensued and were witnessed by all'.

'Fire, and pillars of smoke and luminous light, rose up bodily in our midst; men and women and even stammering children were seized speaking with new tongues and uttering prophecies. Prayers and exhortations were poured forth in abundance, and many of the congregation broke out into the most marvellous and heavenly singing.'

Manifestations of this sort continued at other meetings conducted by Mr Crapsey. The majority of those affected seem to have been young persons between the ages of ten and thirty. Sometimes the disturbances were so violent that the house would 'rock about as if in a gale of wind, although the air outside was as still as death', and the pupils in the school room, which was beneath the meeting room, had to be sent home because 'they could not write and feared to remain upon the premises'.

The general public were greatly disturbed by the excitement caused by these outbreaks, and Mr Crapsey was asked to leave the district. When he refused, his enemies had him arrested on the charge of assaulting persons in his congregation. This charge could not be proved. His opponents now attempted to bribe him to leave, and when this also failed they resorted to violence. Crapsey and his congregation were refused admission to any building in the district and when they held their meetings in the open, attempts were made to break up their meetings, and disturbers even went to the extreme of firing the wood in which the meeting was being held.

Many disturbers seem to have been converted by the phenomena they saw when attempting to break up a meeting; these included flashing lights, rocking trees, trembling of the earth, the appearance of angelic beings and of the spirits of the dead.

As news of Spiritualism reached the district, the greater extravagances of the movement died down, and Mr Crapsey's congregation seem to have channelled their activities into a more normal form of Spiritualism.

Spread of the Movement across the Continent

The news of the occurrences in the eastern states spread rapidly across the continent, and in many places Spiritualist groups developed to try the truth of the reported phenomena. There is no doubt that similar phenomena had occurred spontaneously in some places even before the date of the Rochester rappings, but the significance of these does not seem to have been understood until reports of the Rochester events arrived. An example of the spontaneous development of phenomena occurred in Cincinnati where a number of cases of rapping and 'demonical' possession were reported as early as 1845. The nature of these happenings were not however realized until news arrived of the similar events in the east. The first public demonstrations of Spiritualism in Cincinnati were given on 26th September 1850 by Mrs Bushnell who had developed mediumistic powers after having had experiences in the circles in New York State. In 1851 interest in Spiritualism in the city was greatly stimulated by the visit of the Fox sisters, and some three years later the Cincinnati *Daily Times* reported that at least fifty-nine seances were held regularly every night in the city, that hundreds of circles were held occasionally, and that there were at least 310 practicing mediums. The circles were not restricted to any one class of society, nor to a particular religion. 'Christians, Jews and Infidels are earnest in their inquiries. The number of investigators can be estimated only by tens of thousands.'

In Columbus, Ohio, Spiritualism started early. Circles were developed by several prominent citizens who had attended the Rochester investigations. Considerable opposition was put up by the Churches, who called for united prayer meetings to ask for deliverance from the devil. The Foxes visited Cleveland, Ohio in 1851 and during their visit a number of mediums were developed. Among these was an orphan girl, Abby Warner, who suffered from a number of physical defects which made her helpless and unsightly. On Christmas Eve 1851, Abby and some friends attended a service at St Timothy's Church. During the service a number of loud rappings occurred. The minister requested that these knockings should cease, but instead the rappings became louder than before. Abby Warner was charged with having caused the disturbance and brought before the court on 27th December. The court was unable to find sufficient evidence to show who was responsible for the rappings, and Abby was discharged. The persons sitting near her during the service had been unable to detect her making the raps, which in any case seemed to come from many parts of the church. The Spiritualists claimed that the noises were caused by invisible spirits. Abby's mediumistic powers were subsequently investigated by a committee of prominent persons, who proclaimed them to be genuine. The trial of Abby Warner greatly stimulated the growth of Spiritualism in Cleveland and in the Western Reserve of the state generally. It was at this time that Abraham Lincoln's name was first associated with Spiritualism, and Lincoln is said to have later become a convinced Spiritualist.

It was reported that by 1857, in the Western Reserve of Ohio, the majority of the inhabitants were Spiritualists. In many places orthodox churches were deserted; for example at Newton Falls three out of six churches were closed and the other three almost deserted. Everywhere Spiritualist meetings were crowded.

In 1850 at Millfield Township, Athens County, Ohio, a remote mountain district, there lived two farmers Jonathan Koons and John Tippie. In 1852 Koons became interested in Spiritualism and discovered that he and his eight children were all endowed with mediumistic powers. Under the direction of the spirits he built a log cabin 16ft by 12ft, some short distance from his house. This cabin was to be used exclusively for holding seances. In Koons' Spirit Room, as it became known, many extraordinary phenomena were experienced and the room was visited by many interested persons. Tippie, who was a neighbour of the Koonses, also developed mediumistic powers at about the same time, and built a similar Spirit Room near his house.

The phenomena in these spirit rooms continued to manifest with great force for some years, but eventually died down. Koons and Tippie travelled, demonstrating their mediumistic powers and by 1859 we find that Koons had settled in Jefferson Co., Illinois and Tippie in Lynn Co., Kansas.

An attempt to repeat the experiences of Koons' Spirit Room

was made at Laporte, Indiana. A Mr Poston who rented a farm there, built a spirit room on the same plan as Koons'. Very soon powerful manifestations occurred, and the rooms were visited by the Hon. Charles Cathcart, an ex-congressman. Cathcart himself developed mediumistic powers, and constructed his own Spirit Rooms in 1854 where regular meetings were held.

St Louis was early the scene of experimentation in animal magnetism. The first spiritual circles were formed by a Mr Hedges, who had become acquainted with the movement while visiting New York. Again interest was increased by the visit of the Misses Fox. In 1852 in that city a Spiritualist paper *'Light from the Spirit-World'* was published with Peter Bland as the editor. Public lectures were first given regularly in the same year, and continued to be given until 1861 when they were interrupted by Civil War.

At Hannibal, Missouri, Spiritualism was introduced in 1857 by a settler from Salem, Massachusetts, who invited Mrs E. Hardinge down to give lectures. She was coldly received, but she reports that when she re-visited the town two years later, her entry was in her own words a 'perfect ovation'. In 1853 great excitement was aroused in St Louis by the trial of Mr Henry Stagg before the pastor and officers of the Second Baptist Church, on a charge of heresy, for believing in Spiritualism. As a result of this investigation Mr Stagg was expelled from the church.

St Louis was also the home of Dr Hotchkiss, who was widely known as the 'colour doctor'. He held that colour was the key to health and that the absence of good colours or the presence of bad colours was the primary cause of disease. Part of his treatment involved allowing his patients to leap up and down on his prostrate body. After this performance Hotchkiss would get up and go through a series of weird ecstatic dances similar to those performed by Eastern dervishes. These performances seemed to induce hypnotic conditions in his patients, which enabled him to diagnose their diseases by their reactions to colours which he presented to them. He used not only colour in his treatment but also dancing and snapping of the joints. Hotchkiss seems to have practised with some success in St Louis for over twenty years.

Opposition to Spiritualism was extensive, and in addition to ridicule, led to many cases of the persecution of individuals.

A case of this sort which caused great interest throughout the country occurred in 1852 in Chicago.[17] A certain Ira B. Eddy, a wealthy citizen of that town, became converted to Spiritualism. He decided to invest his money in a bank run by a Spiritualist friend and also to build a room for the holding of Spiritualist meetings. On hearing of his intentions certain of his relatives and friends had him seized and incarcerated in a Lunatic Asylum at Hartford, Connecticut. A number of Eddy's friends however obtained his release as a result of a court action, for it seemed that neither the superintendent of the Asylum nor the examining experts could find in him any signs of insanity. A similar case occurred at Waukegan, Illinois where a Presbyterian minister, the Rev. Packard, had his wife certified and incarcerated in a lunatic asylum, where she remained for three years before being able to escape. It was also at Waukegan that in 1855 Miss Grace Davis was expelled from the Congregational Church for holding Spiritualist beliefs.

Opposition was general from the churches and the press, but it was strongest in the southern states. Mrs Hardinge tells that during her stay in Memphis, Tennessee, in 1859, she met with much hostility, her public lectures were interrupted and on one occasion a large stone was thrown through the window of the room in which she was lecturing; on another occasion a lecture had to be cancelled because a gang led by a number of 'clerical gentlemen' had threatened to lynch all those concerned if they dared to carry on with the lecture. The campaign seems to have been led by a Presbyterian newspaper, the Memphis *Inquirer*. In reply to the abuse and misrepresentation published in that newspaper, Mrs Hardinge wrote to the editor, and it is to his credit that he published her letter. This letter aroused great interest among the readers of the paper, and from then on the paper seems to have ceased to campaign against Mrs Hardinge.

The campaign against the Spiritualists in the south reached a peak in January 1860, when, alarmed by the growth of the movement in spite of opposition, the Legislature of the State of Alabama passed a Bill declaring that any person giving a public demonstration of Spiritualist phenomena should be liable to a fine of 500 dollars.

A stronghold of Spiritualism in the south seems to have been

[17] E. Hardinge, op. cit., pp. 377 et seq.

New Orleans, where many circles were held not only by the white but also by the coloured population, and many coloured persons were found among the mediums. Dr Barthet who became a leading spiritualist in the city was known to have experimented with animal magnetism in the early eighteen-forties, and Dr Valmour, a free creole, attained great celebrity as a healing medium.

In Georgia the centre of Spiritualism was at Macon where the cause had the support of the editor of the *Georgia Citizen*, Dr L. W. Andrews, who also published a paper for the Spiritualists called the *Christian Spiritualist*.

Early in 1860 Mrs Hardinge visited North Carolina, where she was well received at Wilmington, but her visit to South Carolina had to be cancelled because of the threat of lynching. The Charleston *Courier*, was virulent in its attacks on the 'incendiary practices of the abhorrent Spiritualists'.

The main cause of the great antagonism which Spiritualism aroused in the southern states arose from the fact that Spiritualist teachings were favourable to equality and liberal thought, and consequently spiritualists in general disapproved of slavery. In addition to this, Spiritualism spread among the negro population, and the spirits disregarded the colour of a man's skin, for they often 'chose mediums' from the ranks of the slaves.

The growth of Spiritualism in the south was further hit by the outbreak of the civil war. The regular Sunday meetings which had been organized in Macon, St Louis, Memphis, New Orleans and some other places were suspended. The *Christian Spiritualist* ceased publication.

Spiritualism spread rapidly across the continent and reached the Pacific coast. As we have already mentioned, Dr Gardner's visit in 1849 gave the movement its first start in California, and circles were started in that state. Much of the phenomena that occurred in that state during the eighteen-fifties seems to have been of a weird and startling nature.

Spiritual Circles developed not only in the cities and villages of the settled states of America but also in the camps and settlements in the undeveloped territories of the west, and a number of well-known mediums braved the dangers of these lawless frontier districts to spread knowledge of the movement.

From the United States the movement spread rapidly to many

parts of the world. By 1850 it seems to have been known in Canada, and in a short time spread through that country. In 1853 we read of Circles being formed in Guatemala, where Spiritualism met strong opposition from the Catholic Church. By 1854 it had made its first appearance in Cuba.

Community Movements within Spiritualism

The early nineteenth century saw the establishment of many settlements and communities in America based on Socialist and Communist principles. These were often based on the ideas of Charles Fourier and took their name of 'Phalanx' from his books.[18]

In addition to the socialist ideas and practices of these communities many of them were also based on strong religious beliefs and were held together by the religious fervour of their members. Of this type of organization were the Shakers, who claimed to have experienced an outbreak of psychic phenomena some years before the Hydesville episode.

It was not long before a number of Spiritualist communities were set up. The first of these developed from the Spiritualist circle at Auburn which had been initiated by the visit of Kate Fox to the home of Mr Capron. In 1850 Mr Capron claimed that there were between fifty and 100 mediums in Auburn. One of these, Mrs Benedict, formed a circle, which had a number of Second Adventists among its members. This circle claimed to be under the spirit direction of St Paul, St John the Divine, the prophet Daniel and other apostles and prophets. In recognition of its spirit directors the circle was called the 'Apostolic Circle'. A number of messages from the Apostles and Prophets were published, which however were not only puerile but also ungrammatical and brought disrepute on the movement.

In 1850 the spirits sent Mrs Benedict to New York to summon the Rev. James D. Scott, a Baptist minister, to come and lead the movement, and soon after he was joined by the Rev. Thomas L. Harris. After their arrival it was noted by Mrs Hardinge that the literary quality of the messages from the Apostles improved. These messages were now published in a paper called '*Disclosure from the Interior and Superior Care for Mortals*'.

[18] Alexander Gray, *The Socialist Tradition*, London, 1946.

The claims of the Apostolic Circle and of Scott and Harris in particular were never accepted by the Spiritualist movement as a whole even in Auburn, for it was felt that such extravagant assertions brought disrepute on the whole movement. In 1851 it seems that the saner Spiritualists of Auburn hinted to the 'Apostles' that they were no longer welcome in Auburn and at the same time Scott had a vision which revealed to him that a community should be set up. Scott, and about a hundred of the faithful, left Auburn and set up a community at Mountain Cove, Fayette Co., Virginia. Here all things were held in common and the community submitted itself to the complete control of Scott, who now claimed to have soared above the Apostles and to be in direct communication with the 'Most High'. In consequence it became sacrilege to question any of Scott's statements. At first most of the members seem to have believed that he was 'divinely inspired', but it was not long before charges of licentiousness were made against him. These charges were suppressed but strife and contention continued at Mountain Cove. In February 1852, payments on the land could not be met, and it was returned to its original owner. Scott went to New York and there induced a number of wealthy persons to join the Community; the money they brought in was used to re-purchase the land. Harris joined Scott and together they continued to make the most extravagant claims. The members gradually became disgusted by their assumption of divine power and holiness, and in 1853 the community broke up.

Harris resumed his place in the working world and later became famous as the author of several volumes of Spiritualist poems.

Another Spiritualist community known as the Kiantone Movement was established in 1853 by John M. Spear, a Universalist minister who had become a medium. In the valley of the Kiantone, in Chautauqua Co., New York, a spring having healing power was discovered, and some of its water was sent to Spear for psychometrical examination. Spear and some others at once tried to purchase the land on which this spring stood. In this they were unlucky, but they succeeded in purchasing the adjoining farm, where there was another similar spring. On this land, they established a community having communism and free love as well as Spiritualism as its basis. This community seems to have soon collapsed as a result of the disapproval it met in the practice of its free love principles.

A similar community was formed at Harmony Springs, Benton County, Arkansas in 1855. Here an ex-Methodist minister, T. E. Spencer, who claimed the title of doctor, and his wife founded the Harmonial Society, and together with about forty other persons settled on about 480 acres of land.

Each member of the society was required upon joining to give up into the treasury of the society all the money and property he possessed, and Spencer induced at least thirty wealthy persons to join his society.

Free love and a frugal vegetarian diet were, Spencer said, laid down as rules by the Angels. He further declared that only a select band of humans survived death, and these were of course the members of the society. These members submitted to an extremely arduous life, with hard work, little food and a set of strict rules. The Spencers however, as the reward of attaining angelic perfection, ate, drank and behaved as they pleased.

After some time some of the members began to realize that they were dupes of the Spencers, and violent contentions broke the 'angelic peace' of the community. At first their questionings were quietened by the Spencers' revelations from the Angels, but eventually certain members determined to attempt to regain the property they had given to the society. The Spencers heard a rumour of this move and fled, taking with them all that they could lay their hands on. One member who had invested $5,000 in the settlement pursued them and had them thrown into prison.

Many of the other socialist communities of this period had connections with the Spiritualist movement. Brook Farm was a Swedenborgian community. Hopedale was founded by the Rev. Adin Ballow, a prominent spiritualist. Warren Chase, another well known spiritualist, had in 1844 been the founder of a socialist community in Wisconsin, which was named Ceresco in honour of the goddess Ceres. This was one of the most successful of such projects and lasted for six years.

Horace Greeley, another well-known spiritualist, was Vice-president of the North American Phalanx. The Modern Times community founded in Long Island in 1851 also had several Spiritualists among its members.

The Excess of Spiritualism

While the vast majority of Spiritualists seems to have been sincere, respectable and moderate people genuinely convinced of the truth of the cause they promoted, the movement was also afflicted by a number of cranks and charlatans. The cranks, while they were probably sincere in their beliefs, held beliefs which were unreasonable and considerably in excess of what the generally accepted phenomena of the movement would justify. An example of the sort of cranks thrown up by the movement was to be found in the Mountain Cove community, and in particular in its leaders James Scott and T. L. Harris, who claimed not only divine inspiration but direct communication with God.

Another of the cranks was John M. Spear, who claimed to be in communication with a council of 'highly-exalted' spirits. In 1853 these spirits announced that they were forming among themselves seven associations of spirits whose general aims were to help humanity on earth. These associations were the Association of Beneficents; the Associations of Electrizers; of Healthfulizers; of Educationizers; of Agriculturalizers; of Elementizers, and of Governmentizers. In the following year S. C. Hewitt, the editor of *New Era*, disclosed that the 'electrizers', through the mediumship of Spear, had given instructions for the contruction of a machine which was to provide the world with a continuous and unfailing supply of motor power. The 'New Motor', although it was constructed of metal, was to be a living organism. It is reported that in order to endow it with a living spirit, a female disciple of Spear's spent some time with the machine, during which time she experienced 'pangs of parturation for two hours' while elements of her spirit animated the machine. After this the movements of life were reported to be present in the motor.

The majority of Spiritualists, including A. J. Davis, the philosopher of the Movement, held that Spear's claims were excessive, and that while the spirits had inspired Spear to construct the motor, these spirits were lacking in practical knowledge of mechanics. Spear moved the motor to Randolph, New York, where, he claimed, it would work more efficiently because the supply of terrestrial electricity was better there. Soon after he reported that a mob had broken in and destroyed the 'New

Motor'. The spirits are said to have refused to have allowed him to rebuild it because mankind was not yet ready for such a revelation.

As we have already seen, Spear was a founder of the Kiantone Movement, and was one of those responsible for advocating free love in the Spiritualist movement. The association of free love ideas with the movement brought Spiritualism into great disrepute.

An eccentric organization, 'The Order of the Patriarchs' originated in Cincinnati in 1854. An inhabitant of that city, whose name seems nowhere to have been disclosed, received an 'impression' one day, which instructed him to visit a certain locality in the city. When he arrived at the place indicated he was amazed to see a large mansion, which seemed to have sprung up as if by magic, where he had never seen a house before. He went to the door, where he was met by an old gentleman who told him to go home and that there he would find further instructions. When he reached home he found that a box had been delivered to his house; inside was a marble-slab, honeycombed with perforations. This gift puzzled him until he received another 'impression' which instructed him to consult a leading Spiritualist in the town. The spirits declared that the perforations on the stone were a form of language and gave the key to the transcription of this language. When the inscription on the stone was translated it was found to be instructions for the creation of a secret organization to be called 'The Order of the Patriarchs'. The slab gave the secret knowledge which was to be taught to the members as they progressed, from degree to degree. The writing on the slab seems to have changed from time to time, thus making endless the mysteries that could be revealed. The teachings of the order included the advocacy of free love.

The order seems to have been a typical mystery society which pandered to the very human desire of some people for an hierarchical system in which some persons may indulge their feelings for superiority, not only over the general public, but also over their fellow initiates. Such orders also flourish on another common human failing, that of awe in the face of spurious mystery, which in certain circumstances replaces love of truth revealed. This Order seems to have only flourished for a few years on the wave of credulity aroused by the Spiritualist movement as a whole. Such movements were condemned by the great majority of spiritualists, not only because their extragavances led the whole movement into disrepute but also because the concept of a secret society was contrary to the free disclosure of spiritual knowledge, which the movement generally practised, and to the ideas of equality which were prevalent within Spiritualism.

Somewhat later, in 1862, Spiritualists became aware of a similar organization which seemed to be growing rapidly particularly in New England. This was 'The Sacred Order of Unionists'. The members of this order were said to teach and practice immorality, which one gathers is mainly to be interpreted as free love. In May 1862 the Boston Spiritualists called a meeting at the Lyceum Hall at which the activities of this secret society were exposed. A number of former members seem to have taken part in revealing the secrets of the society, and although the Order continued to exist for a time, its power was ended by the opposition of the vast majority of Spiritualists.

In addition to the cranks the great success and popularity of Spiritualism in the eighteen fifties encouraged a number of dishonest persons to 'cash in' on the movement by pretending to have mediumistic gifts, and to make a dishonest living by deceiving the public by producing by trickery the effects of psychic phenomena. These fraudulent mediums seem to have flourished in great profusion between 1858 and 1862.

It seems that not only did deliberate frauds take up Spiritualism but that some persons with genuinely mediumistic gifts, who had taken this activity up as a profession, also practised deception in order to maintain their income and reputation when genuine phenomena failed to appear.

Some exposures had taken place from the early days of the movement, but during this period a considerable number of mediums were detected in trickery and exposed as frauds. In many cases it seems to have been the Spiritualists who were responsible for exposing the frauds. Nevertheless the revelation of the possibilities of fraud on such a large scale so disillusioned a number of Spiritualists that they severed their connection with the movement and recanted their views on the subject. The numbers were obviously extensive, since even Mrs Hardinge (who as a Spiritualist attempts to play down this period in the history of the movement), refers to it as the 'recantation movement'.

Recantation Movement

By 1850 Spiritualism had spread widely throughout the eastern states of America, and in the course of the next five years it had spread across the continent and had been introduced into a number of other countries.

The movement aroused an immense amount of interest throughout the country. The newspapers regularly, though not always sympathetically, reported the fantastic happenings of the Spiritualist circles. The Spiritualists themselves built up an extensive and flourishing press, and by 1854 had ten publications, devoted entirely to the propagation of the movement.

The supporters of the movement were not drawn from any one class or sector of society. It was not, as were many enthusiastic Christian sects, a religion of the poor or of the oppressed. Many of the supporters of the movement were men of distinction such as J. Fennimore Cooper, the novelist, W. C. Bryant, the famous poet, Governor Tallmadge, and a number of judges and eminent lawyers and generals. It even included a few scientists, and Abraham Lincoln was interested, at least for a time.

The movement seemed to have reached a high water mark around 1854–55, but from then on it declined and although there was a revival in the eighteen seventies and again in the eighteen nineties, it has never since recovered the popularity it achieved in its first six or seven years.

In 1854 Partridge said that the movement had the support of 'over a million' persons; Governor Tallmadge claimed that there were two million supporters, and a non-spiritualist, writing in the *North American Review*, estimated that there were 'nearly two million' Spiritualists in the country. The Roman Catholic Church was particularly concerned about the rapid growth of this new religion, and a speaker at a Catholic congress at Baltimore estimated that there were eleven million Spiritualists in America. This was a fantastic figure considering that the total population of the country at that time was only twenty-five million, but it reflects the concern that the movement was causing its opponents. Even though it certainly never reached a figure of membership as high as this, the movement must have been extraordinarily successful during this period.

In the later eighteen fifties a decline set in in the movement as a result of what Mrs Hardinge calls the Recantation Movement. This movement started as a result of the disillusionment of many supporters at the exposure of some fraudulent mediums. The process of decline was also accelerated by the emergence of cranks and of the association of certain elements in Spiritualism with such radical teaching as socialism and free love. The fact that only a minority of Spiritualists were active participants in these eccentric practices or even believers in those teachings did not prevent the whole Spiritualist movement from being condemned by public opinion for the excesses of a few.

Public interest waned during the later years of the fifties and the increasing wonders of Spiritualist manifestations failed to stimulate the same furore that the movement had aroused in the earlier years of the decade.

In 1857 occurred the famous investigation into Spiritualism by the professors of Harvard College. Some two years previously Frederick Willis, a student of divinity at the college, had discovered that he had mediumistic powers, and had during those two years given a series of private seances. Early in 1857 Professor Eustis, a lecturer at the college, attended two of these seances, and denounced Willis as an imposter.

Willis was called before the Faculty of the Divinity School, and was expelled from the college without any proper consideration having been given to his case. This injustice brought a number of protests and aroused interest in the impartial investigation of the subject. The *Boston Courier* offered 500 dollars for the production of certain phenomena, in the presence of a committee of professors from Harvard College. Dr Gardner accepted the challenge and gathered together a number of well-known mediums, including Catharine and Leah Fox and the Davenport Brothers. The result of this investigation was a complete failure, for no satisfactory manifestations appeared. The opponents of Spiritualism suggested that this proved that when supervision was strictly enforced the fraudulent production of phenomena was impossible. The Spiritualists on the other hand contended that the atmosphere of hostility in which the seances were conducted was sufficient to prevent the sensitive mediums from attaining the necessary psychological state for the manifestation of spirit phenomena. This investigation seems to have discouraged many supporters of the movement, and to have been an important factor in the decline of Spiritualism.

Spiritualism had not recovered from the Recantation movement, and a long series of exposures when the quarrel between the south and the north which had attracted much attention for some years developed into the Civil War. The outbreak of war in 1861 caused a great deal of disruption of Spiritualist activities; many of their members left to play an active part in the war effort and their absence was particularly felt since the Spiritualists had never developed a regular form of organization which held together the more orthodox religious denominations.

The disturbing effect of the first total war in modern history, coming as it did immediately after the disillusionment of the 'recantation movement', resulted in a serious decline in the whole movement. Public activities seem to have ceased almost entirely during the war, and in the south the situation was worse than in the north, for Spiritualism was associated with the Anti-slavery movement.

In 1864 the first attempt at establishing a national movement was made when a National Convention was held in Chicago. During the next few years other National Conventions were held at various centres in the north, but as Warren Chase says, 'this experiment to establish a national and central organization was premature'. A permanent national organization was not formed until 1898.

In 1865 A. J. Davis was instrumental in forming in St Louis the 'Society of Spiritualists and Progressive Lyceum', whose constitution proved a model for many other local associations which were established later.[19] The following year the 'First Society of Spiritualists' was founded in New York, and the movement began to re-establish itself after the disruption of war.

It was not long before state associations began to be organized; one of the first was the New York State Association which was formed in 1867.

In 1869, we find the first instance of the ordination of a Spiritualist minister. In January of that year the Indiana State Spiritual Association issued a certificate conferring the powers of a minister upon James H. Powell.

Writing in the same year Mrs Hardinge stated that in the two previous years '600 spiritual associations' had been formed in America, and she looked forward with great confidence to the

[19] Warren Chase, *Forty Years on the Spiritual Rostrum*, p. 198, Boston, 1888.

triumph and 'irresistible success of Spiritualism'. Her hopes however were confounded, for never again did Spiritualism regain its hold on the American public. Formal organizations came too late to prevent a decline, and were unable to recover many of the great losses that had already been sustained.

Chapter Two

THE PHENOMENA OF SPIRITUALISM

In our review of the rapid rise and decline of Spiritualism in America between 1848 and 1870 we have only made brief mention of some types of phenomena that were commonly experienced within Spiritualist circles.

Before attempting to trace the sources of Spiritualism and the causes of its sudden rise to popularity in America, we must examine rather more closely the forms of manifestation that were known at that time.

It was the nature of these manifestations that distinguished Spiritualism from all other religious organizations and sects, and the doctrines and teachings of the movement were derived, in the main, directly from the manifestations that were experienced at their circles.

As we have seen, during the period of most rapid expansion there was no central organization of Spiritualists and there were very few local organizations of any permanence. The movement in this period was virile and fluid in the extreme, consisting of local groups of enthusiasts who seldom formalized their organizations into anything like a church.

This fluidity of organization was associated with a corresponding fluidity of doctrines, both of which were not unconnected with the variability of the phenomena and with the sort of information that was received from the 'Spirit World'.

Beyond a vague belief in the existence of God, the immortality of the human spirit and the ability of spirits to communicate with the living, there was little agreement on a doctrine.

The spirits themselves had various opinions regarding the nature of God and varied answers to other theological and natural problems. This was not strange to Spiritualists though since they believed that the human soul does not become all wise on entering the spirit world, but takes with it all its earthly preconceptions and beliefs. Only gradually do the spirits acquire further know-ledge. It is therefore not strange to find that in their beliefs about God the Spiritualists varied from the agnostic position through Unitarianism to conventional Christian beliefs.

During the first ten years of its existence, the Spiritualist move-ment developed almost all the different types of phenomena that are familiar in the movement up to the present time. The only major phenomena which did not appear at that time were com-plete physical materializations and spirit photography.

A survey of all the forms of manifestation known at the time appeared in *The Spiritual Magazine* in 1860, and we shall use the classification made in that article as a basis for our analysis.

The first type mentioned is:

1. 'The Rappings, Table-tippings and other sounds and movements of ponderable bodies'. This was the type of pheno-mena that first appeared at Hydesville and may be connected loosely with poltergeist manifestations. It remained the most frequently practised form of communication throughout the early period of the movement.

2. 'Spirit Writings and Spirit Drawings'. These consist of writings and drawings made without the conscious volition of the medium, the hand appearing to write autonomously, and consequently such productions are often now described as automatic writing or drawing.

3. 'Trance and Trance Speaking'. In this form of mani-festation the medium passes into a trance condition and speaks the messages from the spirits. Some mediums are apparently able to reproduce the voice of the spirit communicating through them.

4. 'Clairvoyance and Clairaudience'. Some mediums claim to be able (either in trance or in a 'normal' condition) to see or hear spirits, and can then describe them or pass on their messages to the sitters.

5. 'Luminous Phenomena'. At many seances illuminous objects have been seen to float around in the darkness.

6. 'Spiritual Impersonation, or the representation or repro-duction in a medium of the actions and manner, gait, deport-ment, and other peculiarities which distinguished the actuating spirit in his earth-life'.

7. 'Spirit-Music – represented both with and without the instruments'.

8. 'Visible and Tactual Manifestations, such as the appearance and touch of Spirit-hands'.

9. 'Spirit intercourse by means of the Mirror, Crystal and Vessel of Water'.

The author lists other phenomena associated with Spiritualism, but which were less frequently met with. These included:

10. 'Apparitions of the Departed'.

11. 'Visions and previsions'.

12. 'Dreams'.

13. 'Presentiments'.

14. 'Spirit Influx by which ideas and sentiments are infused into the mind'.

15. 'Involuntary Utterance (including "Speaking in Tongues")', and

16. 'Possession'.

We now give a series of eye-witness accounts of the phenomena experienced at the time. The first is an account by Mrs Fox of the events at Hydesville which started the whole Spiritualist movement.[1]

> On the night of the first disturbance we all got up, lighted a candle and searched the entire house; the noises continued during the time and were heard near the same place.
>
> Although not very loud, it produced a jar of the bedsteads and chairs that could be felt when we were in bed. It was a tremendous motion, more than a sudden jar, which continued on this night until we slept. I did not sleep until about twelve o'clock.
>
> On 30th March we were disturbed all night. The noises were heard in all parts of the house. My husband stationed himself outside the door while I stood inside, and the knocks came on the door between us.
>
> We heard footsteps in the pantry and walking downstairs, we could not rest, and I then concluded that the house must be haunted by some unhappy, restless spirit. I had often heard of

[1] Quoted from *Prediction*, London, April, 1937; the statement quoted by E. W Capron in *Modern Spiritualism* differs in a few details from the version given here.

such things, but had not witnessed anything of the kind that I could not account for before.

On Friday night, 31st March, 1848, we decided to go to bed early and not permit ourselves to be disturbed by the noises, but try and get a night's rest.

My husband was here on all these occasions, heard the noises and helped to search.

It was very early when we went to bed on this night – hardly dark. I had been so broken of rest I was almost sick. My husband had not gone to bed when we first heard the noise on this evening. I had just lain down when it commenced as usual. I knew it from all other noises I had ever heard before.

The children, who slept in the other bed in the room, heard the rapping, and tried to make similar sounds by snapping their fingers.

My youngest child, Cathie, said: 'Mr Splitfoot, do as I do', clapping her hands. The sound instantly followed her with the same number of raps. When she stopped the sound ceased for a short time.

Then Margaretta said, in sport: 'Now do just as I do. Count one, two, three, four, striking one hand against the other at the same time' – and the raps came as before. She was afraid to repeat them.

I then thought I could put a test that no one in the place could answer. I asked the 'noise' to rap my different children's ages successively.

Instantly, each one of my children's ages was given correctly, pausing between them sufficiently long enough to individualize them until the seventh – at which a longer pause was made, and then three more emphatic raps were given, corresponding to the age of the little one that died, which was my youngest child.

I then asked: 'Is this a human being that answers my questions correctly?'

There was no rap.

I asked: 'Is it a spirit? If it is, make two raps.'

Two sounds were given as soon as the request was made.

I then said: 'If it was an injured spirit, make two raps', which were instantly made, causing the house to tremble.

I asked: 'Were you injured in this house?'

The answer was given as before.

'Is the person living that injured you?' – answered by raps in the same manner.

I ascertained by the same method that it was a man, aged thirty-five years, that he had been murdered in this house and his remains were buried in the cellar; that his family consisted of a wife and five children, two sons and three daughters, all living at the time of his death, but that his wife had since died.

I asked: 'Will you continue to rap if I call my neighbours, that they may hear too?'

The raps were loud in the affirmative.

My husband then went and called in some neighbours, whose questions were answered accurately.

A friend, Mr Duesler, then asked: 'Were you murdered?'

Raps affirmative.

'Can your murderer be brought to justice?'

No answer.

He then said: 'If your murderer cannot be punished by law, manifest it by raps.'

The raps were made clearly and distinctly.

In the same way, Mr Duesler ascertained that he was murdered in the east bedroom about five years ago and that the murder was committed by a Mr ——— on a Tuesday night at twelve o'clock; that he was murdered by having his throat cut with a butcher's knife; that the body was taken down to the cellar; that it was not buried until the next night; that it was taken through the buttery, down the stairway, and that it was buried ten feet below the surface of the ground.

It was also ascertained that he was murdered for his money, by raps in the affirmative.

'How much was it – one hundred?'

No rap.

'Was it two hundred?' etc. – and when he mentioned five hundred the raps replied in the affirmative.

Many called in, who were fishing in the creek, and all heard the same questions and answers.

Many remained in the house all night, but I and my children left. My husband remained with the neighbours.

On the next Saturday the house filled to over-flowing.

There were no sounds heard during the day, but they commenced again in the evening.

On Sunday the noises were heard throughout the day by all who came to the house.

On Saturday night, 1st April, they commenced digging in the cellar; they dug until they came to water and then gave it up.

The noises were not heard on Sunday evening nor during the night; Stephen B. Smith and his wife (my daughter Marie) and my son David S. Fox and his wife slept in the room this night.

I heard nothing since that time until yesterday.

In the forenoon of yesterday there were several rappings answered in the usual way. I have heard the noise several times today.

I am not a believer in haunted houses or supernatural appearances; I am very sorry there has been so much excitement about it. It has been a great deal of trouble to us. It was our misfortune to live here at this time, but I am willing and anxious that the truth should be known and that a true statement should be made.

I cannot account for these noises; all that I know is that they have been heard repeatedly.

I certify that the foregoing statement has been read to me and that the same is true and that I should be willing to take my oath that it is so, if necessary.

(Signed) Margaret Fox

April 11, 1848.

The second account is of two seances held in Koons' Spirit Room in 1854. This account is extracted from a letter written by Stephen Dudley to the Editor of *The Age of Progress* in 1854. In this account we read of several of the different types of phenomena we have classified above.

Prior to our arrival, arrangements had been made for a public circle that evening, hence there was quite a crowd composed principally of near neighbours, the chief part of whom were sceptics. We, being strangers, were by the politeness of Mr Koons provided with comfortable seats in an eligible position.

It was easy to see from the first, that it was a very inharmonious party; nevertheless the spirits performed all they had promised to do. After we were seated, Mr Koons gave a short but very appropriate address, at the conclusion of which the spirits announced their presence by a tremendous blow on the bass drum. It sounded like the discharge of a cannon, and was succeeded by noises equally startling occasioned by what was called 'the charging' of the electrical apparatus by the spirits.

In this process, the large table and the log house itself shook like a tree in a gale of wind. A reveille was then beaten by the spirits on the tenor and bass drums with tremendous power and almost distracting effect. Mr Koons then took up one of the two violins that were lying on the table before us and drew his bow across it. Immediately, the other was sounded, and presently the full band of all the instruments, of which there must have been quite a dozen, joined in, keeping time, tune and concert.

After the instrumental performance, Mr Koons asked for a vocal accompaniment from the spirits, which they at once complied with, and I think if anything can give an idea of heaven upon earth, it must be the delightful music made by that angelic choir.

All this time there was a most extraordinary exhibition of spiritual pyrotechnics, seeming to consist of luminous bodies flying about with the swiftness of insects, yet moving in orderly time to the music. In shape they resembled different-sized human hands.

The next exhibition was that of a spirit hand as perfect as any hand of flesh and blood. It moved about amongst us, dropping pieces of sand-paper steeped in phosphorous, prepared by Mr Koons according to the direction of the spirits.

The object of these motions seemed to be for us to pick up these pieces, so that the hand might come, and by their light, be seen to take them from us. This was repeatedly done. In taking the piece from me the spirit hand seemed to linger in contact with mine, in order that I might feel and examine it. It differed nothing from a human hand, save in its excessive coldness. After some conversation with the spirits, which was conducted in a human voice through a trumpet, they bade us 'good night' and thus ended the public circle. About two hours after its dismissal Mr Koons, the chief medium, and myself, went into the spirit room alone, to see if we could learn what would be the order of the proceedings for the next evening. The medium put the trumpet on the table, when it was instantly elevated about the height of a man's head, and gave us 'good-evening', to which we responded.

I then commenced a conversation with them, asking if my wife and other dear departed relatives were present. They said they were, and some very satisfactory evidence ensued of their presence. I told them we had come a long distance to see them, and were desirous of witnessing some of the more wonderful manifestations of their power, of which we had heard so much. They replied that they knew how far we had come, and if all things were favourable, we should be gratified before our departure. Upon inquiring what they meant by 'things being favourable', the leading spirit replied that he meant 'a harmonious circle and not such a one as we had previously that evening'. After some further conversation we were dismissed with 'good-night'.

The next evening, at seven o'clock, Mr Koons, his wife, son, our party of four and two gentlemen, investigators – nine in all – repaired to the spirit room.

All being seated and quiet, the single startling concussion on the drum announced that the spirits were ready to commence the performance of the evening. Again the table was charged with the convulsive rattlings and tremblings before described. The tremendous reveille was beaten, Mr Koons commenced playing on the violin, joined not only by the whole band of instruments, but also with a large harmonica which stood in the room and on this occasion was played on, in a most masterly manner. Again they were asked for a vocal entertainment, which was given by several voices in such delicious strains, and in such exquisite harmony, that I must be permitted to say if it was done by the 'devil', then is that worthy fit to lead a choir of angels. At an interval in the music I asked Mr Koons if he would request the spirits to write for us. Without hesitation or delay, they supplied themselves with the paper and pencils which we had taken in and lain on the table. And here let me state that I had brought with me printing paper, unsized and unruled, hence unlike any that could be procured in that part of the country, or indeed, anywhere but from a printing office; also I brought with me, purposely, one of Flesheim's Buffalo pencils. They placed the paper on which they were going to write immediately before me. Then, what appeared to be a human hand holding a pencil was plainly visible over the paper and immediately commenced writing with a rapidity that no mortal hand can equal or come near to. The paper, the hand and the pencil, were so near to us, and so plainly visible by the luminosity of the hand, that we could all three have touched them, and we were able to inspect them at our leisure with the most perfect ease. My next neighbour was so intent upon the examination that he got his head immediately over the pencil, whereupon the hand made a sudden move upwards and hit his nose with the pencil, which gave him such a start that he drew his head back with considerable speed. When anyone expressed a wish to see the hand move more plainly as some did, the writing would cease, and the hand was displayed, extended opened and shut, as if to show the flexibility of the joints and the kindly compliant disposition of its owner. One of the ladies, who was not so near as we are, expressed a wish that she had been more eligibly seated. Immediately the hand and paper moved to the corner of the table nearest to her, wrote there a few lines and then returned to its former position.

When it had written both sides of the sheet full it handed the pencil to me, which proved to be the same Buffalo pencil which I had placed on the table. The spirit had then folded the paper and placed it in mine. I took it, and was subsequently instructed what to do with it. On receiving the paper, I found it too was the same that I had placed with the pencil.

After this the hand was presented to each one in the room, and shaken by all save one who was too timid to receive it. As before, it was deathly cold, but firm, and as solid, apparently as a human hand.

After a few words of conversation through the trumpet they dismissed us with the usual 'good-night'.

Our next account, taken from a letter to the *Boston Post* describes the movement of physical objects and the levitation of the medium.

The room was now darkened, when the following pheno-mena occurred: The table was forcibly drawn up to the ceiling, leaving the dents of its legs on the ceiling; it then came down, having adhered to the ceiling with such force as to drag down the plaster-dust with it. It was raised some twelve or fourteen inches from the floor whilst the whole party had their hands on its upper surface. Whilst six of our party strove to hold it by main force, it was wrenched from our grasp and thrown some six or eight feet upon the bed. The medium was lifted bodily from the floor at various distances, whilst we held him by either hand. He was lifted from the floor and placed, standing, on the centre of the table and again stretched upon his back thereon. Being seated in his chair, himself, chair and all, was elevated several inches and hopped about the room like a frog. Suddenly it was lifted, medium and all, into the centre of the table. Again it was drawn up so high that the medium's head touched against the ceiling; and finally the medium was thrown out of it upon the bed, whilst the chair was hurled upon the floor.

Clairvoyance is the subject of a brief quotation from an article by Professor Whipple published in *Sunbeam* of New York.

Whilst lecturing in Marrow County last winter, I attended a circle one evening composed of about twenty persons, and there, for the first time met a young man, a medium, who had no acquaintance with me, and knew nothing of my history. He was controlled to give tests to different individuals.

At length he turned his attention to me; said he saw a young man, a spirit, by my side, whom he described very particularly.

The description answered exactly to my brother, he compared his features with mine, said we greatly resembled each other, and that he appeared to bear the relation of brother to me. 'Now' said he, 'I will see if I can tell how old he is'. He paused a moment and then exclaimed, 'Why, he says he is neither older nor younger than you'. 'Very true', I answered, 'for he is my twin brother'.

An unusual phenomena, writing on the body of the medium, is described in a letter published in the *Spiritual Telegraph* in 1853.

. . . A lady medium of this vicinity, Mrs Seymour, when entranced, is in the habit of writing communications on her arms with the point of her finger – first on the left arm with the index finger of the right hand, and then vice versa. The

D

writing is for some minutes illegible, but soon it begins to appear in raised letters that can be both seen and felt distinctly.

At first these lines have a whitish appearance but afterwards become a bright red, and can be as plainly seen and deciphered as chalk marks on a wall. When examined by the sense of feeling, they impart the same unyielding impression to the finger as the ridges, inflicted by the stroke of a whip, though the finger in writing is passed over the surface very lightly and rapidly. To the eye they look like a burn, or not unlike erysipelas. They remain thus distinct and legible for fifteen or twenty minutes, causing no pain or even unpleasant feeling, and then gradually fade away as they came, leaving the skin natural, smooth and uncoloured.

Dr. Dexter in his book on Spiritualism describes how he developed a talent for automatic writing.[2]

When in pursuance of this design I attended circles my hand was seized and made to write. At first the sentences were short and contained a single idea, but as I became developed they wrote out many pages, embracing various ideas and subjects. . . .

Every meeting, however at which I was present, something new was always developed and the handwriting of the spirits manifesting assumed peculiar and distinct character, thus identifying the individual who wrote through my hand. The earlier attempts we were hardly able to decipher but after some practice, the writing was rapid, bold and easily read. From the first essay of the spirits to influence my hand to write, it was the medium by which many, both friends and strangers communicated with the circle; but when the design was apparent that they had developed me for a special object, my hand was controlled by two spirits, whose names will be found recorded in this book as Swedenborg and Bacon.

During the whole time, from their earliest endeavour to write, they have used my hand as the instrument to convey their own thoughts, without any appreciation on my part of either ideas or subject.

I know nothing of what is written until after it is read to me and frequently, when asked to read what has been communicated, I have found it utterly impossible to decipher it.

[2] Edmonds and Dexter, *Spiritualism*, vol. 1, p. 93.

Not only is the thought concealed, but after it has been read to me I lose all recollection of the subject, until again my memory is refreshed by the reading.

Judge Edmonds describes in a letter dated 27th October 1851 how his daughter was able to speak in languages which she did not know in a normal way.

On another occasion some Polish gentlemen, entire strangers to her, sought an interview with Laura (Miss Edmonds) and during it she several times spoke in their language words and sentences which she did not understand but they did; and a good deal of the conversation on their part was in Polish, and they received answers, sometimes in English and sometimes in Polish.

. . . The incident with the Greek gentleman was this: One evening, when some twelve or fifteen persons were in my parlour, Mr E. D. Green, an artist of this city, was shown in, accompanied by a gentleman whom he introduced as Mr Evagelides, of Greece. He spoke broken English, but Greek fluently. Ere long a spirit spoke to him through Laura, in English, and said so many things to him that he identified him as a friend who had died at his house a few years before, but of whom none of us had ever heard.

Occasionally, through Laura, the spirit would speak a word or sentence in Greek, until Mr E. inquired if he could be understood if he spoke in Greek. The residue of the conversation, for more than an hour was on his part entirely in Greek, and on hers sometimes in Greek and sometimes in English. At times Laura would not understand what was the idea conveyed either by her or him. At other times she would understand him, though he spoke in Greek, and herself when uttering Greek words. . . .

He goes on to describe a further case of speaking in tongues.

'November 3rd, 1852. There was a special meeting of the Circle of Hope last evening to meet some of our friends from Albany. . . . Mr Amtler was soon thrown into the magnetic state. . . . After he came out of the trance state Mrs Shepherd was affected and spoke in several languages. . . . And she continued for an hour or two thus to speak in some foreign language. It seemed to us to be in Italian, Spanish and Portuguese. . . . Mrs Mettler was then thrown into a trance state and she was developed for the first time in her life to speak in diverse tongues. She spoke in German and what seemed to be Indian.

And the two, i.e. Mrs Shepherd and Mrs Mettler then for some time conversed together in these foreign languages.

The only important phenomena we have so far not mentioned is Spirit healing. Healing has always been a common and familiar practice among Spiritualists and also in many 'enthusiastic' Christian sects. The methods and theories of healing are many and varied. In some sects it is assumed that the healer has special powers; others hold that the spirits, usually of doctors, work through the body of the medium, while others insist that God heals through the mediumship of the 'healer'.

Chapter Three

EARLY SOURCES OF SPIRITUALISM

Psychic phenomena have not been restricted to the modern
Spiritualist movement but have appeared in all known human
societies throughout history and are found in all existing societies.
In fact psychic phenomena appear to be one of the few universal
elements in human society. The universality of belief in the
existence of spirits led Sir Edward Tylor, the nineteenth century
British anthropologist, to suggest that a belief in spirits, which
he described as Animism, constituted the minimum definition of
religion.

Tylor argued that the belief in spirits arose from two types of
common experience; from the experience of dreams and visions
on the one hand and on the other from the observation of the
difference between a dead and a living body. Men frequently
dream of having waking visions of those who are dead and this
leads them to conclude that the dead are in fact alive in some spirit
world in some other order of existence. It would seem that psychic
experiences are commoner among primitive peoples or perhaps we
should say among people who live in non-urban-industrial
societies. Perhaps this is because in such 'rural' societies men live
closer to nature and are less alienated from the psychic sources of
life than are those who live in the artificial environment of
industrial societies. The observation of the difference between a
living and a dead body further leads men to believe that at death
the animating element, spirit or soul leaves the body.

Tylor's theory of animism as the source of religion has been
criticized by many later writers and in particular by R. R. Marett,
who suggested that the animistic stage of religious belief was
preceded by a more primitive stage which was described as pre-
animistic or animatistic religion. Marett pointed out that many
primitive peoples believed in an impersonal supernatural force
which is usually termed Mana, from the word used for the

concept by the peoples of Melanesia, where it had first been observed by R. H. Codrington.[1] Andrew Lang and Wilhelm Schmidt also showed that many of the most primitive peoples had beliefs in a 'High God', and that these High Gods showed few signs of being derived from a belief in spirits. There is however no proof that a belief in Mana or in High Gods preceded a belief in spirits, since those people who have beliefs in Mana and High Gods also believe in spirits. The theory of the origins of the belief in spirits has also been criticized, notably by Emile Durkheim, who argued that the theory was too intellectualist and untenable because 'religion cannot be based on an illusion but must be rooted in a concrete basic fact of experience'.[2] As Alexander Goldenweiser points out, the experiences to which Tylor attributes the origin of spirit beliefs can scarcely be called illusions.[3] Dreams and visions are facts of human experience, as also is the observed difference between a live and a dead body, and these are as important to those who experience them as any other form of experience. The criticism that the theory of animism is too intellectualistic is based on the strange assumption that primitive man was incapable of thinking logically about his experiences.[4]

If Tylor may be criticized it is for not emphasizing that experiences of a psychic nature, whatever their ultimate cause, have important effects on those who have them.

The belief in the existence of spirits is naturally parallelled by a belief that these spirits may appear to the living in the form of ghosts. A ghost may be defined as a spontaneously appearing spirit, that is to say a spirit which manifests itself without any conjuration or the intervention of a 'medium'.

The ghost story is popular not only in sophisticated circles in the modern world but is enjoyed also by primitive peoples, and has been a distinct literary form at least since the time of Homer's *Odyssey*.

The belief that spirits have the power to appear to mortals and to influence their lives very soon develops into the idea that such

---

[1] R. R. Marett, *The Threshold of Religion*, 1909; R. H. Codrington, *The Melanesians*, Oxford, 1891.

[2] E. Durkheim, *The Elementary Forms of the Religious Life*, 1961.

[3] A. Goldenweiser, *Religion and Society: A Critique of Emile Durkheim's Theory*, in W. Lessa and E. Vogt, *Reader in Comparative Religion*, New York, 1965.

[4] A. E. Jensen, *Myth and Cult among Primitive Peoples*, Chicago, 1963.

spirits may be called up or communicated with, through specially endowed persons or through special rituals.

In primitive society men are generally more concerned to avoid the spirits than to communicate with them. Their belief in the powers and influence of the dead are often very real, but since they usually attribute misfortune to the envy and malice of the departed, they tend to fear and avoid them rather than to love and seek to communicate with them. Such communication as they undertake is usually only for the purpose of propitiation or exorcism.

The raising of spirits and communication with the dead is often known as necromancy and is a widespread and ancient practice, often carried out in order to discover from the spirits a know-ledge of future events or to diagnose a disease, for disease is often considered to be the result of the evil influence of an animistic spirit.

An interesting account of an animistic religion is given by Margaret Mead in her study of the Manus. When she first visited them, they had a religion which 'is a special combination of spiritualism and ancestor worship. The spirits of the dead males of the family become its guardians, protectors, censors, dictators after death' . . . . 'The Will of the spirits is conveyed to mortals through seances, women with male children acting as mediums. The spirit child acts as a messenger boy upon the spirit plane. He speaks through his mother's mouth, in a whistling sound which she translates to the assembled questioners. At her bidding he goes about interrogating the various spirits who may be responsible for the illness, misfortune or death, or he collects the bits of purloined soul-stuff and returns them to the sick person'.

The Tiki people of the island of Fatu-Hiva in the Marquesas group were animists before the Christian religion was introduced by the French. They believed in the immortality of the soul and that the spirits could return to punish wrong-doers. Their 'medicine-men' were chosen solely on the basis of the medium-istic powers they possessed.

Similar practices and beliefs are found in many other parts of the world wherever animism is a significant force in the religious life. The concepts of animism have survived to some extent in all religions even to this day, and form the basis not only of many superstitions but also of a belief in a separate and surviving soul.[5]

The human instruments through which spirit communication takes place and around which psychic phenomena focus are known as mediums. Such persons, who are liable to fall into trance states and have ecstatic experiences, are found in all societies and seem to belong to the same type wherever they are found; little work has so far been attempted in the direction of a psychological or physiological study of mediums and consequently very little is yet known of the causes of 'mediumistic' powers.

As Ruth Benedict has pointed out in her book *Patterns of Culture*, in some societies mediums are highly valued. She reports that 'some of the Indian tribes of California accorded prestige principally to those who passed through certain trance experiences'. Among the Shasta tribe the shamans were chosen exclusively from women. This is by no means always the case, in fact in most societies the shamans are male.

Shamanism is one of the most widespread of religious institutions and the one which, although found among primitive peoples, most closely resembles modern spiritualism.[6]

The shaman is a medicine man whose prime function seems to be the cure or causing of disease. In order to carry out this function he must communicate with the spirits, either the spirits of the dead or nature spirits, although in some cases there are other reasons for communicating with the dead. Communication with the spirits is often carried out under conditions that closely resemble those at a western spiritualist seance. The shaman goes into a trance state, usually in a dark hut, and produces spirit voices and sometimes physical phenomena.

Shamans are mediumistic persons, often of an unstable type, who are chosen solely because of their peculiar gifts, although there are doubtlessly fake shamans as well as fake mediums, and probably more of them, for shamanism is a source of social prestige in many primitive societies.

Shamanism is found throughout the Americas from the Eskimos in the north to the tribes inhabiting the tropical forest of South America, and few of the native peoples in the Americas are unfamiliar with the practice of the shaman.

---

[5] There is an extensive literature on Spirit possession amongst primitive peoples – *see* bibliography.

[6] M. Eliade, *Shamanism*, 1964.

In Asia the practice is very widespread. It is particularly popular in Eastern Siberia and Manchuria but is also found in Tibet, China, India, Japan, Korea and Indonesia. It is found as far west as eastern Europe, among the Finns, the Lapps, the Estonians and the Magyars.

Similar practices are found in many African tribes.

Among the Eskimos the shamans are known as Angakoks. They usually become possessed by their spirit helpers, when giving their performance, and speak a private spirit language.

Among the South American tribes the shaman is looked on as an intermediary between the spirit world and the community. The cure of sickness and the foretelling of the future are two of their functions.

The trance is usually induced by heavy smoking, but they may also use parica snuffs or drink decoctions of ayahuasca or floripandio.

In Asia the trance is self-induced, usually by drumming and dancing.

The Voodoo cult of Haiti and the West Indies is an example of a complex religion which has developed from the contact of the animistic beliefs of the negroes from West Africa with Christianity and native Indian beliefs. Possession by spirits of the dead, by discarnate nature spirits and gods forms a regular and essential part of the practices of Voudoun. The ecstatic condition necessary to possession by the spirits is often induced by rhythmical drumming and dancing, and the spirits speak through the mouths of the possessed.

The cult of the dead and a belief in the after world may be traced, by inference at least, to prehistoric times. In Ancient Egypt concern with the after-life dominated the religious thought of the people. In Egypt also the diagnosis and healing of disease was a major function of the priest and magician. The healer first sought to discover the name of the demon whose presence caused the disease and also the name of the particular god who had power over the demon. Then he would either summon the presence of the god and get him to expel the demon or effect the same result by disguising himself as the god and so deceiving the demon into leaving the afflicted person. In some cases magical devices rather than the direct invocation of the gods were used in the process of exorcism.

In Ancient Greece many sick people sought healing at the temple of Asklepios at Epidaurus. Here the sufferers underwent incubation. They slept in the temple and in the night had visions of the god who appeared to them and healed them. The many inscriptions found in the temple at Epidaurus prove that this treatment was at least as efficacious as the healing in more recent times at such Christian shrines as Lourdes or the tombs of many times.

The oracles of Greece seem to have been 'mediums' who in trance or while possessed were able to utter prophecies.

The Chthonian element of Greek religion was at least partially a cult of the dead, for the Chthonioin were spirits who lived in the dark recesses of the earth. The mystic Orphic cults were concerned with the ways in which men might obtain immortality through initiation.

In the official religion of both Greece and Rome there was singularly little psychic content. This was found in the popular cults of the ordinary people and both in Greece and Rome these cults only arose to any prominence in times of trouble.

Among the Jews, as recorded in the Old Testament, there were many occurrences of healing, prophecy and the miraculous mani-festations of physical mediumship. The clearest indication that necromancy was well known is found in the story of King Saul's visit to the Witch of Endor and in the strong condemnation of witchcraft.

The founder of the Christian religion and His apostles practised healing and prophesy, and many other psychic manifestations are recorded in the New Testament.

The practice of communing with spirits and all the other 'gifts of the spirit' mentioned by St Paul continued to be practised for two or three hundred years in the Christian churches.

All these gifts are reported as being practised at the end of the second century by Irenaeus, who was martyred in A.D. 202.

The followers of the heretic Montanus who flourished at about the same time had among them a number of mediums.

Tertullian, in *De Anima*, tells of a prophetess who commonly fell into a trance during the religious service and communicated with angels and performed healing.

The regular practice of the 'Gifts of the spirit' seems to have gradually died out in the orthodox branches of the Christian church, with the exception of particularly gifted individuals; of these there were many hundreds.[7]

During the middle ages individuals having psychic powers were often accepted by the church and might attain great prestige and later be canonized. The Roman church still consider carefully reports of the miraculous when they appear within its own organization. It accepts visions of the saints and communication with saints and angels, but rejects communication with the un-sainted dead. The phenomena of stigmata which closely resembles certain of the physical phenomena of Spiritualism has been accepted as genuine in many cases by the Catholic Church, at least since the times of St Francis of Assisi.

One of the most startling phenomena of modern Spiritualism, levitation, is also found in the records of the Christian saints. An outstanding example was that of St Joseph of Copertino, who is reported to have flown for considerable distances. Similar feats are reported to have been performed by St Mary Magdalen de Pazzu, the Blessed Martin de Porres, Christina of Saint-Trond and others.

Levitation is also reported to be one of the accomplishments of the Buddhist adepts of Tibet and also of Hindu adepts. In the *Buddhaghosa* are listed the miraculous powers which the practitioner of Buddhism may acquire. These include the power to become invisible, to walk through solid objects, and to control his body functions, as well as to levitate.

The ability to appear in any shape he desires is another power of the adept, who can also obtain knowledge of another persons's thoughts, has the ability to hear things from a distance (telepathy?) and to recall his former lives. Phenomena of this type are particularly prominent in the Tibetan version of Buddhism.

Even in a strictly monotheistic religion such as Islam, room has been found for a belief in angels and djinns and mystic cults have developed.

A form of manifestation that is closely allied to Spiritualist phenomena is that of the poltergeist. The word poltergeist comes from the German and means 'noisy spirit', and it is used to designate cases in which unexplained noises are made or in which

---

[7] As M. Weber pointed out, the Romans avoided ecstasy in religious activities and this attitude influenced the developing Catholic church which took steps to control and routinize ecstatic expression. *Sociology of Religion*, 1965, pp. 180–1.

objects are moved without any apparent human agency. Cases of this sort have been reported throughout history and Hereward Carrington has analysed 375 cases mainly from western Europe which have occurred between A.D. 355 and 1949.

There is an extensive literature devoted to poltergeists in modern times, and some of the most valuable studies have been carried out by the Society for Psychical Research and have been reported in their *Proceedings* and *Journal*.

The universality of the appearance of psychic phenomena of course does not necessarily indicate that such phenomena are objective. Such phenomena, although they undoubtedly occur, may be the result of delusion, but if so, this form of delusion is common to all human societies.

Psychic phenomena are common to human society as are artistic phenomena or criminal behaviour. Like these phenomena, they are not universal to all human beings. Not all men are artists or criminals but no human society exists that does not include art and criminality among its activities. So no human society exists without some psychic phenomena, though there are certainly individuals in all societies who do not experience such phenomena. The proportion of individuals who experience such phenomena varies considerably from society to society and only rarely is it the case that the majority of individuals within a society have personal experience of such occurrences.

The Forerunners of Modern Spiritualism

There were a number of developments in thought during the eighteenth century which prepared the ground for the emergence of Spiritualism in the nineteenth century and the later appearance of the scientific study of the human mind and of psychic phenomena.

Probably the most important of these developments was the growth of animal-magnetism, which arose mainly from the teachings and studies of Franz Anton Mesmer. Mesmer was born in the village of Iznang on the shores of Lake Constance in Austria in 1734. At first he intended to enter the priesthood and studied at the Jesuit University at Dillington and at Ingoldstadt University. In 1759 he went to the University of Vienna where he at first studied law, but he soon abandoned this for medicine. He qualified in 1765 and three years later he married a wealthy widow whose social connections enabled him to establish a practice amongst the best social circle in Vienna. He seems to have practised mainly on cases which today would be defined as psycho-neurotic, and developed a system of treatment which led to some remarkable cures.

Mesmer's theory of animal-magnetism was based on an analogy with the theories of magnetic force that had developed shortly before that time from the work of Volta and Galvani. Magnetism was supposed by many people to be caused by a mysterious fluid which was stored in certain metals. He held that human beings could be influenced by the application of magnets and that cures could be affected by the use of this fluid.

We find that the term magnetic did not originate with Mesmer, but was familiar before his time among mystical philosophers and in particular by practitioners of the sympathetic system of medicine. Paracelsus is thought to have been the founder of this school of philosophy, and although he uses the term magnet usually in a metaphorical sense, he also used the magnet itself in the treatment of certain diseases. The magnet was considered to be able to exert an influence from a distance by virtue of a force or fluid which radiated from it.

A similar force was thought to radiate from the stars (hence the basis of astrology) from the human body, and indeed from all material objects, which were thus constantly influencing each other. These forces could be directed by the power of the spirit, but the forces were dual, and in constant conflict with each other.

Mesmer contributed little to the development of this philosophy but merely claimed to have discovered a way of applying it to the practice of medicine.

In 1778 Mesmer went to Paris, which at that time was the centre of intellectual ferment. There he at first had great success and converted many to his theories, among them M. D'Eslon.

Mesmer and D'Eslon used a piece of apparatus called a 'baquet' in their treatment. This consisted of a circular tub from which projected a series of iron rods. The patients sat round this and applied the ends of the rods to their bodies. During these performances music was played and the patients became worked up until they had convulsions or collapsed. The climax of this process was called the 'crisis' and was alleged to lead to the curing of the disease from which they suffered. The baquet was claimed to be an apparatus for containing and concentrating magnetic force.

The work of Mesmer caused such a stir in Paris that the French government appointed a Commission to investigate animal magnetism in 1784. This commission reported unfavourably on Mesmer's theories and recommended their legal suppression.

In spite of this report, animal magnetism continued to be popular among the aristocracy. Many cures were said to have been made and societies for the study of the subject were established in six French provincial cities and at Turin, Berne, Malta and the French West Indies.

In the course of treatment applied by animal magnetists many patients fell into what de Puysegur described as the somnabulic sleep. This and similar conditions observed by magnetists were described as 'rapport'. When in this condition the subject could hear no voice except that of the operator and would be under his influence. This somnambulic sleep seems to have been the condition known subsequently as hypnotic trance, and such cures as were effected seem to have been the result of suggestion given by the hypnotist and not of magnet fluid as claimed by the magnetizers.

The practice of magnetism spread rapidly through Germany and Scandinavia and it was in Sweden that the abnormal phenomena that often occurred in connection with the somnambulic or magnetic trance was first interpreted as being the result of supernatural influence. In May 1787 the Societé Exegetique et Philantropique of Stockholm carried out a series of experiments in which it was claimed that spirits of the dead communicated through the somnambule.

It seems that a Spiritualist interpretation of the unusual aspects of magnetic phenomena arose first in Sweden as a result of the influence of the teachings of Swedenborg, and the Stockholm society which conducted these experiments seems to have been founded mainly to propagate Swedenborg's doctrines.

The spirit interpretation was advocated in France by Dr Billot. The somnambules used in his experiments communicated with spirits who claimed to be the guardian angels of the mediums; amongst other phenomena that occurred were the 'apport' of flowers. Billot's work was mainly carried out between 1819 and 1833.

Alphonse Cahagnet in January 1848 published an account of spiritual communications received through the somnambulic trance.

It was however in Germany that the spirit interpretation of trance phenomena was first widely accepted. The founder of this school seems to have been J. M. Jung-Stilling, who was born in 1740. He became a Professor of Political Economy at the Universities of Marburg and Heidelberg. In the later years of his life he wrote a book *Theorie der Geister-kunde* in which he advanced a theory to explain ghosts, prophecy and second sight.

In the early part of the nineteenth century many cases of spirit communication were reported from Germany. Among these were the cases of Auguste Muller of Karlsruhe, of Fraulein Romer, and of Frau Frederica Hauffe who was known as the 'Seeress of Prevorst'.

The Seeress, who died in 1829, produced most of the phenomena that later became familiar in America. Not only did she communicate with the spirits in trance, but raps and physical phenomena appeared in her presence, and on at least one occasion a materialization seems to have been produced.

The practice of 'animal magnetism' was first introduced into England in 1785 by Dr Bell and for about ten years it aroused considerable interest but the craze died down by 1798. In all probability the advent of the long French Wars diverted the interest of the public, for it was not until 1828 that we find mesmerism again being demonstrated in Britain. Interest soon faded and it was not until 1837 that the movement became established in Britain. In that year 'Baron' du Potet came to London. He interested Dr Elliotson who practised mesmerism on some of his patients at University College Hospital. The hospital authorities requested him to discontinue the practice of mesmerism and in 1838 he left the hospital to devote his time to the propagation of mesmerism. In 1843 Elliotson and another doctor named Engledene produced a magazine called *The Zoist*, which was devoted entirely to the study of mesmerism. In the same year another periodical *Phreno-Magnet* was also published.

During the eighteen forties and fifties considerable interest was aroused in Britain by the mesmerists; they were mainly concerned with healing, but many cases of clairvoyance and thought transference were reported. These phenomena were interpreted as manifestations of a physical force or fluid, and the supernatural interpretation does not seem to have been popular in this country. In Britain and America mesmerism became closely connected with the new 'science of phrenology' which H. G. Atkinson in Britain and Buchanan, Collyer and Laroy Sunderland in America claimed to have discovered. The phrenologists claimed to have discovered 'organs' in the human brain which were the seat of all human faculties.

Knowledge of mesmerism and the somnambulic trance seem to have reached America about 1837. In that year Dr Larkin of Wrentham, Mass. first became interested in the investigation of animal magnetism. After some years he found, in 1844, a good subject for his experiments in Mary Jane, a servant girl in his house. Through her mediumship, raps and teleports occurred and spirit messages were received. Reports of his experiments caused a considerable stir, and in 1847 their phenomena were investigated by a local committee. This resulted in Mary Jane being charged with 'necromancy' and imprisoned for sixty days in 1849. Larkin was expelled from his church and persecuted by his neighbours until he signed a declaration saying that he did not believe in 'communion with spirits'.

In 1839 the Rev. Laroy Sunderland, who, as we have seen, was at first a phrenologist, made experiments with the mesmeric trance. In 1842 he founded a magazine called *The Magnet*. He later rejected phrenology and the magnetic interpretation of trance phenomena.

There were reports of Spiritualist type phenomena in America as early as 1829–30 but this was in no way connected with animal magnetism. In that year members of the Shakers, a mystical sect, were possessed and fell into trances in the course of which, they claimed, prophecies were made of a great discovery of material wealth and outpouring of spirit-truth, which would occur in 1848. In 1848, gold was discovered in California, and the Spiritualist movement was given its start by the Fox family. Unfortunately the Shakers did not make public their experiences until after 1848.

One man, however, played a major part in preparing the American public for the advent of Spiritualism, and that was Andrew Jackson Davis. Davis was born in a rural area of New York in 1826. In 1838 he was taken to Poughkeepsie by his father who was a weaver and shoemaker. He was given very little education and in 1841 was apprenticed to a shoemaker named Armstrong. In 1843 Professor Grimes gave a series of lectures on animal magnetism in Poughkeepsie. This aroused great interest and a tailor called Levingston experimented with Davis and succeeded in throwing him into a trance. For the following two years Davis practised as a professional clairvoyant, with the assistance of Levingston. In 1844 he claimed that while alone in the country he fell into a spontaneous trance and communicated with Galen and Swedenborg. Some time later he met a Dr Lyon and the Rev. William Fishbough, and went with them to New York where he set up as a medical clairvoyant. There he gave a series of trance lectures which were transcribed by Fishbough and were published in 1847 as *The Principles of Nature, Her Divine Revelations, and Voice to Mankind*. This encyclopaedic work included an evolutionary account of the origin and growth of the universe, a system of mystical philosophy, and an account of the relations between the spirit and the material world and a plan for the reorganization of society on socialist lines. The book was a remarkable production for a young and poorly educated man of twenty-one. It enjoyed a great success and went through thirty-four editions in the following thirty years.

A small group gathered around Davis including the Rev. S. B. Britten (a Universalist who later became converted to Spiritualism, and married Emma Hardinge) and the Rev. T. L. Harris, also formerly a Universalist, who was later connected with the Mountain Cove Community. Davis and his group produced a periodical the *Univercoelum* to propagate his Harmonial Philosophy.

Interest in animal magnetism and related teachings was widespread in America during the decade 1840–50 and this interest was aroused and spread by a large body of itinerant lecturers. These lecturers made the American public familiar with the phenomena of the trance, of clairvoyance and healing, and in this way prepared the minds of the public to accept the claims of the Spiritualists.

The second of the influences which stimulated the growth of Spiritualism was derived from the experiences and teachings of the Swedish seer Swedenborg.

Emmanuel Swedenborg was an eminent scientist in eighteenth century Sweden, who specialized in mining engineering and metallurgy, but was also accepted as an authority on astronomy, physics, zoology and anatomy. It was not until he reached the age of fifty-five in 1744 that he developed psychic powers. Swedenborg's powers seemed to resemble those of a modern Spiritualist medium. His main experiences were those of communications with angels who revealed to him conditions in the after-world. He wrote a series of works describing his experiences and also produced a number of theological books in which he re-interpreted the Bible and put forward a new form of theology. Swedenborg claimed that he had been specially chosen as a vehicle for these revelations and that his experiences were exclusive. His followers consequently condemned any claims by other persons to communication with angels or the dead.

The New Church was founded in England late in the eighteenth century by his followers, and by the early nineteenth century had reached America. It had little direct influence on Spiritualism, for it condemned the appearance of such phenomena, but indirectly it had some influence, since dissemination of the teachings of Swedenborg had made many people familiar with the idea of communication with angels and spirits.

A third influence is derived from the long history of Christian mysticism which made familiar the phenomena of trance, healing, stigmata and other miraculous performances. Meditation and a belief in direct inspiration came directly through the mystical elements in Quakerism.

A further Christian influence was that of the 'enthusiastic' Christian cults, which have continued the practices and tradition of the early church up to modern times. In such sects the 'gifts of the holy spirit' variously interpreted, continue to appear. These include the 'gifts of prophecy'; 'of discerning spirits' (mediumship); 'of tongues' (glossolally) and of healing manifestations of this nature which had appeared during the 'revivals' of the early nineteenth century and were regularly practised by sects such as the Shakers.

A non-Christian influence which originated from Europe was that of the tangled and much confused complex of belief connected with witchcraft, black magic and alchemy. These are really three separate belief systems but they have become very much interconnected in popular thought.

The witchcraft cult in Europe is a survival of the fertility religions which existed prior to the introduction of Christianity;

as such it was impregnated with animistic thought. Witches were able, by ritual practices, to develop their psychic powers and to communicate with the spirits and also to perform certain acts of physical mediumships from whence are derived the stories of witch curses and of flying on a broomstick.

Witchcraft found its way to America with the early settlers and appears to have been rampant at least in some places in the seventeenth century, when the infamous Salem witch trials took place. These occurred in 1692, and after that date little is known of witchcraft in America, but it continued to exist and its influence is reflected in certain aspects of Spiritualism, particularly the esoteric elements in the movement.

The secret and mystery cults and brotherhoods also influenced the esoteric elements within Spiritualism. Among these cults the best known were the Freemasons and the Rosicrucians.

All these cults claim to possess secret knowledge which is imparted to their members through a process of training and initiation. This secret knowledge, which is of psychic and spiritual matters, they claim is derived mainly from the Ancient East, with Egypt as a favourite source of inspiration. Their influence is clearly seen in the emergence of certain secret hierarchical cults within Spiritualism, which however lasted for only a short time.

Ceremonial magic, usually called black magic because it was used for evil purposes, has been usually confused with witchcraft, but instead of being a survival, as is witchcraft, it is derived largely from traditions of Judaism and Christianity. It is in a sense an inversion of these religions in which the good God is rejected and the Devil is worshipped. Magicians claimed that by ritual methods they could obtain power over the devils and make the spirits work for them. Their abilities, they claimed, included necromancy and prophecy. They were part of the forces that kept alive a belief in communication with the spirits and fortune telling.

The movements of witchcraft, magic, alchemy and astrology may all be seen as influencing Spiritualism mainly through their prior influence on the lines of thought which led to the development of animal magnetism.

A final influence which may provide a clue to the origin of the movement in America was that of native Red Indian religious practices. The Red Indians had two main systems of belief which forerun spiritualist beliefs and practices.

The first of these is the system of beliefs centreing around the idea of a Guardian Spirit.

Sir George Dunbar quotes Francis Parkman's account from *The Jesuits in North America* of the way in which an Algonquin obtained his personal guardian.

> At the age of fourteen or fifteen, the Indian boy blackens his face, retires to some solitary place and remains for days without food. Superstitious expectancy and the exhaustion of abstinence rarely fail in their results. His sleep is haunted by visions and the form which first or most often appears is that of his guardian manitou – a beast, a bird, a fish, a serpent, or some other object. animate or inanimate. An eagle or a bear is the vision of a destined warrior, a wolf of a successful hunter; while a serpent foreshadows the future medicine man, or, according to others, portends disaster. The young Indian thenceforth wears about his person the object revealed in his dream, or some portion of it – as a bone, a feather, a snakeskin or a tuft of hair. This, in the modern language of the forest and prairie, is known as his 'medicine'. The Indian yields to it a sort of worship, propitiates it with offerings of tobacco, thanks it in prosperity and upbraids it in disaster. If his medicine fails to bring the desired success, he will sometimes discard it and adopt another. The superstition now becomes mere fetish-worship, since the Indian regards the mysterious object which he carries about with him as an embodiment than as a representative of a supernatural power.[8]

Ascetic practices of fasting and self-torture were used to induce visionary experiences, and in this the Indians resemble the Christian and other religious ascetics. In certain parts of America trance states were induced by eating payote, a cactus button containing a drug which produces ecstatic visions.

The second system of beliefs held by most Red Indian tribes and the one which in its manifestations most closely resembles modern Spiritualism is shamanism.

The following account from the writings of Kohl, which was reprinted in W. Howitt's *History of the Supernatural* published in 1863, recounts an Indian shamanistic performance among the Ojibbeways.

[8] Sir George Dunbar, *Other Men's Lives*, 1938.

'Thirty years ago', a gentleman told me, who had lived among the Indians and was even related to them through his wife, 'I was present at the incantation and performance of a jossakid in one of these lodges. I saw the man creep into the hut, which was about ten feet high, after swallowing a mysterious potion made of a root. He immediately began singing and beating the drum in his basket-work chimney. The entire case began gradually trembling and shaking, and oscillating slowly amid a great noise. The more the necromancer sang and drummed, the more violent the oscillations of the long case became. It bent backwards and forwards up and down like the mast of a vessel caught in a storm and tossed on the waves. I could not understand how these movements could be produced by a man inside, as we could not have caused them from the exterior.

'The drum ceased, and the jossakid yelled that "the spirits were coming over him". We then heard through the noise, and cracking, and oscillations of the hut, two voices speaking inside – one above, the other below. The lower one asked questions, which the upper one answered. Both voices seemed entirely different, and I believed I could explain this by very clever ventriloquism.

'Thirty years later, the Indian had become a Christian, and was on his death-bed. "Uncle", I said to him, recalling that circumstance; "Uncle, dost thou remember prophesying to us in thy lodge thirty years ago, and astonishing us, not only by thy discourse, but by the movements of thy prophet-lodge? . . . Now thou art old, and hast become a Christian; thou art sick and canst not live much longer; tell me then, how and through what means thou didst deceive us?" My sick Indian replied, "I have become a Christian, I am old, I am sick, I cannot live much longer, and I can do no other than speak the truth. Believe me, I did not deceive you; I did not move the lodge; it was shaken by the power of the spirits. Nor did I speak with a double tongue; I only repeated to you what the spirits said to me. I heard their voices. The top of the lodge was full of them, and before me the sky and wide lands lay expanded; I could see a great distance round me; and I believed I could recognize the most distant objects." '

It is easy to see the many close resemblances between shamanism and Spiritualism, and these provide some grounds for suggesting that the forms of spiritualist practice have been stimulated by contact with Indian shamanism and guardian-spirit beliefs. Modern Spiritualism arose in a newly settled district and many of the settlers may well have had knowledge and experience of Indian beliefs.

Chapter Four

AMERICA 1840–60

American social life was in a state of extreme fluidity and form-lessness in the middle years of the nineteenth century. A social structure can scarcely be said to have existed. Social mobility was so great that an individual might change his social role frequently in such a way that a stable structure of social norms could not be built up. The ties of social class did not exist and the control of the primary group was broken and as yet unreplaced, at least in the frontier areas, by the control of law. The individual was largely thrown upon himself and left to his own resources.

America had always been a society in which social mobility was an important factor and in which individualism was valued, but these aspects of American life reached their climax during the 'forties and 'fifties of the last century, when the migrations across the continent were in full swing, when immigrants were flooding into the country, and in the east industrialism was beginning to be felt as a force in the economic and social life.

In much of America the mores and folkways of a stable society had not yet established themselves, and in the Atlantic states they were disrupted by the great migration and by the arrival of new immigrants. The great influx of immigrants from many parts of Europe, each group bringing with it its own conflicting social traditions and ideals, led to a greater confusion of differing and conflicting folkways and mores than had ever existed in any one society before.

It is true that each foreign national group gradually became Americanized, but in doing so it contributed something of its own ideas and personality to the building of the total 'American way of life'. The process of Americanization meant that each new group acquired certain basic attitudes and attributes from those who lived in the country before its arrival. To some extent this process can be traced back to the early days of colonization. The first settlers brought with them certain ideas and traditions which set the tone for those who followed. From the first, the colonists consisted, broadly speaking, of two types, the rebels who fled from the persecution of church or state in their homelands, and the adventurers who sought to make their fortunes in the opening up of new land or in trade.

Both the rebels and the adventurers naturally tended to be men of strong individuality who saw in the New World opportunity to create the sort of society they desired, the chance to live the sort of life they wanted or to get rich quickly unhindered by the controls and restrictions imposed by society in the Old World. Developing from such beginnings, and having for its citizens persons of these types of personality, American society tended to grow with a marked bias towards individualism and the general acceptance of an ideal of boundless opportunity for all.

One of the major factors in the establishment, preservation and development of these ideals and their incorporation in the 'American Way of Life', was the long period during which the country was dominated by an expanding frontier.

The frontier may be defined as a thinly populated area having not more than six inhabitants per square mile, in which the pioneers were engaged in the clearing and breaking of the ground and in which they were beginning to settle.[1] When we think of the frontier we usually think of the West, of cowboys, prospectors and Indian wars, but in fact of course the frontier started on the Atlantic coast in the early days of colonization and from there advanced steadily across the continent.

By the close of the Revolutionary War the frontier had moved over the Appalachian and Allegheny mountains into western New York State and western Pennsylvania, into eastern Tennessee and the uplands of Georgia.

The main feature of life on the frontier was the isolation in which the pioneers lived; the nearest neighbour might be some miles away.

Independence and self confidence, together with a belief in equality, were the main attitudes encouraged by frontier life. These qualities, unrestrained by social control, led to the love of liberty being carried to the extremes of licence and to much violence in the name of individualism.

[1] F. L. Paxson, *History of the American Frontier 1763–1893*, New York, 1924.

When the first census was taken in 1790, the population of the United States was about four million, who occupied a territory of less than one million square miles in extent. By the census of 1850, the population had risen to over twenty-three millions, who occupied more than three million square miles of territory.

During the first half of the nineteenth century the frontier moved across the Mississippi and Missouri Rivers into the centre of the continent. Most of this expansion was peaceful though it was marred by a number of bloody and merciless Indian wars. Texas was annexed in 1846, and California, New Mexico and other territories were acquired as the result of a war with Mexico. The land acquired during this period was largely unoccupied or very sparsely populated, and the rate of immigration was comparatively low until about 1845, so that the great increase in population during the first half of the century must be attributed largely to the natural increase of a fertile and virile people.

In the ten years between 1820–29 the average annual number of immigrants arriving in the country was 9,000. In the following ten years immigration increased to an annual average of 35,000. But in the first forty years of the century less than half a million immigrants arrived in the country. In the following twenty years from 1840–69, at least five and a half million people came into the country.

Before 1845 the frontier was advanced largely by a westward flow of the indigenous population of the Atlantic Coast States. The 'Goers' from the Atlantic States, as Turner says,[2] tended to come from the 'come-outer class', that is to say were rebels who differed from the rest of the community, and who sought salvation in a new land where they could build their lives in accordance with what they felt to be right.

The 'stayers' in the old colonies tended to be conservative-minded persons with a respect for the established order.

The frontiersman had to be tough, adaptable and self-reliant, for the life was hard and only persons having those virtues could survive, but as Latourette[3] points out the strong individualism and love of democracy which was distinctive of the American Frontier is not a distinctive feature of all frontier situations. These trends did not arise for example in the Roman Catholic

[2] F. J. Turner, *The United States 1830–50.*
[3] K. S. Latourette, *History of the Expansion of Christianity,* vol. 4, 1941.

frontier areas in South America or French Canada. Latourette rightly attributes this American frontier democracy and individualism to the influence of particular forms of Protestantism upon the settlers, for during the first half of the nineteenth century the majority of frontiersmen along the northern frontier came from New England[4] where Calvinism with its encouragement of individualism and Congregationalism with its democratic form of church government were the predominant forms of religion.

From the South Atlantic states a vast migration proceeded across the south and central part of the country.[5] These migrants were largely of Scottish-Irish descent, who tended to become cattle-men, or of German ancestry, and of a less aggressive type of personality who tended to take up farming. The Scottish-Irish were Calvinists and consistent advocates of liberty. The Germans were generally of Lutheran belief. Both groups came of stock which had emigrated to America in search of freedom.

The great flood of foreign immigration which began about 1845 reached a peak around 1850 but continued to surge in throughout the 'fifties and 'sixties, though it was interrupted for a time by the Civil War. This flood was composed of two main streams, one from Ireland which resulted from the famine of 1845–47, the other from Germany, which consisted of refugees from the persecution which followed the unsuccessful revolutions of 1848. Both these streams were composed largely of Roman Catholics.

These new immigrants had been used to poverty in their homeland, and they were consequently prepared to accept poor conditions and low wages in the new country. The most poverty stricken of these immigrants were unable to migrate to the frontier and settled in the cities of the east coast where they found employment in the new factories.

At this time the industrial revolution was in full swing in America, some fifty years behind events in Britain. Conditions in the slum areas in which these newcomers lived were appalling.

---

[4] F. J. Turner, *The United States 1830–50*, pp. 43–44. 'Between 1790 and 1820 Southern New England lost 800,000 of its people by migration out of the section. By the census of 1850 there were over 450,000 people born in, but residing out of New England .

[5] F. J. Turner, op. cit., p. 148. 'By 1850 about a third of the white and free coloured natives of Virginia and of North Carolina were living in other states and of South Carolina about forty per cent.'

The willingness of these new immigrants to accept low standards depressed conditions generally, and this was resented by native workers. There was considerable conflict between the newcomer and the natives, which even led to the formation of 'Native American' political parties with the primary aim of reducing or preventing immigration. The fact that the newcomers were largely Catholics whereas the natives were Protestants was another source of conflict.

Speaking of the economic conditions of the period, Cochran and Miller tell us: 'The year 1837 was one of panic in the United States; 1857 was another. Between were two decades that, whatever their seasonal and cyclical ups and downs, produced more wealth, more waste, more hope and disillusion than any previous twenty years in the country's history'.[6]

It was during this period that a leisured class having wealth and culture developed in the cities of the east, and the great extremes of wealth and poverty became obvious.

The depression of 1837 was over by 1845 and by 1850 trade was booming. This was the era not only of factory development but of the construction of the railways, between 1850–57 an average of 2,300 miles of track was laid annually. It was thus in a period of booming industry and great contrasts of poverty and wealth that the Spiritualist movement arose and reached its greatest development.

During this period America was predominantly a rural country. As late as 1860 only 16·1 per cent of the population were urban, defining urban as those who lived in towns of over 8,000 inhabitants.

In addition to these social factors there were certain political factors which influenced the social atmosphere of the period. The triumph of the democratic ideas of the west came with the election to the presidency of Andrew Jackson in 1828. The ensuing period was one of widening democratic trends which resulted in a general feeling of optimism throughout society.

This optimism was certainly not without some justification. It was possible for the poor boy to rise to a place of power and influence or indeed to the highest position in the land as was proved by Jackson's rise from great poverty to the presidency. Examples of such rises from poverty to power or wealth were

[6] Thomas C. Cochran and William Miller, *The Age of Enterprise*, New York, 1942.

sufficiently common to give credence to the theory of an age of opportunity.

This period saw democratic trends developing in many directions. In the field of education there was a tremendous growth of public schools and also of higher education. In New England education had always been valued, and by 1850 only 1·89 per cent of the white population were illiterate and the great majority of these were recent immigrants.

The standard of literacy was only slightly less in New York and Pennsylvania. In the north central states illiteracy varied from about two per cent in Michigan and Wisconsin to seven per cent in Indiana. Illiteracy was highest in the southern states, the negro population was almost totally illiterate and in those states to the south of Maryland it was five times as high among the white population as in New England.[7]

Not only was the public school system firmly established during the early part of the nineteenth century, but higher education also flourished and expanded. In 1800 there were twenty-four colleges in the States; by 1860 these had grown in number to 228. These naturally varied widely in standards from those of high academic standing such as Harvard to many local colleges which were no more than high schools.

Nevertheless this rapid expansion of colleges during this period shows the widespread interest in education which was manifested at this time.

In the eighteen twenties and thirties the Lyceum movement developed; this was an adult educational movement which may well be compared with the Workers' Educational Association in England (at a later date). The first mention of the movement appears in an article entitled 'Associations of Adults for the Purpose of Mutual Education', by Josiah Holbrook in the *American Journal of Education* in 1826. In the same year he organized at Millbury, Mass. the 'Millbury Lyceum, No. 1 branch of the American Lyceum'. Within a few months fifteen Lyceums were established in nearby villages. By 1834 some 3,000 Lyceums existed organized under State boards. In 1839 a national convention was held. By that time there were Lyceums in almost every village in New England, and some of the greatest men of the time travelled round the Lyceum circuits lecturing.

[7] In England at that time the percentage of illiterates was about forty-one.

It was in the areas of highest educational standards and the lowest rate of illiteracy that Spiritualism first arose, spread most rapidly, and gained its greatest support.

A further democratic trend was to be found in the field of journalism. A highly literate population created a demand for reading matter. In the eighteen thirties this demand led to the production of a great number of penny newspapers.

The first of these in America seem to have started in Boston in 1830. In 1833 the New York *Sun* was founded, and in 1835 the *Herald*. By 1837 both these papers were selling 30,000 copies daily. There was scarcely a town in the country which did not boast a local paper, and in most cases two or more competed actively for readers.

Between 1830 and 1850 the speed of printing was increased some twenty-fold by the mechanization of the industry. On the 1st June 1850 it was reckoned that there were some 2,800 newspapers and periodicals published in the United States, having a total circulation of about 5,000,000.

The high standard of literacy in the United States combined with the wide readership of the press must be taken as one of the major factors in the explanation of the rapid spread of the Spiritualist movement. There was also a long tradition of religious freedom and toleration which encouraged the growth of new sects.

Many of the early colonists were religious fanatics who had fled to the new world to escape persecution in the old. Fanaticism led to intolerance at first in some of the colonies, though others, in particular Rhode Island, allowed religious freedom from the first. A wide variety of religious sects established themselves in the colonies, from many parts of Europe, as well as from England.

The thirteen colonies with their varied interests, both religious and economic, were united by their common struggle against Britain in the War for Independence. Their common economic interests were sufficient to overcome religious differences and when the constitution of the United States was drawn up religious toleration became a recognized principle in the constitution. The establishment of any church was forbidden though some states which had already given recognition to a particular church continued to retain establishment until early in the nineteenth century.

There were several consequences of religious freedom which are of interest to us in our study of the rise of Spiritualism. In the first place religious freedom resulted in American religious organizations being based upon the principle of voluntarism.

By voluntarism is meant the principle that church membership should be the voluntary choice of the individual, and not, as was the case in countries having a State church, that one was automatically a member of a certain church because one was born in a particular geographical area. Voluntarism also means that the churches are financially maintained by the voluntary contributions of their members.

A second consequence of toleration was the growth of democracy in the government of the churches. This tendency had existed from the first in the predominant churches of the early colonies. The Congregationalists, Baptists, Quakers all practised control of the church by its lay members, and even the more autocratic churches have become more democratic than their European counterparts in the American environment.

Religious freedom naturally resulted in the growth of many denominations. Each individual had the right to seek out the truth for himself, and to join together with others who thought as he did in creating a new organization, if no other suitable organization already existed. So, as there are naturally very many views about religion, there developed a like multiplicity of sects and denominations.

The denominations themselves had no effective power to discipline their members. They could, of course, censure them or as a last extreme expel them from the church, but unlike the State churches in other countries, they had no powers to coerce heretics. This led to many denominations being split, some several times, on what were often points of faith or practice.

The movement of evangelism which in its extreme form was expressed in a series of revivals was a consequence of voluntarism. The churches generally believed that members should not be born into it but brought in 'voluntarily'. The revival was the main technique for recruiting new members. It was in the atmosphere of the frontier that revivals seem to have been most successful and Latourette suggests that this is because frontiersmen are more susceptible to group suggestion.

The first half of the nineteenth century was an age of great religious activity; in 1800, 6.9 per cent of the population were church members by 1850, 15.5 per cent were members. This was still a comparatively small proportion. During this period there was considerable conflict in the churches which led not only to schism and division within many of the existing denominations but to the establishment of new denominations. The spirit of toleration and independence in religion was a factor in permitting and facilitating the growth of the Spiritualist movement.

Chapter Five

SOCIAL CAUSES OF
THE RISE AND FALL
OF AMERICAN SPIRITUALISM

Spiritualism as a movement arose in America and spread with amazing rapidity across that continent within some five or six years of its inception. Never before, or since, has any religion spread so rapidly or become so popular within such a short period.

The causes of this unique event must be sought in the social conditions within the United States during the eighteen forties and fifties, for, as Durkheim insists, the explanation of any social phenomena is to be found in social facts. This theory must not however be carried to the exaggerated lengths to which Durkheim and his followers carried it, for they extended this theory to the point where they assumed that all forms of human behaviour could be treated as social and their explanation sought in antecedent social facts. Durkheim sought to explain the origin of religion as arising from social conditions within the human group.[1] As many critics have pointed out, religion is not an exclusively social phenomena any more than is, for example, eating, and it is as futile to attempt to explain religion as the result of gathering together in groups for ritual purposes as it would be to explain eating as the result of gathering together for meals.

The origins of religion, as of eating, which are not only social but also individual phenomena, are to be sought in the physiological and psychological needs of the individual. It is only the sources of the particular means and methods of satisfying these needs that are rightly to be sought in social facts. The sources of religion lie deep within the psychological make-up of human individuals, but the particular form which religion takes at any place and time is determined by social conditions within the given society.

[1] E. Durkheim, *Elementary Forms of the Religious Life*, New York, 1961.

E

This is true not only of religion in general but also of Spiritualism which is an essential ingredient in all religions. Spiritualism in some form or other is universal in human societies, but only rarely has it come to play an overriding part in religious practice. While it is doubtful whether Spiritualism itself can be explained as a result of social factors since it is not primarily a social phenomena; the extent to which it exists, and its influence within any society are social events and should be explained by reference to social facts.

It is for these reasons that we shall seek the causes of the rise of modern Spiritualism in America in the social conditions of the time.

The social factors we have already briefly considered are:

1. High social or vertical mobility.
2. Extensive horizontal or geographical mobility.
3. A great influx of immigrants with different and conflicting cultural patterns, and
4. The effects of rapid industrialization which led to chaos in the social structure and a failure to develop a coherent and integrated pattern of culture.

In fact the social conditions which existed in America during the 'forties and 'fifties of the last century seem to combine two of the types of society which Durkheim found to produce an increase in suicide in a community.[2]

The two relevant types are Egoism and Anomie. He defines Egoism as a state of society 'in which the individual ego asserts itself to excess in the face of the social ego and at its expense'. It is a state of 'excessive individualism' which as we have seen was typical of America particularly at this period.

A further element in the situation was a degree of social Anomie which may be defined as a lack of regulation in human activities resulting in the breakdown of social control and the absence of social norms. Durkheim considers that Anomie is the result of rapid and sudden economic change. Man can only live if his needs are in harmony with his means. The means at his disposal are normally controlled by society; when the possibilities of sudden wealth or poverty or rapid changes from one state to

---

[2] E. Durkheim, *Suicide*, translated by John A. Spaulding and George Simpson, 1951.

the other increase and are tolerated by society, then harmony between needs and means ceases to be operative and conditions of Anomie ensue.

Such conditions are characteristic of an industrial society and are particularly acute at the point of transition from a Communal society to an Associational society. A Communal society may be equated with Tönnies concept of Gemeinschaft, a society which develops without deliberate intention out of the mere fact of men living together and an Associational society with his concept of Gesellschaft, a society which is based upon relations voluntarily entered into by independent individuals.

The stresses upon the individual are particularly acute at the point of transition from one type of society to another. The frontier was characteristic of an Associational society having very strong Egoistical trends and the transition of the migrant from the more communal societies of New England or even more so of the immigrant from the old world to the chaotic appearing conditions of an Associational society was sufficient to set up great stresses in the personality structure of the individual.

These do not of necessity result in suicidal trends. On the other hand, aggression may be turned outwards upon the community, and this possibility is illustrated by the prevalence of violence not only on the frontier but throughout American society.

The type of Anomie prevalent at the time may perhaps best be defined as Simple Anomie[3] which 'refers to the state of confusion in a group or society which is subject to conflict between valve systems'. Almost every community in America at the time was composed of individuals from many different cultures each bringing with him his own system of folkways and mores. These often conflicted violently with each other, and in the case of immigrants, with the developing 'American way of life'. The existence of simple Anomie would seem to lead to a more advanced form of Anomie in which all value-systems lose their value and a system of 'normlessness' supervenes.

The individual placed in a society lacking clearly defined social norms and devoid of the support of a primary group tends to develop a sense of insecurity. and if he finds none of the means of obtaining security (psychological rather than economic) within the existing social institutions he will direct his search to other

[3] Robert K. Merton, *Social Theory and Social Structure*, Glencoe, Ill., 1957.

methods of satisfying his needs. These methods may be conventional or unconventional, individual or organizational, political or religious.

Much discontent of the period expressed itself in conventional
political forms, in the formation of new political parties, the
Anti-masonic Party, the Workingman's Party, the Locofocos and
the 'Native American' movements. A good deal of insecurity was
relieved by the conventional religious activities of the more
conservative religious bodies. There were cycles of revivalistic
activity which resulted in a considerable growth of church
membership. At the time of the revolutionary war only one in
twenty-five of the population were members of a church and the
people generally were indifferent to religion. In 1800 there were
only 365,000 church members, by 1850 this had increased to
3,530,000.[4]

Among the most interesting and conspicuous of the unconventional political methods were the many communist and
socialist communities which were established at this time; many
of them were also influenced by religious motives and a few as
we have seen had close connections with the Spiritualist movement.

Spiritualism was one of the unconventional religious methods
of solving the problems of individuals confused by the social
chaos of the period, and, at least for a time, a particularly successful
one. This was a period in which many new sects arose and
flourished in an atmosphere of fanaticism. Two other important
sects which arose at this time were the Mormons and the
Millerites. Both these were particularly influential in the district
in which Spiritualism was later born, the western districts of New
York State, which was also the home of fanatical and progressive
movements. The anti-masonic movement arose in this area in
1826. It was in Seneca county in this district that Joseph Smith
saw visions of the Angel Morani, who told him where the Book
of Mormon could be found. In 1827 Smith dug up the book,
which was written on gold plates, translated it, and had it printed
in 1830. It formed the bases upon which the Mormon movement
rapidly developed. In 1831 Smith and his followers left for Ohio.

About the same time William Miller in New England predicted
that the second coming of the Lord and the end of the world was

4 H. K. Rowe, *History of Religion in the United States*, New York, 1924.

at hand. He fixed the date for March 1843. The Millerite movement became popular and one of its chief centres was in western New York. When Miller's predictions failed the movement collapsed but never completely died, for many followers continued to believe in the imminence of 'the end' though they no longer put an exact date to it.

This area of New York State, as Sweet points out, had a background of revivalism and disturbed economic conditions. It was known as a 'burnt-over district' as a result of the waves of revival that had swept across it. The area had been settled in the early years of the century by two waves of migrants who were mainly from New England. The first wave were rough, and, Sweet says, 'of unsavory fame'. The second he describes as of an 'intelligent industrious class from Eastern New York and New England'. He goes on to say the 'mingling of these two classes gave a peculiar psychological character to the people, producing, on the one hand, sane and progressive social movements, and on the other, tendencies towards fanaticism'.[5]

We find both of these tendencies were existent in the early days of the Spiritualist movement. Many of the leaders of the movement were highly intelligent, educated and honest men, who we find on occasion complained of the credulousness and fanaticism of some members of the movement.

This western district of New York, although the frontier had only recently passed across it, was easily accessible from the established areas on the east coast since the Erie canal had been built through the district in 1825. The canal had been commenced in 1817. Prior to that date there were no settlements along its route west of Rome, but by 1830 the whole area had been developed. New waves of migration passed up the Mohawk River and along the canal to the Great Lakes and the west. In the early 'forties, a series of railways were driven through this country from Albany to the Lakes. This again accelerated the development of the country and increased the flow of settlers into, and migrants through, the district.[6]

It is in the social conditions of western New York that we must seek the cause of the rise of these movements and the reason why these ideas became popular at that particular time.

[5] W. W. Sweet, *The Story of Religions in America*, New York, 1930.
[6] R. Whitney Cross, *The Burned Over District*, New York, 1950.

All the conditions which we have considered with respect to the United States as a whole were present, but they were exaggerated in this area, because, of all areas of the country, change was probably more rapid in this area than in any other. Within twenty years this area had changed from a frontier settlement to the beginning of industrial development.

The insecurity of life in a rapidly changing society produces psychological and physiological stresses in the individual which have an important effect in the formation of his ideas and behaviour patterns, though it is only recently that the importance of such conditions have been realized and studied.

The older forms of religion with their belief, ritual and organization suited to a more stable and authoritarian structure were unable to adapt themselves sufficiently rapidly to the changes in social structure. In rejecting authority and an hierarchical system in society, men rejected the authority both of the dictatorship of God and of the leaders of the church. They demanded democracy in religion as in the state. They sought independence and the preservation of their individuality in the spiritual sphere as well as the material. They sought freedom for the individual to choose his path and rejected the determinism of Calvinist doctrine. All these demands of the common man were met by the rise of the Unitarian and Universalist movements, but both these movements lacked a warm emotional content, and were also unable to offer proof of their claims.

The 'Common Man' was not attracted by these movements; they were too intellectual; he needed emotional reassurance, but this they did not provide. The spirit of the age was one which demanded proof. Men of strong individuality sought the assurance that this individuality was not snuffed out by death. Only Spiritualism could offer this proof or give emotional content to the liberal theology of the day.

The effect of rapid technical and economic changes on the cultural pattern of societies and the mental health of individuals has been studied extensively in recent years, in particular in the effect of the impact of modern technology on more primitive forms of society. It has been found that even comparatively small technical modifications may cause considerable disruption or even a complete breakdown in the traditional cultural pattern of a primitive society.

In the words of the UNESCO report on 'Cultural Patterns and Technical Change,'[7] 'The culture of each people is a living unity in the sense that a change in any one aspect will have repercussions in other aspects. This is true even in those cultures which, while in the process of very rapid change, are torn by conflicts and contradictions.'

'As each human individual embodies the culture through which he lives, discrepancies, inconsistencies, different rates of change of parts of culture, will have their expression in the personality organization of the individuals who live within changing cultures.'

'Any significant change in the life of an individual tends to introduce some degree of instability or disharmony in the way his life activities, his beliefs and attitudes are organized.'[8] This in turn creates a state of tension in the individual.

'The existence of such tensions will be accompanied by changes in the individual's behaviour which tend to reduce the original tension; the dissipation of such tensions may take a considerable time or may not be successful. If the dissipation of the tension is not successful, the individual remains in a state of maladjustment or frustration.'[9] The report goes on to say that even when changes are painful, the revolution is more likely to take place, and will occur more quickly when the individual has a strong wish to change. Not all frustrations are harmful since they may provide just the stimulation which is required to provoke progressive development.

On the other hand, 'When frustration persists and is intensified, consequences not at all beneficial tend to occur. These consequences generally reduce the individual's tension, but while so doing, impair the healthy functioning of the whole personality and disrupt his successful adjustment to the society within which he lives. Of the many such consequences the following are important in understanding social behaviour:

(a) Return to old forms of behaviour. . . .
(b) The individual's behaviour may become less mature and

[7] UNESCO, *Cultural Patterns and Technical Change*, Margaret Mead (Ed.), p. 28, New York.
[8] UNESCO, op. cit., p. 271.
[9] UNESCO, op. cit., p. 272.

more childish; his feelings and emotions may be more poorly controlled, or new forms of dependency may develop.

(c) The accumulated tensions may find expression in aggressive acts, such as feelings and actions of anger and rage. . . .

(d) The individual may withdraw psychologically or physically from the frustrating situation. . . . Withdrawal may be into apathy, into substitute activities such as alcoholism, drug addiction, or gambling or into nativistic cults in which the former state, now seen as a golden age, is acted out symbolically. . . .

(e) The individual may reduce his tensions by preventing the occurrence of a tension-provoking reaction. Partial prevention is even more common. It then happens that the unresolved tensions find expression in diverse and often unrelated ways, such as chronic fatigue, preoccupation with one's state of health, compulsive ritual, new activities which are socially approved, redefinition of the situation in a way that is more acceptable to oneself, assigning blame for the situation to others, retreat into endless thinking about the situation without any attempt to check the thinking with reality.'[10]

In primitive societies all these forms of individual reaction may occur, and the effects of change on a primitive society may vary from acceptance and adaptation to complete social disintegration and the destruction of the group, as for example many Red Indian tribes and the Tasmanian and Australian aborigines.

We are concerned with only one manifestation of social change, namely its stimulating effect upon the rise of new religious cults.

In many cases relief from the tensions brought about by social change of a rapid or extreme type appears to be sought in new religious activity. The 'comforts of religion' are sought to provide security in an unstable or insecure situation.

Even in a situation in which religious cults arise, religious activity is not the only way in which relief from tension is sought. The exact form in which relief is sought by any individual depends upon the social environment in which he finds himself and his own personality organization.

A religious revival or new cult arises or reaches prominence when a great number of persons react to social stresses by

[10] UNESCO, op cit., pp. 274-5.

religious activity, but even in such circumstances many individuals may react in other ways, apart from those who welcome and make good use of such change. Others may react by seeking to effect social reforms or by political activity; by anti-social or criminal behaviour; or by lapses into a psychotic or neurotic state. The religious reaction is thus only one of several alternative (or simultaneous?) reactions to the stress of sudden change.

The predominant form of reaction in society at any given time depends on the predominance of certain social factors in the environment. Little is known at present about which factors are responsible for determining that a religious rather than any other reaction takes place at any time, and a great deal more research is needed to uncover these factors. It is impossible to do more than suggest a few hypotheses.

The most outstanding example of the rise of a new religion as a result of the impact of social change on primitive communities in recent times has been the appearance of 'cargo' cults in many parts of Melanesia and the South Seas. Studies of these have been made by Margaret Mead, Peter Worsley and others.

Cargo cults are millenarian movements. Their members believe that in the near future the existing order will be overthrown and God or their ancestors will come bringing a 'Cargo' of all the material things the people want. In preparation for the arrival of the 'Cargo', religious rituals are developed and storehouses built, often existing property is destroyed or thrown into the sea. A certain amount of enthusiastic phenomena such as possession, prophecy, shaking and communication with spirits are connected with these movements.

A similar series of cults arose in America during the nineteenth century among the Indian peoples. These became known as the Ghost-Dance Religion, and sought to revive the religious rituals which had been lost as a result of the culture-contact and conflict with the white man. These practices were based on dream and trance revelations given to the medicine man by the spirits of the ancestors.

Examples of religious movements arising as a result of social change and disorganization may be found not only in the records of cultural anthropology but throughout history. To mention a few such cases; Judaism was revolutionized as a result of the effects of the Exile in Babylon; not only did a revival take place but the concept of God as a universal creator emerged from the traumatic experiences of this period.

In the period of Republican Rome many cults arose in times of trouble. About 496–93 B.C. a famine led to the development of the cults of Ceres, Liber and Libera; a plague in 399 B.C. led to the introduction of new religious ceremonies and another outbreak of pestilence in 293 B.C. was followed by the introduction of the Cult of Asculapius. The Hannibalic Wars led to the growth of religious activity and the subsequent development of individualism resulted in the outbreak of Dionysiac orgies in 186 B.C.[11]

The Fall of the Roman Empire, one of the periods of extreme social disruption in history, was a period of great religious activity; so too was the end of the middle ages when the Reformation followed the disruption of the stable feudal system and modern capitalism emerged.[12]

In most cases the form of religious movement which emerges in such times of change are 'enthusiastic' rather than formal, are mystical or 'spiritual' rather than ritualistic. They emphasize individual inspiration rather than the acceptance of authority, and in many cases phenomena similar to those found in modern Spiritualism are familiar.

Niebuhr[13] following Troeltsch[14] suggest that 'creative religion is more the work of the lower strata', and that the new sects tend to rise to meet the needs of the religiously neglected poor. This is true in many cases and on the basis of our previous analysis it is easy to see why this should be so. The stress of change is more likely to affect the poor, the economically depressed and the socially disinherited, and they are less easily able to find other methods of adjustment in periods of social disruption.

The civil war period in England threw up movements among the poor such as Millenarians, Anabaptists, Ranters, Diggers, Levellers and Quakers. The Industrial revolution was accompanied by the spread of emotional revivalism and the growth of the Methodist movement.

At periods when social disruption reaches an extreme condition,

[11] W. Ward Fowler, *The Religious Experience of the Roman People*, 1911.

[12] R. H. Tawney, *Religion and the Rise of Capitalism*, 1938; M. Weber, *The Protestant Ethic and the Rise of Capitalism*, translated by Talcott Parsons, 1930. N. Cohn, *The Pursuit of the Millenium*, 1962.

[13] H. Richard Niebuhr, *The Social Sources of Denominationalism*, Henry Holt, 1929.

[14] E. Troeltsch, *The Social Teachings of the Christian Churches*, 1931

as at the end of the middle ages, all classes are seriously affected by stress and may seek security in religious activity.

As we have seen, the middle of the nineteenth century in America was a period of acute stress for the majority of individuals in that country, for they were involved in a series of rapid changes unparallelled in history. This resulted in the rise of many movements whose latent function was the relief of tension; such movements included political organizations such as the 'Know Nothing' Party, the Locofocos and the Anti-masons, such reform movements as the Temperance movement and the Abolition movement, as well as religious revivals and the rise of many new and often extravagant sects and cults.

Spiritualism was one of these cults, and during the eighteen fifties was probably the most successful of all the movements which arose from the chaos of social change.

The extreme individualism of the American led naturally to a concern for the future of the individual. The individualist finds it very difficult even to imagine the extinction of his own personality; he is an easy convert to the preacher who promises immortality. Many persons in America at that time were unable to accept the teaching of heaven and hell propounded by the orthodox churches These concepts were too crude and too nebulous. The educated and intelligent sought proof to support a reasonable theory of human survival. These they found in the philosophy and practice of the Spiritualist movement.

In recent years there have been some attempts by psychologists and physiologists to uncover the sources of sudden change in the religious conviction of individuals.

In his discussion of the techniques of religious conversion William Sargant[15] points out that the evangelist attempts to create emotional tension in the potential convert. Such tension is built up until a breakdown occurs. The evangelist also simultaneously offers a route of escape from the tension he has created.

It is not always necessary to create such tension by artificial means. In certain circumstances social conditions may produce sufficient tension and stress to cause the breakdown of some individuals. Certain types of individuals break more easily under stress than others. Pavlov[16] who studied the reactions of dogs

[15] William Sargant, *Battle for the Mind*, 1957.
[16] I. P. Pavlov, *Selected Works*, Moscow, 1955.

and men to conditions of stress concluded that there were four basic temperamental types which differed in their reactions to stress and conflict.

The first two types:

(1) the strong excitatory and
(2) the lively,

both reacted to stress by showing increased excitement and more aggressive behaviour, but they differed in that whereas the strong excitatory tended to become uncontrollable, the reactions of those of lively temperament showed purposeful and controlled reactions.

The two other types:

(3) the calm imperturbable and
(4) the weak inhibitory,

both tend to show a passive response to stress, but where the calm imperturbable were stable in their responses, the weak inhibitory rapidly developed a state of brain inhibition in which they were paralysed by fear.

All four types showed that when the stress was increased to a certain point breakdown would occur but the (1) strong excitatory and (4) the weak inhibitory types broke down more rapidly than did the other two types.

Pavlov's typology appears to be equally applicable to human beings as to dogs, for human beings appear to react to stress in similar ways. When the brain is in danger of damage from stress (or fatigue) a protective reaction takes place which has been called 'transmarginal inhibition'. In this condition suggestibility is heightened and sudden total changes may occur in ideals and behaviour patterns.

Techniques of applying artificially created stresses have long been used to produce religious and political conversions, and it is probable that many of the spontaneous forms of religious and political enthusiasm are the result of similar stresses which have arisen naturally from the effects of social conditions upon the individual members of society.

Examples of these forms of spontaneous reactions to stress are to be found in the religious 'dancing manias' which swept through

Europe in the fourteenth century, and the series of religious revivals which were particularly conspicuous in Britain and America during the eighteenth and nineteenth centuries.

The Nazi movement in Germany was a typical example of a political movement which exploited for its own ends the search for security.[17]

The particular form in which the consequence of stress express themselves and the type of movements which arise are determined by historical factors. The rise of such movements depend upon such factors as the type of ideas which arise or which become popularly known at the particular time. They are also influenced by the level of education of the people and the adequacy of leadership.

Psychic phenomena have always been known in human society and have in the past also provided the basis of movements, as for example in the mystery cults of Ancient Greece and the witchcraft cult of Mediaeval Europe. In the first half of the nineteenth century, as we have seen, such phenomena, or at least very similar phenomena have been familiarized by the propaganda efforts of the Mesmerists.

When the events occurred in the Fox family at Hydesville and Rochester they aroused the immediate interest of the populace of the surrounding district. The phenomena differed to some extent from that which had been practised by the 'magnetic' practitioners, and the educated members of the community, once convinced of the genuine nature of the manifestations, were quick to perceive their implications.

The manifestations, if genuine, gave proof of the survival of the human personality beyond the event of death. The appeal of such proof would be tremendous particularly to those persons who were unsure of their religious beliefs, as well as to certain religious persons who saw in them the possibility of providing proof of the beliefs they already held.

The leadership of the new movement was composed largely of religious persons mostly from the more liberal sects such as the Quakers, the Unitarians and the Universalists, but the bulk of the membership of the movement seems to have been drawn from persons who were not closely associated with any religious denomination, or were sceptics. The majority of the people in

[17] E. Fromm, *The Fear of Freedom*, 1942.

America at this time were unconnected with any church for in 1850 only 15·5 per cent were members of a church.

The high standard of education and literacy made many people discontented with the orthodox teaching of the churches. Such persons were unable to accept the crude teachings of hell-fire and consequently did not respond to the efforts of conventional revivalists. Among the more intelligent, the teachings of Unitarianism and Universalism had become popular, but many people had lost their belief in Christianity and consequently their faith in a future life. It was to such persons that Spiritualism with its promise of proof of survival particularly appealed.

The lack of restrictions on thought which resulted from the social conditions led to many popular enthusiasms not only of a religious and political nature but also to efforts at social reform. Campaigns against the use of alcohol, tobacco and pork and others in favour of free land, free love, universal peace and the equality of the sexes were popular. At this time too occurred a revival in American socialism, and a number of communities were established on the basis of Fourier's ideas; many of these were connected with the Spiritualist movement, and Spiritualists were also closely connected with many of the other reform movements of the time.

Another factor which promoted the growth of the movement was the fact that the phenomena reported were accepted as genuine even by many non-spiritualists and opponents of the movement. Although the movement was denounced by the conventional churches this was not because they doubted the occurrence of the phenomena, but because they condemned such manifestations as the work of the devil, which they did because the teachings and practices of Spiritualism undermined their own authority and their teachings.

The manifestations were also accepted as genuine by many non religious persons who only rejected the Spiritualist interpretation and held that they were caused by the operation of a physical 'odylic-mesmeric' force or that they were the result of the subconscious working of the human organism.

The previous existence of mesmerism in America helped the growth of Spiritualism in three ways. Some Somnambulic clairvoyants, for example Mrs Tamlin and Mrs Bushnell began to include spirit rapping in their seances. Mesmerism had provided a ready made philosophy and prepared the minds of the public to accept the wonderful manifestations of Spiritualism. Finally the mesmeric movement had the support of many intelligent and educated persons who were experienced as editors and lecturers; many of these came over to Spiritualism and helped to spread the movement by lecturing and the production of Spiritualist papers and pamphlets.

The Causes of Decline

On a superficial level of analysis the Spiritualist movement declined as a result of the exposures of fraud and deception which were made on a large scale during the later fifties. These exposures combined with the excesses of certain elements in the movement, led to the disillusionment of a number of the intellectual supporters of the movement, and made the conversion of such people more difficult.

The trend towards free love in certain parts of the movement was abhorrent to the conventional thought of the period. It disgusted the morally narrow-minded who, confusing the part with the whole, tended to leave Spiritualism alone as a morally doubtful movement.

The association between Spiritualism and the socialist and community movement was also contrary to the individualistic ethics of the times and raised suspicion in the minds of all 'good Americans', who saw in their country the hopes of endless opportunity for the individual.

The churches from the first attacked Spiritualism as the work of the devil and kept up a campaign against the movement in their numerous newspapers and magazines. The fact that Spiritualism in America was never wholly Christian and at times and places was even anti-Christian aided the propaganda efforts of the churches, and turned many nominal Christians against the movement.

The press in America at the time was a powerful weapon which on the whole was turned against Spiritualism. The newspapers, eager for sensation, reported the phenomena of the movement but generally rejected the Spiritualist interpretation.

There was no active persecution by the State except in the south where, as we have seen, the public demonstration of Spiritualism was forbidden by the State of Alabama. In the south also there was much private persecution including the threat of 'Judge Lynch'; and private persecution was not unknown even in the generally tolerant north. The pressure of antagonistic public opinion, while not carried to the extent of active persecution, was felt by many Spiritualists.

The interests of many people were diverted also by the growing problem of the abolition of slavery and of the relations between the north and the slave owning states of the south. These problems aroused a tremendous amount of emotion at this time and diverted men's attentions from more spiritual matters. The outbreak of war in 1861 resulted in heightening the existing feelings and diverted attention to the achievement of material aims.

The war not only diverted men's attention; it occupied their time; it took them away from home and in so doing it completely disrupted and in many places destroyed the existing Spiritualist organizations.

The orthodox religious churches and sects survived the war and in many cases during the war made progress, at least the northern churches, because they had developed national organizations.

It is not too much to say that Spiritualism failed to maintain its early promise and to survive the events we have mentioned because of its failure to develop either organization, ritual or doctrine.

Spiritualism during this period never developed any organization beyond a few local and temporary Associations. The majority of the activity was carried on in private circles meeting irregularly in the houses of members; these circles usually gathered around one or more mediums. They tended to have no formal organization or leadership. A great deal of activity depended on the itinerant lecturers or mediums who toured the country holding irregular public meetings and demonstrations wherever they could attract an audience.

In the larger towns associations existed which organized regular weekly meetings and frequent and regular seances, but there were few such organizations.

Before the Civil War there was nothing that could be described as a church. There were no state or national associations. The movement was in fact (except for the communities) too private and individualistic. There was a great amount of contact with Spiritualists in other parts of the country mainly as a result of the extensive geographical mobility of the population, but also because of the travels of the itinerant lecturers and the extensive, though often short-lived, Spiritualist journals. Nothing in the nature of a formal leadership, let alone a ministry, arose.

When difficulty and disruption hit the movement and its informal leadership was removed by the exigencies of war, the movement tended to collapse as a result of the lack of the stabilizing influence of organization and formal leadership.

Not only did Spiritualists fail to develop an organization, they failed to develop anything in the nature of a common ritual of the sort which holds together religionists even in the absence of any formal organization. It is true that certain common features could be found in any Spiritualist group, but just as the medium was too charismatic a figure to build an organization around, phenomena such as table tapping or the trance were too uncertain to develop the required formal certainty of a ritual.

There was also a complete failure to develop a coherent and comprehensive doctrine. The only common belief to be found among spiritualists was the belief in communication with the spirits of the dead. Even immortality was not universally accepted, at least one group holding that only its own members and a few others could survive death. Beliefs ranged from extremely orthodox Christian, to Unitarian and Universalist, while many spiritualists were non-Christian. There were wide differences on all points of doctrine, and each group tended to support its own teaching by claiming that it had either derived its teachings from the spirit world or had obtained the approval of the spirits. The dead it seems are as individualistic in their beliefs as the living and taught varying doctrines to different groups. Warren Chase[18] tells us that a number of spiritualists 'backed out' into Christianity; most of these joined the Unitarians or Universalists, but some Christian Spiritualist churches were formed.

Chase and a number of other Spiritualist leaders were anti-Christian, and Chase in particular campaigned violently against the churches all his life. He held that Spiritualism was not a religion but only proved scientifically the survival of the

[18] Warren Chase, *Forty Years on the Spiritual Rostrum*, Boston, 1888.

individual beyond death. This 'scientific' spirit of many American spiritualists may also partially account for the loss of enthusiasm in the ordinary member and the decline of interest among the general public.

Part Two

SPIRITUALISM IN BRITAIN

Chapter Six

MOVEMENT AND ORGANIZATION

The Spiritualist movement which had swept through the eastern states of the U.S.A. reached England in 1852 when Mr Stone, an American lecturer on animal magnetism, brought the medium Mrs Hayden to this country.

The public in Britain had been prepared for the introduction of Spiritualism not only by news of the events in America, but also by the activities of the 'mesmerists' or 'animal magnetizers', many of whom had turned to the study of psychic phenomena and had adopted a 'Spirit' interpretation of the phenomena they had observed. There were some native mediums in Britain before 1852, and one of these, Georgiana Eagle, gave a demonstration before Queen Victoria at Osborn House in 1846. These native mediums, however, did not attract any permanent groups of followers or extensive publicity. The arrival of Mrs Hayden aroused immediate interest. Mrs Hayden was the wife of W. R. Hayden, a Boston journalist and former editor of the *Star Spangled Banner*. She was an intelligent and well-educated woman, who on her return to America graduated as a doctor and practised medicine for fifteen years. During her visit to England Mrs Hayden spent most of her time in London where she gave many private demonstrations of mediumship. The press treated her as an adventuress and many papers poured ridicule on her activities.

Her circles and demonstrations were attended mainly by the members of the middle class who were either scientifically interested in psychic investigation or were simply curious to investigate personally the supernatural wonders that had been reported from America. Among the prominent men of the time who were convinced that Mrs Hayden's demonstrations were genuine was Robert Chambers the publisher, who after attending a seance admitted that he was unable to account for the phenomena. A Royal Physician, Dr Ashburner, defended Mrs Hayden in a letter to the press, and the well known rationalist and socialist, Robert Owen, attended one of her demonstrations and was converted to an acceptance of human survival. He at once proclaimed his new beliefs in his journal, the *National Quarterly Review*, much to the consternation of his fellow rationalists.

Augustus De Morgan, the famous mathematician, who for many years was Professor of Mathematics at University College, London, and for eighteen years Secretary of the Royal Astronomical Society, was also interested in this type of investigation. He had already carried out an investigation of a clairvoyant, Ellen Dawson, in 1849, and had been impressed by what he had discovered. De Morgan carried out a series of investigations of Mrs Hayden in his own home. The result of these investigations was published in 1863 by Mrs De Morgan.[1] The book was published anonymously because De Morgan feared that his career as a scientist might be affected by declaring his conviction of the truth of the Spiritualist interpretation. He says in his introduction to his wife's book, 'My state of mind, which refers the whole either to some unseen intelligence or something which man has never had any conception of, proves me to be out of the "pale of the Royal Society".'

The majority of scientists of course remained unconvinced. In a letter to *The Times* of 30th June 1853, Michael Faraday attacked the Spiritualist interpretation of psychic events and advanced the theory that the movements of the table and the 'tapping' that formed the main type of manifestation at these early seances could be explained by unconscious muscular pressures exerted by the sitters. The explanation was welcomed by sceptics and critics of Spiritualism and was used as a main argument against the Spiritualist interpretation for many years. The opinion of Faraday carried considerable weight in spite of the fact that he had never investigated the phenomena he claimed to explain.

In an effort to promote the movement W. R. Hayden produced the first English spiritualist paper, *The Spirit World* in May 1853, but the attempt was premature and only one issue appeared.

Mrs Hayden returned to the U.S.A. in the autumn of 1853, but her place was taken by two more American mediums, Mrs Roberts and Miss Jay, who visited this country in that year. These

[1] Anon, *From Matter to Spirit: The Result of Ten Years Experience in Spirit Manifestations*, 1863.

three ladies concentrated their activities largely in London, giving demonstrations of mediumship, usually of the type known as table turning or 'tapping'. An epidemic of table turning and tapping spread through the country, though whether as a result of the work of these American visitors or of the influence of mesmerism from Europe it would be difficult to say.[2]

The author of an article published in 1856 in *The Yorkshireman* said, 'Some two or three years ago there was not an evening party which did not essay the performance of a spiritualist miracle . . . In those days you were invited to "tea and table moving" as a new excitement, and made to revolve with the family like mad round articles of furniture.' These early circles were composed largely of groups of friends who met to investigate the phenomena of which they had heard or read. They were often stimulated simply by curiosity, and many of them took the subject lightly as a form of entertainment.

During the eighteen fifties and sixties there was little sign of formal organization among Spiritualists, except in the Keighley area of Yorkshire, and even there the greater part of the activity was carried on in private circles. In this period Spiritualism was almost entirely a matter of private meetings in the homes of believers and investigators. There were few professional mediums and amateur investigators gathered together with their friends to study the subject. These circles were generally of a temporary nature, breaking up when interest declined, though some went on to develop a permanent structure and later become societies with a formal organization.

There appears to be two ways in which the Spiritualist movement spread in the early period. A group might form around the charismatic figure of a spontaneous medium, or on the other hand a group of friends might decide to investigate Spiritualism and create an informal circle to carry out their studies.

An example of the first type of group was the Spiritual Circle that gathered round the Nottingham visionary J. G. H. Brown in 1854. Brown claimed to have been chosen by the spirits to establish the 'Universal Church of Christ'. He was a healer and seer who published his message to the world in two books and sought to propagate his ideas further by publishing a paper, *The Communities Journal and Standard of Truth*, and by founding in 1857

[2] F. Podmore, *Modern Spiritualism*, 1902.

the 'Great Universal Organization' which had social rather than spiritual aims. A further example of this type of organization was the Croydon Circle founded by Fred Hockley in 1853. Hockley claimed to be in touch with a group of very elevated spirits controlled by the Crowned Angel of the Seventh Sphere. The first Spiritualist organization in London, The Charing Cross Spirit Circle, was established in January 1857. It appears to have been stimulated by the visit of an American trance medium, P. B. Randolph. The organization changed its title in July of the same year to the London Spiritualist Union, but difficulties soon arose. The Union was split by the activities of a new medium, Jones, whose followers formed a new group known as the 'Circle of Spheral Harmony'.

The majority of circles seem to have been formed to satisfy the curiosity of investigators of psychic phenomena and not around the activities of a charismatic medium. In many cases their interest in the subject was stimulated by attending a seance or public demonstration given by a well known medium or by reading an account of such a meeting. If the circle was successful in producing psychic phenomena it would continue to exist as long as its members retained an interest in the subject, and when interest continued over a long period some sort of formal organization might emerge. New mediums discovered their powers at such regular meetings as they do today in the 'Developing Circles' held by Spiritualist societies. Regular attendance at a circle over a long period seems to be necessary to develop latent mediumistic powers. In this way it seems groups may give rise to mediums or to charismatic leaders, though the process by which such groups give rise to leaders requires further investigation.

Some mediums arise spontaneously, having a natural endowment of psychic abilities. These tend to be the most powerful mediums and should logically be capable of giving the most influential leadership. In fact few of these spontaneous mediums have founded organizations which survived the death of their founder. Some like D. D. Home worked entirely outside formal organizations; others have worked entirely happily inside the existing organizational structure. Many have formed independent groups within the movement which however do not survive the demise of their founders; only one, Winifred Moyes, has founded a large scale continuing organization, the Greater World

Christian Spiritualist League, though others, including Madame Blavatski and Mrs Baker Eddy, formed movements which are outside the body of Spiritualism.

The Work of the Medium

We shall examine the life and work of the most gifted and remarkable medium of the nineteenth century, Daniel Dunglas Home, as an example of the influence of the medium at that period.

Daniel Dunglas Home was Scots by birth, having been born at Currie near Edinburgh in 1833, and he claimed that his father, who spelt his name Hume, was the illegitimate son of the 10th Earl of Home. His parents emigrated to America in 1840 leaving Daniel with his aunt, Mrs Cook, who had cared for him from about the time when he was one. When he was nine, Mrs Cook also emigrated to America, taking Daniel with her. Daniel's mother was said to have had the peculiarly highland gift of 'the second sight' and this Daniel seems to have inherited, since from the early age of four he saw visions and had premonitions.

At the age of thirteen he had the first important psychic experience. He saw the spirit form of a friend and this friend, Edwin, indicated to Daniel that he had died three days previously; this proved to be correct. Four years later he had a vision of his mother at the time at which she died some miles away. This proved to be the real beginning of his psychic powers. So many strange and inexplicable events occurred in the Cook house that his aunt, believing him to be possessed by the devil, called in the local ministers. When they proved ineffective she threw Daniel out of the house.

For the next few years he stayed with friends, moving from place to place where he always found a welcome from persons interested in Spiritualism; wherever he went he gave seances and demonstrated his mediumship. He claimed never to have been a professional medium or to have charged for his services but he had many wealthy friends and sympathizers who lavished gifts upon him so that he was never in need.

When he returned to Britain, Home's reputation had preceded him, and he soon found entrance to the highest ranks of society. He was welcomed by Lady Waldegrave, Lady Combermere,

Baroness Grey de Ruthyn and the Marchioness of Hastings. Sir
Charles Isham took him to Lamport Hall and Sir Edward
Bulwer-Lytton entertained him at Knebworth.

Elizabeth Barrett Browning was most impressed by Home but
her husband, Robert Browning, took an immediate dislike to him
and in 1864 lampooned Home in his poem 'Mr Sludge'.

Home did not stay in England long on his first visit, and he
was soon in Italy where for a time he abandoned Spiritualism and
joined the Catholic church. He seems, however, to have soon left
the church, for in 1857 he demonstrated before Napoleon III and
his Empress, who were most impressed, and Home became
popular at their court. During the following year he travelled
widely in Europe and gave seances at several of the Royal Courts.
He visited Russia where he appeared at the Court of the Tsar, and
married the daughter of a Russian nobleman.

In 1859 the Homes returned to England, where they were
again received well. An account of the startling phenomena at his
seances was published by Thackeray in his *Cornhill Magazine* in
August 1860. This article caused a tremendous furore.

In 1862 his wife died in France and Home was soon penniless;
in 1866 he went on the stage for a brief period. Towards the end
of that year his friends established the Spiritual Athaneum in
London, mainly with the idea of finding Home a job as resident
secretary.

About this time he became associated with an old lady, Mrs
Lyon, who gave him a considerable sum of money. Shortly
afterwards Mrs Lyon changed her mind and sued Home, alleging
that he had obtained the money from her by extortion and undue
influence. The case which was heard in April 1868 went against
Home, who subsequently had to refund the money and was left
in considerable debt.

To obtain a living he gave public readings, and he continued
to give seances. In 1870 Home again visited the continent,
returning to attend a series of seances with Sir William Crookes,
who was unable to detect any imposture, and told Home, 'Pray
do not hesitate to mention me as one of the firmest believers in
you'. Crookes was ridiculed for his 'credulity' but he never
changed his opinion about Home.

In fact Home was never detected in fraud, and although he
accepted many gifts from his wealthy friends he never practised

professionally or accepted money for exercising his gifts of
mediumship.

He married again in 1871 and soon after retired to live a private
life. He died in 1886. Home created no organization and depended
for his influence entirely upon his 'charisma' which derived from
his unique display of mediumistic powers.

Forming a Circle

During the eighteen sixties considerable publicity was given to
the Spiritualist movement by the press, and although much of the
press comment was hostile it drew the attention of many people
to the startling and more sensational aspects of psychic phenomena. Public meetings at which lectures and demonstrations were
given by visiting mediums also attracted popular support. But
those whose attention was attracted to Spiritualism found it
difficult to carry on their investigations since at least up to 1867
there were only two public mediums in the country, and in most
districts there were no Spiritualist organizations that they could
join and even informal groups were rare and difficult to find.
Those who became interested in the subject were consequently
often reduced to the expedient of conducting their own experiments and investigations, frequently with little guidance in the
techniques involved. This situation is illustrated in a letter from
a non-professional medium, John Jones, which was published in
the *Spiritual Magazine* in February 1862. Jones had taken part in
a discussion of the subject of Spiritualism in two newspapers,
The Star and *The Dial* during the summer of 1861 and as a result
had received a large number of letters from enquirers asking to be
allowed to attend meetings of his circle. He pointed out that even
if he gave up his profession and devoted his full time to Spiritualism he could not possibly deal with all enquiries. He advised
enquirers to form their own family circles. 'Let the members of
the family sit round a good-sized table, in a calm but cheerful
spirit and in a child-like manner ask the privilege of witnessing
the phenomena – to sit at a certain hour three times a week for a
month or two and I am sure that in ninety-five cases out of 100
the result would be the occurrence of spirit action in their own
families.'

There was a feeling amongst Spiritualists that many enquirers needed further and more detailed advice on the formation of circles and the conduct of inquiries, and advice was reprinted in several of the early issues of *The Spiritualist* in 1869 and 1870. These instructions on 'How to form Spirit Circles' are very revealing of the attitudes and interests of these early Spiritualists. In the first place they repeat the advice given earlier in John Jones's letter, and show their conviction that all persons are potentially psychic. 'An experimental trial at home among family, friends and relatives often gives the most satisfactory evidence of the reality of spiritual phenomena.' 'At the same time', they point out, 'As no fully developed medium is present among those who have never obtained manifestations before the probability is that there will be no results. Nevertheless it is a very common thing for striking manifestations to be obtained in this way at the first sitting of a family circle.'

These spiritualists were aware of the possibilities of deliberate fraud and went on to warn inquirers of the dangers to be avoided in their investigations.

There are in England several very interesting circles for physical manifestations, where the spirits speak with audible voices, but unfortunately, total darkness is a necessary condition. Non-spiritualists who are inquiring into the subject should have nothing to do with dark seances, which should be held only by those who know each other since they offer so many facilities for fraud. . . . There are plenty of mediums or people who fancy themselves mediums, who can rarely show anything satisfactory, and with whom an inquirer might waste much time. He should then get, say, two sittings by daylight in his own house with each of four mediums, because the power varies in strength at times with every medium; at the end of the eight sittings he is sure to be thoroughly interested in Spiritualism, and to have thrown over the imposture theory, which is the clumsiest and most superficial one of all. . . . At present there is very little imposture mixed up with the Spiritualist movement in Great Britain and there are only four or five paid mediums in all London. . . . Where there is real foundation for suspicion, the best plan is to go often to the medium, accompanied by witnesses, detect the imposture, and prosecute the medium for obtaining money under false pretences. . . . There are few public or semi-public spirit circles at work in London and the pressure for admission is so great where the manifestations are good that the best plan for novices is usually to try to get manifestations at home among their friends.

These passages reflect the confidence of early Spiritualists. They were not afraid to face any investigation and welcomed the exposure of imposters. This attitude displays the scientific bias of the movement in the early period.

The Development of Formal Local Organizations

During the eighteen sixties the movement remained largely a matter of private circles and there were many private mediums, but up to October 1867 at least there were only two known professional mediums in London, Mrs Marshall and Mr W. Wallace. The best known of the private mediums were Mrs Everett of Pentonville, who became a medium in 1855. Edward Childs, and the infant prodigy of mediumship, Master Willie Turketine, who gained extensive publicity for the movement between 1867 and 1869.

The first Mrs Guppy was a private medium who produced her own theory of Spiritualism which she gave to the world in 1863 in a work entitled, *Mary Jane or Spiritualism Chemically Explained.* The second Mrs Guppy, who before her marriage was Miss Nichol was also a medium, and it was she who was the first to produce the phenomena of materialization in Britain in 1872. Her fame however rests upon her claim to have been transported across London by psychic means and to have arrived at the end of her journey in the presence of witnesses.

Public meetings were occasionally held and series of lectures, services and meetings were promoted at various places during the 'sixties. These events were usually promoted by individuals or temporary committees, and permanent organizations only developed slowly.

As time went on, successful private circles began to form themselves into more permanent organizations. The development of societies in Clerkenwell and East London was typical of the process in which private circles developed into public seances and these in turn evolved the formal organization of a society. In 1855 a Mr E. L. Blackwell and a group of friends, who were mainly members of the Phoenix Friendly Society had their curiosity excited by a series of lectures on Spiritualism given by a herbalist, Mr Hardinge, who had a business in the City Road. They met to conduct seances at the Star coffee house, Golden Lane, and at the Cannon coffee house, Old Street. Interest declined after a short time, but in 1859 a Mr Cresswell persuaded Mr Blackwell to allow him to organize regular meetings in Finsbury Hall, Bunhill Row, of which Mr Blackwell was the proprietor. These meetings were open to members of the public, and as no charge was made for admission, the meetings attracted the rough elements looking for entertainment, and were often quite rowdy. In the Spring of 1860 Finsbury Hall was destroyed by fire, but was rebuilt in time for the Spiritualists to renew their meetings later in the same year. The meetings took a new form; most regular attenders had become convinced of the truth of Spiritualist claims and had decided that they wanted to give more serious attention to the matter. In order to be able to do so they decided to restrict the meetings to regular members, who paid a penny a week. A religious element was introduced, as the meetings were opened by hymn singing, Bible reading and prayers. The meetings were discontinued in 1861, since, as a contemporary observer noted, 'The meetings became unruly by reason of strong physical manifestations of a low type'.

Later, in 1861, the meetings were revived at the Alliance Hall in Old Street, where Mr Cresswell formed a society called the Christian Spiritual Enquirers, with himself as Secretary. This society remained in existence for three years and held regular seances on Friday and Sunday evenings.

In the same year a series of seances were held at St John's Hall, Corporation Row. These meetings suffered many interruptions by opponents of Spiritualism who sometimes exploded fireworks to disturb the sitters.

After these two series of meetings were discontinued, the serious investigators continued to meet and conduct seances in the homes of their leaders. In 1868 the leaders of these home circles met and formed the East London Association of Spiritualists with Mr Cresswell as the Secretary. The Association organized a series of public lectures at Stepney Temperance Hall in Mile End Road. This meeting place was too far removed from the former meeting places and from the homes of the members, and consequently the Association existed only for eighteen months, its last meeting being held on 7th December 1869. To provide for these 'old spiritualists' a society was formed in Clerkenwell. This met once more at St John's Hall, and became known as the St John's Association. This Association was very active for about five years, but it was disbanded owing to the difficulty of finding officials who were willing to undertake the work and financial responsibility involved in continuing the organization.

A different type of organization was the Progressive Library and Spiritual Institute established by James Burns in Southampton Row, Holborn, in 1863. For many years Burns' Institute provided a meeting place and centre for Spiritualists in London. The Institute was run as a business and provided a regular programme of developing circles, seances, concerts and social events. Burns appears to have attempted to monopolize the sale of Spiritualist literature at public meetings and services in London. In 1870 he took steps to prevent a rival publisher, E. W. Allen, from selling literature at meetings at the Cavendish Rooms. These meetings were organized by an *ad hoc* committee of which James Burns was a member. When Allen applied for permission to sell papers at these meetings he received a letter from Burns stating, 'Mr Daw informs me that you have applied to sell papers at the Cavendish Rooms on Sunday evenings. I beg to inform you that it is engaged for other purposes and is not at your disposal.'

It seems that at that period many Spiritualist activities were based on business interests. In January 1874 Mr Allen obtained permission from the Tapin Lecture Committee to sell papers at their Sunday meetings. This Committee was described by *The Spiritualist* as 'The first which has been formed in London for a long time independently of trade interests'.

James Burns also met with considerable disapproval as a result of his opposition to the establishment of the National Association of Spiritualists. Many spiritualists believed that his opposition arose from his fear that a central organization would harm his business interests, namely his book shop, library and Spiritual Institute. Burns refused to publish advertisements issued by the National Association, and attacked the formation of that body in his publications. *The Spiritualist*, a major supporter of central organization, replied by publishing several attacks on the activities of Burns. They accused Burns of suppressing letters sent to him for publication in his magazines by supporters of the National Association and of making exaggerated claims for his Spiritual Institute. They pointed out that, 'In his advertisements he states that the alleged Institution is divided into the Library Department, the Financial Department, the Publishing Department, and the General Business Department, thus further conveying the idea to people out of London that it is a great public establishment, the truth being that all the "departments" are comprised in an ordinary little shop with a counter eight or ten feet long.' Burns, they argued, gave the impression that his shop was the centre of a great organization by describing it as the 'central office' of the Spiritual Institute, whereas it was the sole office he possessed.

National Organization

The first attempt at establishing a national organization was made in 1865 when a 'Convention of Progressive Spiritualists' was held at Darlington. The meeting lasted two days and was attended by twenty-five people who included visitors from London, Newcastle, York, Richmond Yorks., Monkwearmouth, West Hartlepool and Sunderland. The Convention was promoted by the small Spiritualist group at Darlington who seem to have felt isolated and who sought by this means to contact other Spiritualists in order to promote social relationships and the exchange of ideas. The meeting was attended by non-Christian Spiritualists and was pointedly ignored by the Spiritualist press, who were not represented at the meetings. The well known London Spiritualist, James Burns, was incensed by this, and made a speech accusing the Spiritualist press of being sectarian. He declared they excluded 'Any articles tending to explode theological errors', and that while they might be useful in promoting a 'Respectable' form of Christian Spiritualism, they were useless as a means of promoting truth and progress'. He proposed the establishment of a new periodical, which in fact appeared almost two years later in April 1867, as a monthly entitled *Human Nature*. This journal remained, throughout its existence, the main mouthpiece of non-Christian or Progressive Spiritualism.

The Convention set up a permanent organization, 'The Association of Progressive Spiritualists of Great Britain', with the object of holding a meeting at least once a year, 'for the purpose of social communion, interchange of sentiment or opinion to record and catalogue our united experience, and the progress which spiritualism is making in and around us; to devise means for propagating and diffusing among our fellow men and women the principles and soul saving truths of this Divine philosophy by the distribution of the best tracts and books'.

In the following year the British Association of Progressive Spiritualists, as it was then called, held its second convention at Newcastle. Interest had increased, and the attendance was much larger than in the previous year. The convention made little progress in spite of lengthy discussions on the principles and organization of spiritualism. This time the Association's activities were not ignored by the Spiritualist press. *The Spiritual Magazine* in a brief report condemned the Progressive Spiritualists for being too narrow and for favouring the anti-Christian type of spiritualism then prevalent in America.

The attendance was again up at the third Convention held in London in June 1867 and included representatives from America, France and Germany.

During 1867 a number of local associations of Progressive Spiritualists were formed, but their connection with the national association was tenuous, since the British Association appears to have been composed of individual members and not of representatives of local groups or associations. The Wolverhampton association formed in January 1867 was described as a branch of the British association, but it is difficult to see in what sense it could be so described since the only function of the British association seems to have consisted of holding annual conventions.

At about the same time a Spiritualist organization was formed at Sheffield, and an association was established at Manchester. The Manchester association was immediately successful, and during its first six months held weekly seances, and some sixty circle meetings; its annual meeting was attended by sixty members. Its activities continued after the collapse of the national association, and it was responsible for holding a convention in Manchester attended by 250 people in 1869.

The British association collapsed after the fourth annual convention, held in London in 1868, as a result of a decline in interest in its activities. This convention attempted to interest British Spiritualists in an ambitious scheme for a World Spiritualist

H

Convention to be held in London, which had been proposed by the American National Convention of Spiritualists. They were unsuccessful in arousing interest in this project among British Spiritualists, and the proposal was abandoned.

This first attempt at national organization failed for a number of reasons. In the first place the majority of Spiritualists at that period distrusted and were opposed to any type of organization. In addition, the majority of English Spiritualists were Christians, and they refused to co-operate with Spiritualists who were non-Christian or anti-Christian in their views.

The association consisted of individual members; it was not securely based on local groups or organizations, which would have given greater continuity to the work of the Association and could have provided stability by providing continuing foci of loyalty for members. The Association did little work apart from organizing annual conventions, and lacked a permanent organization capable of initiating and implementing the other aims of the Association. The Association was frequently in financial difficulties; this has been a not uncommon problem among Spiritualist organizations, since Spiritualists have often been reluctant to contribute adequately to the financial support of their organizations.

Opposition to Organization

From the early days of the movement there has been a strong element of resistance to formal organization among Spiritualists. The opposition was particularly strong in the early period, but suspicion of formal organization continues to the present day amongst certain sections of the movement.

The anti-organizers in the eighteen sixties expressed their opinion mainly in *The Spiritual Magazine*. In an article reprinted from the American magazine *Banner of Light*, the *Spiritual Magazine* summed up the views of opposers of organization in that period. The author of the article admits that organization can be useful. He points out that organization, 'Enables those engaged in the promotion of any cause to work more efficiently for certain ends'. Movements such as Catholicism and Methodism he admits are strong and efficient, 'Largely due to the thoroughness and compactness of their organizations'. 'But', he says, 'do not the members of those communions pay a fearful price for the benefits derived from their compact organizations, in the loss of individuality and intellectual freedom?'

Organization would destroy the spontaneity which most Spiritualists felt to be essential to the life of Spiritualism. Mediums are notoriously difficult to organize, since they must be free to express any teachings that come through them from the spirits.

The development of organization would lead to bureaucracy and the rise of an oligarchy. The movement would be 'Controlled by the lower stratum of minds – minds that live and work almost solely for the interests of organizations' – 'Should Spiritualists organize thoroughly, there are thousands', said the writer, 'who would enlist in their ranks for the purpose of leading the organization, now unknown to most faithful pioneers'. It is interesting to note that the author of this article was aware of those trends in democratic organizations leading towards oligarchy which were demonstrated fifty years later in the work of Robert Michels.[3]

Even at this early period many Spiritualists recognized the dangers inherent in the process of development from cult through sect into a church type organization, oligarchy being one of these dangers, and strongly resisted such a trend. This general distrust of organization continued to hamper the spread of the movement for a long time. The distrust of organization was not restricted to the fear of the growth of national bodies, but also existed at local level. Many of the local societies that were formed failed to survive as a result of the individualistic attitude of Spiritualists, and the casual and ineffective type of organization these societies were enforced to adopt in order to appease the libertarian and anarchistic views of many of their members.

The Second National Organization

In the Summer of 1872 a second attempt was made to form a national organization. A so-called National Conference of Spiritualists was held at Darlington. It was quite unrepresentative of spiritualists in general, since the fifty people who attended came largely from the Darlington district. The attempt was unsuccessful, but throughout the following winter the need for a national

[3] R. Michels, *Political Parties*, Glencoe, Ill., 1958 (First Published 1915).

organization became a frequent subject of discussion in the Spiritualist press and *The Spiritualist* newspaper actively promoted the idea in a series of editorials and articles.

In June 1873 the Liverpool Psychological Society, the most important spiritualist group in that city, decided to promote a National Conference to be held in Liverpool in the August of that year. The proposal was welcomed by Spiritualists in many parts of the country.

The conference, which lasted for three days, was attended by official and unofficial representatives from societies, and individual Spiritualists from the major towns in the country. Mr John Chapman of Liverpool argued 'that organization was necessary for the welfare and further progress of Spiritualism, and order was necessary for great achievements'. 'We should', he said, 'band ourselves together to give a wider spread to Spiritualism and its philosophy, but not to make them into a creed or formula'. He also thought that organization could be used to prevent or resist, 'the legal persecution', of Spiritualists. His arguments were supported by W. H. Harrison, editor of *The Spiritualist*, who also pointed out that a National organization could help the growth of the movement by providing aid and support for new local associations, or for those associations that were experiencing difficulties.

The eloquence of the supporters of organization was successful in persuading the Conference of the need for a national body, and it adopted the proposal of J. J. Morse that the conference should form itself into a National Association. An executive council was elected and given the task of drawing up the rules and constitution of the new association.

Opposition to this move towards central organization came from some prominent Spiritualists. James Burns was a violent opponent, but many people felt that this was largely because he feared the effect of such a move on his business interests in the Spiritual Institute. Opposition based on idealistic principles centred around the personality of W. Howitt, a well known and influential Spiritualist author of the day. Howitt objected to central organization as such, and repeated most of the old familiar objections. He suggested that there was no need for a national organization, since Spiritualism had grown extensively and was still growing without the aid of any such body. In the second place he argued that all organizations tended to become tyrannical and to repress individual thought. With particular regard to the National Association, he held that this body was ill-founded since the only authority for such an association would be derived from a mandate given as a result of a universal election by all Spiritualists. No such election had been held, he pointed out, and thus the 'National Association' had no legitimate authority. He raised no objections to local organizations, which he thought were indeed useful in the promotion of the movement.

The editor of *The Spiritual Magazine* was also opposed to attempts at central organization, but was more cautious and moderate in his criticisms of this particular attempt. He pointed out that 'Hitherto all attempts at national organization whether in America or England have met little or no success, generally leading to a more complete disorganization, by bringing out more conspicuously the wide and fundamental differences on important subjects which divide spiritualists and which vitally affect their conceptions of the spirit and objects that should be aimed at in any movement for its more general diffusion'. He went on to point out that, 'The new association hopes to escape the difficulty by avoiding theological discussion, disallowing collective responsibility for religious opinion or belief, but leaving its members and speakers free to express and advocate any views on the subject they may individually entertain'.

The dispute between the supporters of Howitt and the members of the National Association was not only based on the question of organization but also on what Howitt and Enmore Jones, writing in *The Medium* and *The Christian Spiritualist*, interpreted as an attack on the Christian elements in Spiritualism. In 1874, the National Association published a 'Declaration of Principles and Purposes', which included the statement, 'The Association, while cordially sympathizing with the teachings of Jesus Christ, will hold itself entirely aloof from all dogmatism or finalities, whether religious or philosophical, and will content itself with the establishment and elucidation of well attested facts, as the only basis on which any true religion or philosophy can be built up'. This statement angered Christian elements by dissociating the Association from Christian dogma, and in an effort to placate Christian opinion and to unite all Spiritualists the Association dropped the 'Declaration' from its constitution.

In the Spring of 1874 the British National Association of Spiritualists, to give it the full title, began holding social meetings for members, and public meetings and demonstrations in London. The annual conference was also convened in London in August that year, by that time the association had 190 ordinary members, fourteen vice-presidents and forty-nine members of the Council. The membership was composed of individuals and during the first year only one local society, The Liverpool Psychological Society, had become affiliated to the Association. The work of the Association was hampered by the lack of financial resources.

Two other local associations (The Dalston and the St John's) both in London, discussed affiliation at this time, but decided against it, largely because the majority of the members of both these associations feared that their organizations would be submerged in the National Association. Both these groups were flourishing, and their members could not see that any advantage could be gained from affiliation. The very term affiliation came in for some criticism, and was felt to be a barrier to closer relations between groups and the national body. A number of local societies felt that by affiliating to the National Association they would create the impression that they were subject to that body. In consequence of these criticisms, the National Association dropped the term affiliation and suggested that instead local societies should become allied with the national body. In spite of this change, only one local society was persuaded to become 'allied' during the following year. This was the Brixton Psychological Society, which was formed early in 1875, and became allied to the National Association in August of the same year.

The defence of Spiritualists was one of the aims of the Association, and in 1875 a contribution was made to the Defence Fund of the Newcastle Society, which was involved in a law action for assault against certain of its members. Some financial aid was also given to the Marylebone Society, and to a Mr Cogman, who was doing pioneering work in the East End of London, but the amount of such aid was very small because of the limited funds available.

During 1875 the Association also acquired a house in Great Russell Street as its headquarters; it contained a library and reading room, and accommodation for a resident secretary to take charge of the premises, where seances and meetings were also held. By the time the annual conference was held in May 1875 the membership had risen to 403, and societies at Brixton, Dalston, Cardiff, Brussels and Budapest had become allied to the Association. Mention of the last two places indicate that the Association had made contact with continental Spiritualists, and in June of the same year a Spanish society become allied. Later a South American society also became allied to the Association. In 1876 occurred the first of a series of controversies that led to serious dissensions between the members of the Association, which later resulted in the organization tearing itself apart. The fears of the anti-organizers were realized; the leadership of the Association rapidly developed into an oligarchy. A small group attempted to gain control of the Association by the rigging of proxy votes at a Council meeting. News of the move however leaked out and the attempt was defeated. The attempt was exposed by W. H. Harrison in his journal *The Spiritualist*, and Harrison was attacked at the next Council meeting by Mr Rogers, one of the group concerned, who accused him of misrepresentation and publishing biased reports in that paper. A majority of the Council supported Rogers in insisting that Harrison should be asked to publish reports of the meetings as drawn up by the Secretary and approved by the Correspondence Committee. At a succeeding meeting the Council went further in an attempt to prevent what they called misrepresentation, by agreeing that in future a report of the proceedings of the Council should be printed upon the agenda and circulated to members of the Association. In order to prevent any rigging of meetings, they also decided to abolish the proxy system of voting, and decided that every member should give in his own vote at elections of members of the Council.

A wave of prosecutions of mediums distracted the attention of the movement from the problems of organization in the autumn of 1876 and during 1877, and all Spiritualists united to defend the mediums.

The controversy was revived by a proposal made at a Council meeting in December 1877 to appoint a member to help the Secretary in drawing up the minutes. Harrison saw in this proposal an attempt on the part of the authoritarians on the Council to extend their control over the Secretary, who was a paid official. He also revived the controversy over the powers of the Correspondence Committee, which vetted all correspondence addressed to the Council. He objected to the way in which the powers of the Council were being delegated to committees which could be more easily controlled by a small clique than could the whole Council. In particular he objected to the establishment of a new committee to plan the work of the Council for the coming year; this he thought should be undertaken by the whole Council. He objected to the fact that much of the work was conducted in secret by committees, and argued also that the voting record of members of the Council should be published, since in any democratically run organization members have the right to know how their representatives have voted.

Harrison followed up these criticisms in the next issue of his paper, where he criticized the fact that the Association had delegated to individuals the power of printing matter in the name of the Association which had not been directly sanctioned by the Council. An example of this had appeared in the latest agenda, where approval had been expressed of some mediums who had not been tested by the Association. He pointed out the danger to the reputation of the Association if any of these mediums should subsequently be proved to be frauds.

These criticisms very soon bore fruit. In February 1878 the Council abolished completely the Correspondence Committee and replaced the Progress Committee with a General Purposes Committee. Harrison however was not satisfied, and continued to criticize the Association by attacking the new form in which it had decided to publish its monthly agenda. This was now to be entitled 'Proceedings of the National Association and Allied Societies, containing also various information For Spiritualists and Inquirers'. Harrison argued that the last part of the title made possible the publication of matter not approved by the Council. The Council, however, supported the action of its committee in choosing that title. Harrison, who was a member of the Council, continued to press for more democratic procedures. He proposed at the September 1878 meeting of the Council that the voting of members in committee should be recorded in the minutes, which should be open to inspection by members of the Association. His proposals were rejected, and the Council on the contrary passed resolutions which declared that the proceedings of committees should be only open to inspection by persons who were not members of the Council if they had obtained the express permission of the Council. They also resolved 'That it be considered a breach of privilege for a member to make public comment on the proceedings of its committees and on the action of individual members on those, except as they are brought before the Council by their own reports or otherwise'.

This appeared to be an attempt to muzzle Harrison, who continued to press for the repeal of these resolutions and for the acceptance of his proposals. He became increasingly disillusioned about the possibility of introducing democratic reforms, and in an address directed to those members who had elected him to the Council said, 'I am tired of standing up for the public rights all alone, with not a single supporter or sympathizer present'. In February 1879 Harrison resigned from the Council; at the same time two vice-presidents, Mr C. C. Massey and Mrs Makdougal Gregory, resigned their positions, and two ordinary members of the Association also resigned. Another well known Spiritualist, N. F. Dawe, had already resigned from the Association and Harrison's resignation was followed a month later by the resignation of another vice-president, C. Blackburn, three Council members, and three more ordinary members. Miss Kislingsbury, the permanent secretary, also resigned.

The National Association was clearly now beginning to break up. The Annual General Meeting in May 1879 was only attended by thirty-three members and shortly after this Dr Blake was expelled, with the result that several other members of the Council resigned. An attempt was made to save the Association by a group of members, who presented a petition to the Council requesting changes in the Constitution. They requested that a ballot of members be taken to decide whether a change in the Constitution was desired by a majority of members, and suggested that the Council should be reformed by reducing its numbers from the 'present seventy' to a maximum of twenty, who should all be elected at a general election by members. The large size of the Council meant that there were often more vacancies than candidates, so that members of the Council could usually retain their seats and so in effect become 'life directors', and they could also get their friends made members of the Council. In this way the control of the Association had fallen into the hands of a small group of persons, most of whom were unknown to Spiritualists in general. Many well known Spiritualists left the association because of the dictatorial behaviour of this ruling clique. In view of these circumstances it is not surprising that the Council refused to have anything to do with the petition presented to it, and thus passed the last chance of saving the Association.

The breach with Harrison ended the close connection that had existed between *The Spiritualist* and the National Association since the foundation of that body. The Association transferred its advertising to the journal *Spiritual Notes*, which also published the Proceedings of the Association.

The National Association continued to decline. It had in fact never been a representative national organization, and its claims to be such an organization were increasingly resented by provincial associations particularly as its prestige waned. Its work had from the first been concentrated in London, and it was thus in fact only one of the more important London societies. The members of the Association were gradually forced to admit the truth of this situation, and in 1882 they decided to re-constitute the Association under a new Constitution with the name of the Central Association of Spiritualists. The Central Association took over the premises and membership of the National Association. (the membership at that time was 294), but in fact little had changed except the name. This seems however to have attracted the attention of some provincial Spiritualists, for during the following year four more societies became allied to the Central Association, making a total of twenty societies in alliance. There was in fact little association between these 'allied societies' and the Central Association. The affairs of the Association continued to decline in London, and in October 1883 a special conference decided to 'Liquidate the affairs of the society', and set up a committee to consider a scheme for the formation of a new society which had been proposed by Stainton Moses. The committee announced the formation of a new society in the following March to be known as the London Spiritualist Alliance. The new society made no pretence of being a national organization. As Stainton Moses announced, the Alliance was based on the principle: 'In essentials unity; in non essentials liberty; in all things charity.'

Chapter Seven

THE GROWTH OF ORGANIZATION

The Mission Field

The most important developments in organization within Spiritualism in the eighteen seventies and eighties had their origin in the provinces and took the form of the growth of district organizations. The first district association was established in 1875. This was the Lancashire Association for the Promotion of Spiritualism in New Districts. It was composed of individuals from some sixteen or eighteen places in that county, and was set up with the aim of promoting meetings and distributing literature in places where Spiritualism was weak or did not exist. This first attempt at deliberate missionary activity soon produced results; by the end of the year activities had been started in eight new places in the district. By February 1877 it was possible for a letter to appear in *The Spiritualist* reporting that 'There is scarcely a town or village in the district which the Lancashire Committee has not already visited and sown the first seed'.

This work was carried out by a body with a very loose organizational structure. The Lancashire District Spiritualist Committee, as it was soon known, consisted of an executive of six members, two secretaries, a treasurer and a general body of about forty district representatives, who all resigned quarterly and had to be elected at quarterly conferences of representatives from societies scattered through north, east and mid Lancashire, north Cheshire and north Derbyshire. The executive, which was elected by these representatives, met at least once a month to arrange public meetings, to appoint representatives to organize these meetings at the local level and to provide speakers for such meetings. The Committee had no constitution or formal rules.

The success of this Committee led to attempts to copy its methods in other districts. In the Spring of 1876 a conference at Halifax established a Yorkshire District Committee, but this organization was a dismal failure. In the following June, a conference called by the Newcastle Society of Spiritualists set up 'The North of England Spiritualists Central Committee', the council of which consisted of representatives from societies in seventeen towns and villages in Northumberland and County Durham. This committee was also unsuccessful. We may largely agree with a contemporary observer who suggested that these district committees failed, 'Simply because the existing local societies were sufficient for the work'. Members of local societies seemed to feel that their first duty was to their own groups, and gave little support to a committee whose aims were the extension of the movement, but which would provide no benefits to existing groups. The same writer argued that 'There is a normal ratio of extension that can never be successfully accelerated for any length of time', and it would certainly be true to say that with given limited resources the rate of expansion would also be limited. He also pointed to the other major restraining influence, the fear of organization, which he rightly argued had led to weak forms of organization even in local organizations. 'Where societies have failed,' he said, 'it has been because the rules were subordinated to personal egotism.' Though to impute egotism to those who seem to have been concerned solely with the preservation of liberty and spontaneity of religious expression is rather unfair.

In October 1878, a Midland District Committee was established at a Conference held at Derby of representatives from Sheffield, Leicester, Walsall, Belper, Derby, Nottingham and Birmingham. This committee seems to have had only temporary success. The Lancashire Committee continued to do pioneering work for some years, but it underwent another change of name, becoming the Lancashire Association of Spiritualists. By May 1878 this association was large enough to support the publication of its own monthly paper, *The Spiritual Reporter*. It was estimated that there were some 2,580 Spiritualists in the Lancashire district in 1878, and that of these, 560 belonged to societies working in association with the Lancashire Association. Their work continued to take the form of organizing meetings throughout the district. The extent of their work can be seen from the report of work given to the conference in November 1878, when it was stated that during the previous quarter 102 meetings had been held, attended by an estimated total of 9,000 persons.

The Lancashire Committee made an attempt to create a new national organization. In October 1880 they sponsored a General Conference of Spiritualists, which was held at Manchester with the aim of discussing means of organization and co-operation between Spiritualists. It was not a great success, since it was attended by only thirty-five representatives, and these were mainly from Lancashire and Yorkshire, though representatives were also present from London and Newcastle. The conference agreed that the National Association was unrepresentative and restricted largely to London, though some representatives felt that it could still be revived as a truly national body if more provincial societies would affiliate to it and thus exert their influence in its policy. The conference urged all societies to form themselves into district committees. The Conference however appears to have had little influence on the future development of the movement.

In July 1879 a conference held at Sowerby Bridge revived the Yorkshire District Committee. This was the only one of these early organizations to have an extended existence.

District Organization

The early district committees of the eighteen seventies were largely concerned with missionary efforts to extend the work of the movement into new areas. In the late eighteen eighties a new form of district organization arose, based on the aim of promoting the common interests and furthering the expansion and work of existing societies, though the missionary ideal was not completely abandoned.

The development was stimulated by a competition organized by the magazine *Two Worlds* in 1888. This magazine offered a prize for an essay on 'The Best Means of Advancing Spiritualism in Great Britain'. The prize was awarded to Phillip Seymour of Nottingham, who advocated the establishment of district organizations. Seymour urged spiritualists to

Unite into an organization, and so render yourselves a powerful influence. Let those scattered and isolated societies now existing in different parts of England be invited to send representatives to a spiritual conference to be held in some central town. The object of the Conference to be to determine upon what basis these various societies will be able to unite and constitute themselves an organized brotherhood. Those societies seeing their way clear to such an amalgamation should map out the country into districts, . . . each consisting of so many local branches. . . . The societies' work should be mapped out in detail at least a month in advance, and each member possess either a written or printed list of it.

The editress, Mrs Hardinge Britten, supported Seymour's ideas and added her own suggestion that a national conference should be held in London. This however did not lead to action until two years later. In the meanwhile great interest was stimulated in the possibility and the potential advantages of district organizations. The first positive move was taken in Newcastle, where a conference of local societies met on the 31st July 1888 and agreed to the establishment of the 'North-Eastern Federation of Spiritualists', to the quarterly conferences of which each local society was to be entitled to send one representative for each twenty-five (or part of twenty-five) members. These representatives elected an Executive Committee which held office for one year only.

At about the same time steps were being taken towards the establishment of closer relations between societies both in Lancashire and London. The old Lancashire Committee had ceased to exist and early in August 1888 a number of Lancashire Spiritualists met and decided to call a conference to promote a national confederation and 'to consider on what basis a permanent Lancashire District can be formed'. The conference met at Manchester on the 19th August and agreed to the establishment of a 'Lancashire and District Confederation of Spiritualists'. The aims of this body were largely of a missionary nature, though it also set out to 'aid affiliated societies'. Its membership was to consist not only of representatives of societies but also of individuals, and a central committee was elected annually by the representatives.

In October of the same year, representatives from many London societies met at Copenhagen Hall and set up a council to draw up plans for a London federation. A few weeks later the inaugural meeting was held at Goswell Hall, when it was decided to form 'The London Spiritualist Confederation'. All of these federations were short lived.

The Yorkshire District Committee, which had existed in some form from 1876, was stimulated by the growing interest in district organization, and increased in strength and influence. In 1893 it re-organized itself under the new title of 'The Yorkshire Union of Spiritualists and Spiritualist Societies'. Its work consisted of organizing the supply of speakers for its member societies, conducting propaganda meetings and distributing information about Spiritualism. It grew steadily from thirty affiliated societies in 1896 to thirty-five in 1898 and forty-two in 1902.

In 1906, the Union decided that in view of the large area of the county, a number of District Councils should be set up to carry out the work of the Union in their own areas; in the autumn of that year the first of these, the North West Yorkshire District Council, was set up. This was not a popular move and no more district councils were established. In the following year the Union reversed this policy of decentralization and the North-West District was merged with the parent body. Early in March 1915, J. Collins proposed that the Yorkshire Union should be wound up as its days of usefulness had ended. This proposal was rejected but a drastic re-organization of the Union was agreed. The new organization was known as The Yorkshire Spiritualist County Council. The county was divided into four districts, each with its own district committee. The existing and formerly independent Sheffield District Committee became one of these new district committees of the Council and new committees were set up in Leeds, Bradford and the Huddersfield and Halifax area. De-centralization had become necessary for several reasons. The growing number of affiliated societies had made it impossible for the movable conferences to be held with any frequency at any one given society, and had thus decreased the interest of societies in the work of the Council. The rising cost of living (particularly in war time) made it difficult for societies to afford to send delegates to meetings held in distant parts of the county. The Council had become too unwieldy to deal effectively with its units, and many societies were booking their speakers privately and not using the services of the union for this purpose. Decentralization went some way towards the solution of these problems; during the war years the Yorkshire Council continued to grow and by 1920 there were fifty-three affiliated societies. In that year a new district committee was set up for the east coast of the county.

The success of the Yorkshire Union in the 'nineties and the early years of the present century stimulated interest and led to the growth of many other County and District Unions and Committees whose aims were all similar to that of the Yorkshire Union. They were all mainly concerned with co-ordinating the activities of local societies, and with the provision of speakers and mediums for affiliated societies.

One of the first of these, the Manchester and District Union, was formed in 1894, though a year earlier the Sowerby Bridge, Halifax, West Vale, and Brighouse societies had formed a circle for mutual aid.

The North-Eastern Spiritual Federation was formed in 1896; this was followed two years later by the South Yorkshire District Council which was independent of the Yorkshire Union. In 1902 the Devonshire and District Union, and in 1905 the Midland Spiritualist Union and the South Wales Spiritualist Alliance, were born. The Northern Counties Union was formed in 1906, and the Spiritualist Council of Wales in 1908. In London, an attempt was made in May 1895 to set up a London District Council to replace the London Spiritualist Federation which had become defunct. Four months later two societies were removed from the list of affiliated societies on the grounds that they were not societies but only meetings. Dissensions broke out in the Council, and the organization soon ceased to exist. Early in 1900, a conference held at Manor Park agreed to the establishment of the Union of London Spiritualists.

By 1912 there were fifteen Unions and District Councils in existence;[1] some of these were affiliated to the National Union, while others remained independent. Most of these bodies worked together amicably, and during the early years of the present century their representatives met on several occasions for conferences. The first of these was held in Macclesfield in 1904 and was attended by representatives of the National Union, the North East Lancashire District Committee, the Lancashire Mediums'

[1] The North Midlands District Union; the Manchester and District Union; the Northern Counties Union; the Scottish Spiritualist Alliance; Lodham and District Union; the Yorkshire Union; the South West Lancashire and Cheshire Union; the Midlands District Union; the Sheffield District Union; the North Lancs. Westmorland and West Cumberland District Council; the North East Lancashire Union; the Potteries and District Union; the Union of London Spiritualists; the Southern Counties Union and the South Yorkshire District Council.

Union, the Sheffield District Committee and the Yorkshire Union. This was followed by a series of conferences held to consider ways in which the regional unions could work together to co-ordinate their activities and to minimize any conflict that might arise between them.

The Development of Ideas of Organization

At a conference of Spiritualists held in Manchester in 1904, which had been called to consider the 'centralization of effort' in that city, it was suggested that the Spiritualist movement should adopt the system of organizing speakers used by the Methodist Churches and generally known as the Methodist plan. A similar suggestion had already been made by a writer in *Two Worlds* five years earlier, and indeed a similar idea was behind the creation of many of the District Unions.

The Methodist plan had been evolved as an answer to two problems faced by the Methodist churches; these were the shortage of full time ministers, and the problem of giving laymen the opportunity to take pastoral responsibilities in the church. The Methodists developed the circuit system of organization under which one full time minister would be in charge of a group of churches. He would undertake a full programme of preaching and other ministerial duties but would clearly not be able to conduct all the services at the many churches under his care. These services would be conducted by laymen, known within the Methodist Church as 'local preachers'. The activities of these local preachers were controlled and planned by the circuit committee, who arranged the Sunday programme for preachers and churches within the circuit. This programme was known as the plan.

Few Spiritualists would go so far as to advocate that their churches and societies should follow the Methodists completely in adopting the circuit system with a minister in charge of a group of churches or societies, for they believed that the local society should have far more freedom than was allowed to a Methodist society within the circuit system. The Methodist Society had little say in the choice of speakers allocated to it, whereas the Spiritualists desired to allow as much freedom of choice as possible to the local society. They, however, admitted that the Methodist plan was an effective form of organization and ensured that local societies were supplied with approved and efficient speakers, and many Spiritualists felt that the adoption of some sort of 'plan' would be advantageous to the movement.

The isolated local societies found it difficult to find a regular supply of platform workers, and indeed the early district and county organizations had as one of their aims the supply of speakers and mediums to member societies. Another solution to this problem had been adopted by some of the more prosperous societies in the eighteen nineties. This took the form of the appointment of a permanent speaker who in effect filled the position occupied by the minister in a conventional Christian church. A good many Spiritualists opposed the appointment of a permanent speaker on the grounds that it introduced priestcraft into the Spiritualist movement, which had always been strongly opposed to the existence and development of priestly hierarchical authority. They also argued that this type of leadership would restrict the growth of mediumship amongst the members of the society, since the mediumistic work would be monopolized by the permanent speaker and there would be fewer opportunities for the development of mediumistic gifts by the lay members. Writing on this question in 1899, James Tetlow had suggested that the lack of permanent leadership was one of the causes of the fluctuating membership that was a common feature of Spiritualist societies. People would be attracted to investigate Spiritualism for various reasons and would attend meetings and even join societies, only to lapse from membership within a short period, their places being taken by new members. Tetlow suggested that this happened because no one was appointed to visit members and encourage them or to make them feel that they were wanted by the group. These are part of the duties of a minister or priest in a Christian church and the lack of such a permanent and full time official may indeed have retarded the growth of the movement. There is no doubt that a successful movement must get its members' egos involved, make them feel wanted by the group and ensure their loyalty by getting them fully involved in its activities.

It is perhaps strange that in these discussions of organization there is no mention of the Congregational churches, for these might have formed a pattern on which Spiritualists could have based their own organizations. These movements have much in common from the organizational point of view. In both there is a basic belief in democracy and in the independence of the local group. In both, the local group is central, and there is a fear of the danger of oligarchy, bureaucracy, and the growth of an authoritarian hierarchy that frequently, if not inevitably, follow the process of centralization.

Unconsciously the ideas of Congregational independence formed a part of the tradition of Spiritualism, and consequently the Methodist plan was only adopted with modifications. The District Unions and Committees that became the outstanding feature of the organization of the movement in the early eighteen nineties arose largely to fulfil the planning function of a Methodist circuit while leaving the maximum freedom to the local societies. Member societies would put in their request for speakers and these would be supplied by the District Union, with as much respect being paid to the preferences of the local societies as was possible. The Unions had no powers to interfere in the running of local societies.

The late eighteen nineties was a difficult period for the Spiritualist movement, and local societies also tried various methods of internal organization. These ranged from the extremely open organization to be found at Hammerton Street, Burnley and Bartlam Place, Oldham, where the whole society formed the committee and certain officials were appointed to undertake specific work, to the extremely closed society such as the Salford Society, where] the society was managed by a permanent managing committee and the officials were not elected by the members.

The more successful societies began to acquire many of the trappings of the more orthodox Christian churches, including Gothic style buildings with a Nave and Chancel. An example of this was St Paul's Spiritual Church, Bradford, which was opened in February 1899. Some societies developed choirs at this time, and an Annual Choir Contest was organized. In 1900 six choirs competed at Manchester and the choir from Sowerby Bridge was chosen to be the Spiritualist National Prize Choir for the year.

Mediums' Unions

As early as 1888 the formation of a mediums' benefit society had been proposed by Mr Hopcroft and Mr J. B. Tetlow. This proposal came to nothing, but twelve years later Mr Tetlow played a leading part in the formation of the first mediums' union. This development, like many other new ideas in Spiritualism, originated in Lancashire. It was in 1900 that the Lancashire Mediums' Union was formed, not, as some Spiritualists seemed to suspect, to bring pressure to bear on societies to raise fees paid to mediums, but rather as the 'Aims and Objects of the Union' stated:

To improve the standard of mediumship.
To seek the social, intellectual and spiritual benefit of each member, and
To create greater unity between all platform workers and societies.

The membership of the Union was open not only to professional mediums (of which there were few in Lancashire at that time), but to semi-professional and unpaid mediums, to public speakers and to all members of Spiritualist societies. By November 1900, three months after its formation, the Union had attracted sixty members, and become affiliated to the National Federation of Spiritualists. The Union had considerable success in the north of England, and in 1904 it led the protest against the policy of the new National Union to set up a Certificate system for mediums and other platform workers.

In 1906 the Sottish Mediums' Union was set up to undertake similar work in that country. It was formed by some fifteen to twenty prominent speakers and mediums in Glasgow. In addition to organizing themselves for platform work they decided to open their own mission and to conduct public services and meetings for healing in Glasgow. Later in the year it was reported that this Union was prospering; it had attracted members from other Scottish towns and had sent speakers to address meetings of societies 'all over the country'.

The Lancashire Union had begun to attract members from other areas of England, and in recognition of this fact it changed its name to 'The British Mediums' Union' in 1906. By the May of that year its membership had increased to 130.

The British Mediums' Union consistently worked to raise the standards of mediumship and to protect mediums. It opposed fortune-telling and would not support any mediums who resorted to fortune-telling under the guise of mediumship. It organized classes in a number of towns for developing mediums and for training speakers. It also opposed societies run dictatorially by a single individual, and described these derisively as 'one man shows'. In October 1912, the Union, after a long discussion at its Annual Conference, issued a notice to its members informing them that mediums who continued to serve at 'irregular meeting places' would 'no longer be accepted in membership of the Union'.

While it was true that some of these irregular meetings were disreputable and conducted for money, and were places where the cheaper forms of fortune-telling were practised, there were other such 'irregular meetings' that were quite respectable, and where good work for the Spiritualist cause was taking place. The organizer of one of the 'Meeting places', Mr J. Croasdale, of the Bennett Street Church at Stalybridge, argued that 'It will be a sad day for Spiritualism when our mediums have to go where (and there only) this Union says they must go'. He went on to say, 'It is perfectly true that we have no committee at Bennett Street and that our people will not have one, for, as they say there is harmony, equality, and brotherhood, and no bickering so common in what are known as properly constituted societies'.

Spiritualism and Social Reform

During the period from 1890 to 1914 a number of societies came into existence with specific aims either in the field of Spiritualist propaganda or for the furtherance of the aims of benevolence or social reform.

In America there had been a number of attempts to establish Spiritualist Communities. Nothing quite so extreme was attempted in Britain. The only project that in any way resembled the American communities was the Spiritual Provident Society, which was started by a Mr West in a house at 227 Stirland Road, Paddington, in 1896. The society was formed, 'for the purpose of providing its members with homes, clothing, food, medical aid, amusements, and such employment as will be conducive to a healthy long life after sixty years of age', and also, 'to provide rural holidays.' The organization was based on 'the co-operative principle', members were charged an entrance fee and paid a weekly subscription, and the society had plans to open 'stores' in other districts. This grandiose scheme aroused some interest in the Spiritualist press and was reported in March 1896 to have twenty-seven members and to be holding regular meetings for adults and for children. The scheme was far too ambitious to be successful, and the society must have soon disappeared, for no further mention of it is to be found in Spiritualist literature.

Such efforts at practical communism seem to have little success in Britain, but they reflect the long association that has existed between Spiritualism and Socialism. During the nineteenth century and the early years of the twentieth, many Spiritualists seem to have had progressive political and social ideas, and during this period the relationship between Socialism and Spiritualism was a frequent subject of discussion in Spiritualist journals.

One of the most popular reform movements of the 'nineties and early twentieth century was the Temperance movement, which had the aim of persuading individuals to renounce the consumption of alcoholic drinks. In Britain only a few extremists advocated the legal prohibition of the manufacture and sale of alcohol. Most Spiritualists were in sympathy with the aims of the Temperance movement, and no doubt many of them were individual members of various Temperance organizations. The Spiritualists had an additional reason for advocating and practising temperance besides the moral argument, for it is generally thought that the consumption of alcohol impairs the psychic faculties. In spite of this, the Spiritualist National Abstinence League formed in 1898 seems to have aroused little enthusiasm and to have had less success. Four years later *Two Worlds* announced the formation of the 'Spiritualists' League of Total Abstinence', to be conducted through the columns of that paper by William Stansfield. The League lacked all organization and aroused little interest, though the publicity it gave to abstinence may have persuaded some Spiritualists of the importance of this topic; but of course Stansfield was largely preaching to the converted since at that period most of the readers of the paper would already be 'temperate'.

Many Spiritualists are keenly interested in movements for the prevention of cruelty to animals, and some take this to the point of arguing that Spiritualists should become vegetarians and give up the use of animal products the manufacture of which involve killing or inflicting pain on animals.[2] Lady Dowding, for example, not only suggests that women should give up fur coats, but that they should also give up the use of cosmetics that are made from animal products.

The attiudes of Spiritualists toward animal welfare arose naturally from the belief that animals, like human beings, survive death, though the exact form in which they survive remains a matter for dispute.

Spiritualist opposition to capital punishment dates at least from 1894, and Spiritualists have consistently advocated that criminals should be reformed rather than punished.

Unusual Organizations

An unusual type of organization was the Spiritualist Women's Red Cross Federation. In 1899 the magazine *Two Worlds* started running a womans' column entitled 'Women's Mirror'. The columnist, who wrote under the pseudonym of Kathleen, suggested the formation of this Federation, which was to have the aims of 'banding together Spiritualist women, to visit sick and suffering Spiritualists and others; to encourage each other by periodically publishing reports of work done – and to assist the "National Benevolent Fund".' Those who were interested in such work were asked to send sixpence for a membership card and to write to the magazine about their activities. The Federation had no central (or for that matter local) organization, and there were no privileges of membership. It held no meetings and did not organize the activities of its members. For several months the paper published reports of the activities of members of the Federation in its women's column, and it is clear that at least temporarily it stimulated the charitable activities of a number of Spiritualist women; but clearly the influence of such a movement must have been limited. It was restricted to the readership of the paper, and though members received 'moral support' from 'Kathleen', they lacked the personal contact necessary to maintain and stimulate enthusiasm and loyalty.

Another unusual organization was the Spiritualist Corresponding Society, which was formed in 1891. It had the aims of

---

[2] The first mention I have found in Spiritualist literature is a letter on vivisection in *Light* in 1900.

'assisting inquirers', of assisting in the formation of private circles and of promoting public meetings, and also proposed to supply the press with information and to answer press criticisms of the movement. But its main aim was to provide a connecting link between individual Spiritualists in 'all parts of the world'. The Society at one time had representatives not only in Britain but also in New Zealand, Australia, America, Holland, South Africa, Argentine, Belgium, Brazil, France, Germany, India, Italy, Mexico, Norway, Russia, Spain, Sweden and Switzerland.

After a long debate in *Two Worlds* about the possibility of producing a badge that could be worn as a symbol of recognition by all Spiritualists, the editor announced in January 1894 that a design had been approved; the symbol consisted of a lozenge inscribed with the monogram O.P.S. These letters were said to stand for the 'Order of Progressive Spiritualists', and all who purchased the symbol were invited to enrol in the order. The only positive action taken by the Order was to establish a Sick and Benefit Fund, 'to assist the suffering, the needy and the aged', amongst the Spiritualist movement. The Order was hampered in this benevolent work by the lack of funds. During the year 1895–96 the Sick and Benefit Fund collected only £18 and the Pension Fund £27. By 1899, when these funds were taken over by the Spiritualist National Union Fund for Benevolence, it was seen that these funds had only disbursed about £76 during that financial year. Spiritualists seem to have been reluctant to contribute to their own National benevolent funds, though it is true that many local societies had their own funds to which local members probably preferred to contribute.

Founding the National Union

Proposals for a new national organization appeared in the paper *Two Worlds* in March 1890, and the editor, Mrs Hardinge-Britten, asked those who favoured this idea to write to her. As a result, a meeting of spiritualists was held in Manchester early in April to discuss the question, and a Provisional Committee was set up to organize a National Conference.

The conference met in Manchester on the 6th July, 1890. Delegates came from the north, with the exception of the delegate of the London Federation, though there were also a number of private persons present from London. The conference agreed that it would be useful to hold an annual movable Conference of spiritualists.

The question of a national organization was discussed and the conference agreed 'That considering the number and importance of Spiritualist societies now existing, their federal unity is desirable and expedient, but that such unity shall in no case involve a sacrifice of *local self government or freedom of action*'.

It was agreed that a further conference should be held in a year's time at Bradford and that the existing committee should be re-appointed to carry out the arrangements for that conference. Little further action was taken until the following year, when the Executive Committee prepared a constitution for a National Federation. At the so-called Second Annual Conference at Bradford on the 4th July 1891, this constitution was discussed and accepted, and the Spiritualists National Federation became formally established. Forty-two societies at once affiliated with the federation.

The Federation grew slowly at first and was largely restricted to the north. In 1892 of the forty-five affiliated societies all but four were in the north. During the year 1892–93 the number of affiliated societies dropped to thirty-four. It rose again to forty-four in the following year and to forty-five in 1895; by 1896 there were fifty-eight affiliated societies. At the same time the number of individual associates rose from fifty-two in 1892 to 146 in 1896.

The work of the Federation was restricted to holding propaganda meetings and arranging speakers for societies. The annual conferences held at various towns in the north were great occasions for the Spiritualists and provided opportunities for discussion of common problems and for Spiritualists to get together for social activities. The Burnley Conference, for instance, was preceded by a procession through the streets led by garlanded children from the Lyceums, who marched with banners flying to the music of a Temperance Band.

Spiritualist societies were at that time handicapped by the fact that as societies they had no legal right to own property. In 1896 the Annual Conference meeting at Liverpool appointed a committee to consider this situation and to prepare a deed which would define a Spiritualist society and secure a legal status for such societies. In 1897 this Deed Poll was submitted to the conference at Blackburn but after some controversy it was referred back to the Executive Committee.

Spiritualism could not acquire legal rights without a declaration of principles, and this was difficult to draw up, since beliefs varied widely within the movement, and many Spiritualists would refuse to subscribe to any such declaration.

In the second place it was held that to be eligible for legal recognition any organization must have a body of 'permanent members' who would govern the movement. Many Spiritualists objected to this system of organization as being contrary to the ideas of the National Federation, and restrictive of the freedom of affiliated societies.

However, it was clearly necessary for the movement to obtain some legal recognition in order that it might protect the property of the churches, which was at the mercy of the individuals who formed the committees.

At the conference at Keighley in July 1898, the president reported that a new draft Deed Poll had been prepared and circulated to the societies. The conference discussed the Deed Poll, but decided to continue the discussion at a special conference to be held at Southport in October. This special conference declared that the Deed Poll as amended be accepted, and that the Executive be instructed to proceed to make it legal as soon as possible. Fate, however, intervened and, for reasons that did not become clear for two years, the question was allowed to lapse until 1900.

At the 1900 Annual General Meeting the President reported that 'he had called upon a solicitor . . . and had given definite instructions for the preparing of that draft' of the Deed Poll, but that when he went over the draft he had found that his instructions had not been followed. There was thus no point in discussing the incomplete draft, and the Conference agreed to refer the matter to a special meeting of the Executive Committee. Mr E. W. Wallis asked what had happened to the original Deed Poll which had been approved at the Southport Conference. It was disclosed that after many difficulties had arisen, including the fact that no one knew where to send the Deed for registration, it had eventually become lost in the post while in transit between two of the signatories.

The Deed Poll took a long time to prepare, and when it was published in January 1901 it appeared in the words of the editor of *Two Worlds*, that 'it is not a Deed Poll; it is the memorandum of association, articles of association, and bye-laws of a company to be registered by the Registrar of Joint Stock Companies'. The reason given for the adoption of this method was described in the explanatory addendum as being 'in order to comply with the law as to holding of property, and to save the great expense of a Royal Charter'. The publication of these proposals aroused considerable controversy until 23rd–24th February, when the Interim Conference was held in Blackpool. This conference agreed to the Memorandum and Articles of Association with some amendments and with the addition of a Declaration of Principles that gave a definition of the basic belief of Spiritualism. This declaration stated that belief was accepted in 'The Fatherhood of God, the Brotherhood of Man, the continuous existence of the human soul, personal responsibility, compensation and retribution hereafter for all the good or evil done on earth, and eternal progress open to every human soul'. These have remained the basic principles of the organization ever since. In this way the National Union was conceived.

The annual conference held at Sheffield the following July passed a resolution '. . . that the Federation be incorporated under the Joint Stock Companies' Act with liability limited under guarantee under the style of "The Spiritualists' National Union Limited",' in spite of a last minute attempt of some members led by J. C. Kenworthy to oppose the necessity for legal status as contrary to the principles of spiritualism. (Kenworthy argued that 'the only law that could help the movement was the law of love'.)

The thirteenth and last conference of the N.F.S. which met at Bootle in July 1902 agreed to the bye-laws of the new Union, and upon the adjournment of the Federation meeting the seventy-nine persons who had already enrolled as members held the first General Meeting of the S.N.U. The new Union was not greeted with any great enthusiasm; many feared that its establishment would lead to the end of freedom for the societies and others could not understand the advantages to be gained by legal recognition. Some argued that such an organization would destroy the democratic nature of the movement.

The National Union was soon the centre of a new controversy. The Union devised a scheme for the examination and certification of exponents and demonstrators. The scheme aimed at raising the standard of public speakers and mediums and of ensuring that only qualified persons received the approval of the National Union. This was clearly a move towards the control and routinisation of charisma, and met with opposition from within the movement, though it gradually became accepted.

An Exponents Committee was set up and it devised a set of rules governing the issue of certificates, and invited exponents and demonstrators to apply for certification.

This move, and in particular some of the rules, aroused controversy amongst Spiritualists, and at a meeting held on 9th March, 1904, the Lancashire Mediums' Union passed the following resolution: 'We, the Lancashire Mediums' Union, here assembled, desire to express our opinion that it is not desirable at present to make application for certificates as advertised in the *Two Worlds*'.

The editor of *Two Worlds* commented adversely on the advertisement, but as J. B. Tetlow of the Mediums' Union pointed out, the National Union did not employ speakers; they were employed by the local societies, who therefore had a right to judge what they required for themselves. He also pointed out that the National Union had no 'educational standing' and was not concerned with the training of workers. Therefore, he argued, 'it is putting forward an assumption of power that does not belong to it in anyway whatever, and should be treated with indifference'.

In April the Accrington and Burnley churches in their advertisements stated that they were 'prepared to receive application for engagements for 1905 from Speakers and Mediums *who have made application for the Certificate of the National Union*'. This aroused further protests that these societies were 'boycotting speakers who are not certificate holders'. The North East Lancashire Union supported the National Union on this question, and at their quarterly meeting on 9th April, passed resolutions that the Union representatives at the National Union Conference ask for the names of exponents on the Executive who have *not* applied for their certificates and oppose their re-election; also to urge all societies in the North East Lancashire Union district to engage only speakers who have applied for their certificates.

This action was also attacked in a letter to *Two Worlds* on the ground that it infringed the freedom and toleration for which the Spiritualist movement had always fought.

In a vigorous 'leader' the editor of *Two Worlds* replied to these critics and pointed out that the National Union had no desire to coerce speakers or societies, and that both speaker and societies were free to please themselves in this matter. The violence of this controversy gradually died down, and the principle of examination of platform workers became accepted as part of the work of the national body, though the Conference of the National Union did not approve the issue of diplomas to exponents until 1915.

The Union next set to work preparing a scheme whereby churches could place their property in the hands of trustees appointed or approved by the Union, in such a way that the title of the property should be secured to the Spiritualist church.

Model trust deeds were first presented to the A.G.M. of the National Union in 1905 when they were referred back to the National Council for further consideration. The final scheme was approved in 1907, but the Model Trust Deeds were not published until 1910.

In 1909 the National Union set up a General Building Fund. Under this scheme societies were invited to deposit funds with the S.N.U. so that loans from these accumulated funds could be made to member societies planning to build their own churches. The scheme was not an immediate success, for in 1911 the Trust Property Committee reported that they had received enquiries about advances but no deposits.

The National Union made considerable progress. By 1910 it had 120 affiliated societies and twelve district unions or committees, and in 1911 two new area unions were created for the Midlands and Southern Counties, and the following year two more unions were established within the S.N.U. the North Lancashire, Westmorland and Cumberland Union and the Potteries District. In 1913 the number of societies in affiliation had risen to 141. There were of course still many completely independent societies and societies affiliated to local unions outside the S.N.U. The National Union produced its first Spiritualist Diary in 1910.

Chapter Eight

THE DEVELOPMENT OF RELIGIOUS INSTITUTIONS

The Conflict of Science and Religion

The existence of a basic conflict between religion and science has been asserted by many writers,[1] and this conflict is well summed up in the words of Zenryu Tsukamoto, a Japanese historian, who has recently described scientific rationalism as, 'a resistance movement to God or more precisely to the Christian church'.[2] The concept of a conflict between the attitudes of scientists and the belief systems of the Christian religion receives some support from recent studies of the religious beliefs of scientists.[3] It is also true that since the eighteenth century in the western world there has been much antagonism between men of science and men of religion. Of course not all men of science have come into conflict with religion and the fact that many leaders of the Scientific Revolution of the eighteenth century were Puritans has been used by some authors to support a suggestion that there was a direct connection between the rise of Protestantism and the origins of modern science. Other authors have countered that argument by pointing out that many scientists of that period were Catholics.

The scientific revolution certainly developed first within a Christian cultural system and it has sometimes been suggested that this was a consequence of a particularly Christian 'world-outlook' and that Christianity is essentially more 'this-worldly' oriented than most other religions. It is of course a gross over-simplification to define a religion as 'this-worldly' or 'other-

---

[1] A. D. White, *A History of the Warfare of Science with Theology in Christendom*, New York, 1955 (First Published 1895); J. M. Draper, *History of the Conflict between Religion and Science*, New York, 1896.

[2] Zenryu Tsukamoto, 'Japanese and Chinese Buddhism' in G. S. Metraux and F. Crouzer, *Religions and the Promise of the 20th Century*, New York, 1965.

[3] D. P. Rogers, 'Some Religious Beliefs of Scientists' in *Review of Religious Research*, Winter 1966, Vol. 7 No. 2.

worldly' as there are elements of both basic attitudes in all major religions. It is true that at a given time in history and in a given place one attitude dominates a particular religion, but the relative strength of these attitudes changes over time and one attitude displaces the other as dominant. In Christianity the 'other-worldly' attitude was dominant until the sixteenth century when it was displaced by a more 'this-worldly' approach.

The situation is complicated by the fact that these attitude patterns are not monolithic. The term 'this-worldly' conceals two possible reactions to this world, which we may describe as conservative and reformist reactions.

The 'this-worldly' conservative accepts the world as 'the best possible', both in its material and social aspects, because it is the creation of God or the reflection in materiality of the Absolute Reality. This approach is found in its most typical form in China both in the Confucian and Taoist traditions. Where an attitude of acceptance is dominant men live in 'this world' accepting its social patterns and are not concerned with the scientific study of the material order since this as the creation of God is sacrosanct. The 'this-worldly' reformist sees the material world as imperfect, but only because it is in the process of development towards an ideal state. For the reformist God has not yet completed His creation and man must co-operate in the work of constructing a perfect world. In a non-theistic religion the world may be seen as subject to the impersonal direction of the forces of evolution or development which can nevertheless be influenced by man. Such religions may include the secular religions of Humanism and Marxism. The reformist sees it as man's duty to investigate and study the material world in order to be more effective in it and to extend his control over it.[4]

The 'this-worldly' elements in Christianity were until the sixteenth century almost entirely of the conservative type; since that period the Reformist attitude has continued to increase in importance until by the middle of the twentieth century Christianity has been displaced by science, which has become institutionalized, and the dominant religion (in the sense of belief system) not only in the West but also in the Communist world.

[4] Islam is an interesting example of a religion which has always been predominantly This worldly and for most of its history Conservative This worldly but which during the Abbasid Caliphate had elements of This worldly reformism which appeared in the form of a great interest in scientific studies.

We are not here concerned with settling or discussing in detail the vexed question of the source of the scientific rationalism of the seventeenth and eighteenth centuries. We are however, concerned with the influence of this movement on the state of religious thought and practice in the middle of the nineteenth century and the consequent rise of modern Spiritualism.

Elizabeth Nottingham argues that there are basic differences between religion and science both in the ends they seek and in the means they use to pursue these ends.[5] Religion seeks non-empirical ends by non-empirical means whereas science pursues empirical ends by empirical means. Using these concepts it is possible to construct a series of what Nottingham describes as modes of adaptation. In addition to religion and science as alternative modes of adaptation she also describes magic, which she suggests seeks empirical means by non-empirical means.

She does not pursue the typology, but there is clearly another possible mode of adaptation, one in which non-empirical ends are pursued by the use of empirical methods. This type appears to fit the description of Spiritualism when the movement has not become a religion.

	Ends	Means
Religion	Non-empirical	Non-empirical
Magic	Empirical	Non-empirical
Spiritualism	Non-empirical	Empirical
Science	Empirical	Empirical

Sir James Frazer was among those who noted a relationship between magic and science, though he argued that they were similar both in ends and means, in so far as intentional rather than actual ends and means are concerned. Both magic and science were aimed at producing material results and the magician as well as the scientist believed that he was using empirical means. Magic was thus a primitive and mistaken form of science, for in fact magic is an attempt to use religious means for the attainment of worldly ends. Spiritualism on the other hand appears to be the use

[5] E. K. Nottingham, *Religion and Society*, pp. 34–37, New York, 1954.

132

of scientific methods in the study of certain types of religious experience.

Religion and science in their pure forms as defined by Nottingham are not incompatible, neither need they come into any conflict with each other, for while science is concerned with the empirical investigation of the material world religion is concerned with contact with and experience of a non-empirical spiritual order. Since their ends and means are completely different there is thus no overlap or basis of conflict except that they compete for the time and attention of men. In this context it may be seen that Marx's objection to religion was based on his view that it diverted men's attention from the material world.

If this is the case why has there been so much conflict, particularly in the nineteenth century between religion and science? The conflict has arisen because it has never been possible to keep either religion or science within the boundaries we have described. Both these 'modes of adaptation' become autonomous social institutions that claim validity and assert their authority over a wider sphere than that to which we have attempted to restrict them in our definition. Institutionalized religion has empirical as well as non-empirical ends; it is diluted by magic in so far as it is concerned with the attainment of material ends through an appeal to the supernatural world. This is illustrated by such activities as prayers for victory in war time, for rain in a drought or for any other form of material success. Religious groups not only develop worldly ends for the community as a whole but also for the group itself and seek to perpetuate and promote their own religious institutions and material welfare. They may also adopt worldly means of doing this; religious leaders may assume temporal authority, they may arm their followers and use secular methods of propaganda to spread their ideas. At the height of their power, religious organizations may attempt to monopolize both the ends and means of science as well as those of religion. Scientists may be restricted by the requirement to make their work conform to the theological concepts of the universe. Up to the eighteenth century there had always been a close relationship between science and religion, and it is only in the last two hundred years that it has been possible to draw clear distinctions between them.

Science as a process of consciously directed experimental investigation of the material world seldom appeared as a factor in human society before the sixteenth century. It is true that man had made many technological advances before that period, but these appear to have been the result of serendipity rather than of experimental method. The scientists of the ancient world were more interested in philosophical speculation about the nature of the physical world than in making empirical studies of it, and both in Ancient India and Greece the most important developments for the future of science were in the field of mathematics which is an important tool of scientific method.[6]

The numerous and diverse strands of development of western European thought culminated in an increased interest in the empirical study of the physical creation. At first this cast no doubts on religion as such but only on some dogmatic statements of religious bodies about the nature of the physical world. In fact the rise of science led to the eighteenth century belief that a natural religion could be based on reason and proved by science. It was out of such a belief that Spiritualism arose.

Spiritualism and Mysticism

G. B. Vetter[7] argues that, 'In competition with the scientific point of view and methodology, there is little for religion to do but frankly retreat into mysticism'. In spite of the retreat forced upon them by the advance of secularism the churches have shown great reluctance to seek refuge in what is one of the major sources of religious inspiration.[8] There is however an alternative; an attempt may be made to demonstrate the truth of such religious claims as are amenable to proof. This alternative has also been neglected by the churches and has been the role of Spiritualism, which claims to demonstrate the survival of human personality beyond death and to establish scientifically the validity of the subjective experiences of the medium by showing that those experiences give access to information which can be checked and give rise to powers of performing acts and producing phenomena which most religions would define as miraculous.

Let us consider further these claims of Spiritualism. It has been

[6] R. C. Majumdar, 'Scientific Spirit in Ancient India' and J. Filliozat 'India and Scientific Exchange in Antiquity' in G. S. Metraux and F. Crouzet, *The Evolution of Science*, pp. 77–105, New York, 1963.
[7] G. B. Vetter, *Magic and Religion*, p. 315, New York, 1958.
[8] F. C. Happold, *Religious Faith and Twentieth Century Man*, 1966.

remarked that Spiritualism is singularly unspiritual in that it is concerned to demonstrate its claims by scientific methods and has not produced a great body of spiritual literature. These criticisms are however only partly justified. The experience of the medium, like that of the mystic, is subjective. These experiences lie along a continuum, and the border between them is ill defined. At the extreme of mysticism, for example in Samadhi, the Hindu mystic is conscious only of an ineffable experience of unity with Ultimate Reality, but at lower levels of mystic consciousness the mystic may have visions of gods, angels or saints, hear voices or experience levitation. At the other extreme pole of this continuum the medium may be unconscious while spirit communications are transmitted through him, or be simply an agent for the production of physical phenomena. On the other hand many mediums have conscious experiences, they see visions, hear voices and have other forms of mystical or semi-mystical experience.

A distinction between mysticism and Spiritualism may be made largely in terms of the possibility of subjecting the experience to objective demonstration and scientific proof. It is impossible to offer objective proof of the validity of the experience of a mystic; there is no way of subjecting cosmic consciousness to scientific examination. On the other hand, spiritualists claim that it is possible to validate the experiences of the medium by scientific examination. This can be done in two ways; the messages transmitted through mediums from the spirits and the mediums' clairvoyant or psychometric perceptions can be checked against known facts. Secondly the production of physical phenomena, such as levitation, materialization, dematerialization, aports and healing, can be examined by various scientific techniques.

The Spiritualist movement in its religious aspect has also produced a vast literature of 'spiritual' as distinct from scientific interest. This consists very largely of messages of a devotional, philosophical or spiritual nature transmitted by the spirits through their mediums and either transcribed by a member of the mediums' circle or produced in the form of automatic writing by the mediums themselves. The teachings of Silver Birch, the 'Guide' of Hannen Swaffer's home circle, were transcribed and published and have had considerable influence, as have also the teachings transmitted through the mediumship of earlier workers such as Stainton Moses and Emma Hardinge Britten. The best known automatic writing medium at the present time is probably Geraldine Cummins, whose books on the life of Jesus and the early church have become very popular.

In the past twenty years Spiritualists have tended to emphasize the importance of the higher teaching or philosophy of the movement, and there has been a decrease in interest in the production of physical phenomena and in the scientific study of psychic events within the movement.

Science, Religion and Spiritualism

By the middle of the nineteenth century the rational ideas of the eighteenth century intellectuals had become widely diffused throughout the literate sections of the population in Britain, America and Europe. Science had become a widely accepted belief system, and men looked hopefully to scientific methods to solve all their problems.

It was argued that scientific methods could be used to examine the claims of religion. Certain claims such as those relating to the authorship of the Bible were subject to criticism on the basis of scientific examination. Statements made in the Bible were criticized because they did not fit in with the contemporary scientific theories. A notable example of this occurred later in the nineteenth century when the Darwinian Theory of Evolution was seen as casting doubts on the Biblical story of creation. The miracle stories of the Bible were held to be either inconsistent with scientific knowledge, or attempts were made to explain them as the result of purely physical and material causes.

Spiritualism arose from the need that was felt to apply scientific methods to the solution of some problems that had previously been thought to be the exclusive province of religion. The major problem here was clearly the question of whether the human soul or personality survived the death of the body. Christianity was divided on this question; some Protestants claimed that on the death of the body the soul passed directly to either Heaven or Hell; Roman Catholics held that there was also an intermediate state of the after life, the state of purgatory; while another strong Protestant element believed in conditional immortality, that the soul died with the body, and that only the souls of the saved would be resurrected with the body at the Final Judgment. None of these schools of thought were able to offer any proof that would satisfy the demands of the scientifically minded. Spiritualism claimed to offer proof of human survival that could be empirically tested. It therefore provided a 'half-way house' for those who could neither accept unsubstantiated religious doctrines on the nature of the after life or the claims of materialists that man was a purely material being. Those who accepted the Spiritualist interpretation of psychic phenomena might then proceed to build on this a philosophical or religious interpretation of human life and the nature of the universe.

Spiritualism then appears to be a science in so far as it claims to be able to test its main doctrine, human survival, by the methods of experimental science. In the early period Spiritualism was largely a science, but it gradually became a religion because many people began to accept the claims it made uncritically; but this alone could not make Spiritualism a religion for the theories of other sciences such as physics or astronomy are also often accepted on faith by laymen. An uncritical attitude on the part of laymen cannot transform a science into a religion, and indeed much of what scientists say today must be accepted on faith by laymen for modern science is so complex and technical that it would be impossible for the layman to test experimentally the theories of any scientist.

Spiritualism became a religion largely because there is a close connection in the human mind (at least in the west in the modern period) between the concept of personal survival in an after life and man's relationship with ultimate reality – with the non-empirical which is the basis of religion. The fact of survival, if this can be demonstrated experimentally, tells us nothing about the 'supernatural world' because survival must be a natural not a supernatural event if it can be subjected to empirical study. The fact that death and the after-life had been important topics for religious debate led to confusion of thought. Some people felt that proof of survival, a major claim of religion, gave support to other claims of religion, while the facts of spirit healing and of the physical phenomena of the seance room were said to substantiate the claims made by Christians for the truth of biblical and other miracles. The ideas about the natural and supernatural orders thus became confused and suggestions were made that the phenomena of Spiritualism proved the truth of the claims of religion. A further influence in the development of Spiritualism was that once survival had been proved to their satisfaction many Spiritualists became quite uncritical of the nature and content of the messages they received from the Spirits. These messages, for many non-Christian spiritualists, displaced the authority of the Bible, while for Christians they were thought to complement or supplement the Scriptures. A final influence was the fact that most persons who experimented with Spiritualism were Christian or had at least received a Christian education. Those who had rejected Christianity often had done so regretfully and still had religious feelings which they imported into their interpretation of the psychic phenomena they observed. As D. G. Charlton points out, the majority of persons who rejected Christianity in the nineteenth century did so for moral rather than scientific reasons.[9] Three main ethical objections were made to Christianity. The first was that some Christian doctrines were immoral, the second was that there was little evidence for the alleged goodness of God, and the third was that the practices (both political, social and moral) of the churches were as immoral as their doctrines. Spiritualism provided answers to these criticisms of religion while not defending the orthodox teachings or practices of the traditional Christian churches.

The main Christian doctrine that was criticized as being immoral was the teaching of eternal punishment for those who have not been saved and the allied doctrine of atonement, which argued that Christ had died as a substitute for sinners in order to appease the wrath of God. Such doctrines portray God as a merciless tyrant, and such a picture was totally abhorrent to the growing sensitivities of the nineteenth century which had been reared in the Romantic tradition. A God less loving and merciful than the best that man can conceive could not appeal to such idealists. Spiritualism rejected both of these objectionable doctrines. It taught that vicarious salvation was impossible, the individual was morally responsible for all his actions and must bear the consequences for all his actions and must bear the consequences of these in this world or the next. The evil would bring punishment upon themselves as a natural result of their deeds, there would be no final act of judgment, and there would certainly be no eternal punishment in Hell. Following the Universalists the Spiritualists

[9] D. G. Charlton, *Secular Religions in France 1815–1870*, pp. 19–22, 1963.

believed that no man could be so evil that he merited eternal punishment, and that when suffering had induced in him a change of heart then an eternity of spiritual progression lay before him.

On the other hand Spiritualists rejected the attack on religion by sceptics, who suggested that these doctrines were immoral because it would be clearly unjust to punish a man whose acts are determined by his circumstances. Such critics held that man could not be held responsible for his actions since he has no free will and is not a free agent. Spiritualists stoutly maintained the responsibility of man as a free agent. Spiritualists produced as evidence for their beliefs the teachings of the spirits and their descriptions of life in the next world. To the criticism that there is little evidence of the goodness of God, Spiritualists had many alternative answers. Christian spiritualists would argue that the goodness of God was to be seen in the structure of the universe as a whole which is a spiritual order through which man can progress towards the bliss of unity with the Highest in the Seventh Heaven. Non-Christian spiritualists were not so sure about the personal nature of God, but they felt that ultimate reality was in itself good. The material world might well be cruel and 'red in tooth and claw', but it was only part of the spiritual unity of the universe. Spiritualists were not concerned with the defence of the practices of the Christian churches; they frequently attacked these beliefs and practices and allied themselves with reformist social and political ideals, unlike the orthodox Christians, who tended to support the existing social order.

Science as a Religion

It would appear that science is not able to investigate certain areas of human experience. By this we mean that the scientific method cannot be applied profitably to those areas of human experience which may be classified as moral experience, aesthetic experience, supernatural experience and the experience of ultimate reality. The non-material is not amenable to scientific methods of investigation. The claims of science can only be seen as an attack on religion if one accepts that reality is entirely material, that mental and spiritual phenomena are epiphenominal, that they are merely projections of the material world. Some scientists have made this sort of claim and have said that consequently religion is concerned with and based upon illusions and hallucinations, and that science deals with the 'real' world in the only way in which it is rational to deal with it.

Science as it has become institutionalized has tended to make the same overriding claims as were previously made by religion, to be the 'Truth', and the only correct method of studying the universe. When science takes this step it changes from being an empirical study into a faith or 'religion', since it bases its claims to an exclusive understanding of the truth on a system of beliefs which are themselves not susceptible to empirical testing and are therefore of the same nature as 'religious beliefs'.

Science has become a faith for western man in the nineteenth and twentieth centuries, one of a series of secular religions which include Marxism, humanism and nationalism,[10] and in a similar way Spiritualism has ceased to be the scientific investigation of the psychic and has become a faith in the existence of spirits.

Early Secularism

Spiritualism arose as an attempt to use scientific methods (in a broad sense) to establish the existence of the supernatural. Convinced members of existing religious bodies did not need to have proof of the supernatural world on which to base their religion, since they accepted the existence of such a world by faith and on the authority of the founder and leaders of their religion.

Unquestioning faith of that sort had been challenged, particularly by the rationalism of the eighteenth century,[11] and by the rise of modern science. In consequence many people began to demand proof of any claims made. Authority and faith were no longer unquestionably accepted as the basis for belief. This must now be grounded in science and reason.

In Britain, as previously in America, many of the early converts to Spiritualism were secularists, sceptics and people who were dissatisfied with the churches and had begun to question or reject the orthodox teachings of the Christian religion. Observers were aware of these facts as early as 1862, when a perceptive writer in *The Westminster Review* drew attention to them in an article entitled

---

[10] H. M. Kallen, 'Secularism as the Common Religion of a Free Society', *Journal for the Scientific Study of Religion*, Vol. IV No. 2, April, 1965.

[11] J. M. Robertson, *The Dynamics of Religion (1897)*, 2nd Ed., 1926.

'The Religious Heresies of the Working Classes'. The author of this article was concerned with what he believed to be the growing unbelief or 'secularism' of the working classes.

Secularists appeared to have little organization, but the writer argued that the lack of organization was no proof that they were not influential, for, he says, 'scepticism is negative and does not lend itself easily to organization'.

The churches, he admitted, seemed to be unable or powerless to hold or win back the more intelligent members of the working class.[12] He turned to consideration of the effects of the rise of Spiritualism and points out that,

> It is a very significant fact that modern Spiritualism both in England and America has won the belief of large numbers who were formerly secularists. In Bradford, Bingley, and other Yorkshire towns, there are people once notorious for believing nothing, now equally notorious for believing everything. It is the characteristic of these rude northerners to be afraid of no inquiry, and, out of a love of fair dealing, to be proud to welcome what others excommunicate. Scepticism has always been rife among them, and there is no part of England where preachers have harder to fight or more shrewd heretics to contend with.

The writer of this article then goes on to describe the growth of Spiritualism in Keighley, the home of the movement in the north which illustrates the points he had already made.

> There is a building in Keighley which was originally a chapel for some section of the Methodists, who had separated from the old body because they thought it profane to use an organ in public worship and who were popularly known as 'Noncons'. As the noncons waxed richer they removed to a larger place, and sold their old one to a number of mechanics, weavers, wool combers and small tradesmen. These converted it into a 'Working Men's Hall', and made a platform where the pulpit was. . . . In the remodelled chapel this world took precedence of the other, and Chartism, Socialism, Strikes and

[12] Several recent works have discussed the dechristianization of the working class. The more important are K. S. Inglis, *Churches and the Working Classes in Victorian England*, 1963; and E. R. Wickham, *Church and People in an Industrial City*, 1957.

Atheism were advocated there in turns. Feargus O'Connor and his political followers, Robert Owen, and his anti-theological followers, regarded it as their peculiar property, and there is scarcely a politician or a heretic of any note among working men who has not spoken in it, and looked on it as one of the holy places of unbelief. For years this building was known in Keighley and the neighbourhood as the 'Infidel Chapel', Artisan enquirers from different towns made Sunday pilgrimages thither; while the pious crossed themselves when they mentioned its name, and crossed the street when they met one of its attendants. When Spiritualism was imported from America the managers of the 'Infidel Chapel' offered it an opportunity to show its powers. The offer was accepted and they were converted. Now 'other worldliness' reigned more supreme than it had done in the days of the 'Noncons'. The Sunday evenings, and frequently other evenings of the week also, were devoted to seances, and lectures were given on God and Immortality. Ancient unbelievers deemed themselves favoured with prophetic visions; they held daily communion with saints and angels, and disdained not to acknowledge an occasional acquaintance with devils. A theology half Unitarian and half Swedenborgian gradually grew up, and what they called a 'Free Christian Church' was established. It was never difficult to get sermons, for the great departed were always willing to preach and sometimes dead secularists confessed their earthly errors, and told strange stories of the new life to their companions. The *Yorkshire Spiritual Telegraph* was conducted by men who had been accustomed to look up to Paine and Voltaire as Biblical critics and to see in the Baron D'Holbach's 'System of Nature' an authoritative text book of theology. The secularists who remained unconverted were left without a home; and the itinerant lecturers who had always found a safe haven in the 'Working Men's Hall' struck Keighley out of their lists. During the last four years the surviving heretics of the old time have recruited their forces out of a younger generation and hold meetings again; but they are not what they once were and they have for ever lost the 'Infidel Chapel'.

The author goes on to further illustrate his point by describing the conversion of the socialist-atheist Robert Owen and of his son Robert Dale Owen, who became one of the most important exponents of Spiritualism and who is chiefly remembered for his book *Footfalls on the Boundary of Another World*.

This amusing and sceptical account of the movement in the north demonstrates clearly not only the relationships between Spiritualism and secularism but also the class composition of the movement in that area, where it was mainly upper working and lower middle class. Throughout the north the movement at this time was less Christian than in the south. The anti-Christian elements that later formed the majority influence in the 'British Association of Progressive Spiritualists' came largely from the north. In the south, Christian Spiritualism was dominant.

A close connection can be seen between social conditions, social class and belief systems in Spiritualism at that period. The working class and lower middle class migrants to the industrial towns of the north had been cut off or alienated from Christian influences and many of them were sceptics, hostile to the organized churches. The Spiritualists of the north were recruited largely from these elements, and in consequence they held the view that Spiritualism should not become a Christian sect. The upper and middle classes who were attracted to Spiritualism, often from an interest in scientific investigation, were usually rationalists whose alienation from Christianity was purely intellectual. They often saw the Church as a useful support of the social order, and were emotionally inclined to religion. Such men saw Spiritualism as a means of refuting materialistic attacks on religion, and argued that if the miracles of Spiritualism were true then the miracles of the Bible could also be accepted.

Development of Religious Practices and Institutions

During the eighteen fifties and sixties the activities of societies and groups were mainly directed to the investigation of psychic phenomena, the communication with the dead and to the scientific and philosophical discussion and explanation of these facts. Periodical discussion of the religious implications occurred and attacks from the Christian Churches were frequent and violent. Gradually in the late 'sixties and early 'seventies religious services on Sundays became a part of the activities of some Spiritualist societies. Where this first occurred it is not possible to say, but the practice developed most rapidly in the north. J. J. Morse held Sunday services in Liverpool in 1871 under the auspices of the Liverpool Psychological Society, and the conference held in Liverpool in 1873 to discuss the formation of a National Association agreed that the holding of Sunday services was the best way of promoting Spiritualism, since this gave individuals an opportunity of meeting together for mutual encouragement and for enjoying a 'rational form of spiritual worship'.

In October 1873, the 'Spiritual Church' was holding services at St Georges Hall in London. In 1874 services were being held regularly at the Athenaeum Hall, Temple Street, Birmingham, and two years later we read of services at the Temple of Truth in Liverpool which was heralded as 'the Spiritual church of the future'.

The annual conference of 1877 was given a report of the organization and activities of societies throughout the country. Services were being held on Sundays in London at the East End Spiritual Institution and at Doughty Hall (under the auspices of J. Burns Spiritual Institution); and in the provinces at Bolton and Halifax (where the hall was licensed as a dissenting chapel), at Sowerby Hall, at Keighley, and at the Christian Spiritualist Hall, Nottingham. Later in that year, regular services were also reported at Birmingham, Bradford, Leicester and Stockton.

The *Spiritual Magazine* in February 1866 gave what is probably the earliest report of a discussion on the religious nature of Spiritualism which had taken place at the Darlington conference of the British Association of Progressive Spiritualists. During the discussion it was claimed that Spiritualism was a new religion. The editor of the magazine replied that Spiritualism was not a new religion but rather was the essence of all religions. Controversy continued throughout that year. In the March issue of that magazine an anonymous author widened the argument. 'The unbeliever', he said, 'cannot come to belief by the new facts of Spiritualism. If he appears to do so it is because the seed of belief was in him, and the spiritual facts brought to it light and warmth.' He went on to argue that, 'If Spiritualism cannot create a faith, much less can it form a church'.

The discussion continued in the *Spiritual Magazine* and the well known spiritualist Thomas Brevior in a series of articles argued that Spiritualism is not a new religion but, 'It leads up thereto; it evidences, illustrates, confirms and enforces it; and gives certainty to what in many minds had become doubtful'. He protested against the anti-religious element that was prevalent in America and was he felt beginning to be apparent in British Spiritualism, 'Not destruction, but restoration, not to demolish, but to repair and build up, is the work of Spiritualism'. At this period many sceptics converted to Spiritualism were arguing that religion was inimical to progress; this Brevior denies, 'Religion', he says, 'is the very central principle of progress . . . because it is the keystone of the arch by which all things are upheld and saved from chaos'.

Religious spiritualists seem to have held from the first the view that psychic phenomena not only supported the claims of religion but were at the basis of all religious beliefs, and that consequently Spiritualism was not a new religion but the ground of all religion. Christian Spiritualists saw in the evidence of psychic phenomena proof which would dispel the doubt cast on the miraculous elements within Christianity by the development of science.

With the development of religious practises and institutions, the Spiritualist societies began to call themselves churches. Where this first occurred it would be difficult to say, but the first recorded use of the term 'Spiritual Church' in Britain appeared in 1868 in an address presented to Mrs Emma Hardinge on 10th May, at the Polygraphic Hall, King William Street, Strand at the conclusion of a series of Sunday evening services which she had conducted at that place. The address expressed the determination that 'The Spiritual Church – the Church of the Future – the church you have laboured to build up – must be no narrow communion; must rest on no shifting sands of human opinion, but on principles firm as the earth, eternal as the Heavens, wide as Humanity'. The 'branch of the Spiritual church' at the Polygraphic Hall was however only a temporary organization, but it showed that the idea of Spiritualism as a separate religious sect or church was beginning to take hold of at least a few people in Britain.

Three years later, in 1871, on the conclusion of a further series of meetings conducted by Mrs Hardinge, some newspaper declared that Spiritualism had now become a sect. This brought a protest from the editor of the *Spiritual Magazine*, who commented, 'We hope not, the aim of Spiritualism is not to found a sect, but to demonstrate a truth – the truth of human immortality – a truth which lies at the root of all religions and is professed by all sects, and by vast numbers unattached to any sect'. . . . 'To make this the basis of a sect would then be alike a misapprehension of its nature and a perversion of its spirit'. It would, he thought, be a fatal mistake to add to the sects already in existence and he felt that Spiritualism should unite rather than divide men. The controversy between those who thought Spiritualism to be a religious sect and those who felt that it only demonstrated a fact, continued and is well illustrated in a debate that took place at a meeting of the Psychological Society of Great Britain in 1875. The founder of the society, Serjent Cox, argued that Spiritualism was a religion and a sect. This was denied by Mr Epes Sargent, who pointed out, 'We should hardly call a body of electricians a sect, and the fact that certain investigators of the supersensual phenomena . . . entertain, till they can find a better solution, the Spiritual hypothesis, no more constitutes them as a sect than those persons who hold the Newtonian theory of gravitation are a sect'. 'Still less', he said, 'can Spiritualism be called a religion. We no more impart religion to a man by proving to him that he will continue to exist after the dissolution of his earth body, than we should by proving to him . . . that he would live fifty years after the age of thirty on this planet.' 'Spiritualism is not a sect, a religion or an organization. It is hardly a Science . . . and not even a philosophy. . . . It is . . . the fact . . . that there are spirits.' Such was the argument of a scientific supporter of Spiritualism in the nineteenth century. Spiritualism proved the survival of human personality beyond the event of physical death and nothing more.

The view of the orthodox Christian churches was well represented in a discussion conducted in the columns of the *Hour* newspaper entitled 'Spiritualism *v.* Christianity'. A Christian correspondent held that while the phenomena of Spiritualism were true, they were of an evil nature contrary to the Christian religion. This has remained the main source of dispute between Christians and Spiritualists.

The opposition to the development of Spiritualism as a religion was again revived by Dr J. M. Gully in 1878, who repeated that when a church or sect was formed, 'The responsibility of the individual spirit (will be) merged in that body, and spiritual effort be stupefied in sectarian indolence or strangled bitterness'. In this article he was answering the case presented by Miss Kislingbury, the Secretary of the National Association of Spiritualists, who said that 'Spiritualism differs from mere psychology in that it is a religion as well as a science, and that in proportion as Spiritualists forget this they are helping to weaken its influence as a moral regenerator'.

The religious aspect of Spiritualism continued to grow, particularly in the north, while a scientific approach remained characteristic of the south. When the formation of the London Spiritualist Alliance was announced in 1884 a statement was issued which recognized the useful work carried on by the Theosophical Society at one extreme and the Society for Psychic Research at the other, but argued that, 'Between these poles, Spiritualists pure and simple find their place'. Spiritualism was thus seen as having its base both in the metaphysical and religious approach on the one hand and in scientific method on the other.

As late as the year 1900 the dispute between those who considered Spiritualism to be a religion and the non-religious Spiritualists, and between those who sought to establish Spiritualist churches and those who wished it to remain non-sectarian continued, though by that time it was becoming an academic discussion, for outside London the movement had taken on a distinctly religious colour and most societies had transformed themselves into churches.

Christians v. Religious Non-Christians

In addition to the conflict between the religious and scientific elements within Spiritualism, the religious section of the movement has also been split between those who believe that Spiritualism is an instrument that can be used to revive and stimulate Christianity by supplying evidence to support the supernatural claims of that religion and those who saw Spiritualism as a new religion providing evidence which while challenging many Christian dogmas, supported a generally religious world view.

This conflict first appeared with the formation of the Association of Progressive Spiritualists of Great Britain in 1865. That Association failed largely because it was founded by a group of anti- and non-Christian spiritualists, and as such was feared, avoided or attacked by Christian spiritualists.

In the eighteen seventies the controversy raged between

Christian and non-Christian spiritualists around the organization of the National Association which was also accused of being anti-Christian.[13] But the question was largely obscured during the 'sixties and 'seventies by the disputes between anti-religious and religious spiritualists and between those favouring and those opposing central organizations. These disputes were gradually resolved by the slow development of organizations and the division of the movement into religious and scientific sections.

The way was reopened for the controversy between Christians and non-Christians. In December 1885, *The Medium* expressed the opinion that, 'Spiritualism must assume a religious position', and argued that, 'while it refrains from doing so it is simply feeding the sects, and in its new steps it must avoid the Christian lines'. A reply from the magazine *Light* attacked the anti-Christian attitude of *The Medium*. *Light* however went on to argue that,

> The basis of religious union amongst Spiritualists – whenever that question comes within the range of practical polity – must be broad and catholic. For that reason they must stand outside all sects – strictly unsectarian. Their aim should be in the direction of Universal Religious (not merely orthodox 'Christian', for that is too narrow) unity. Spiritualists . . . will recognize that in all creeds there is an underlying unity of purpose and similarity of doctrine to be traced; that God has sent his teachers unto every age, to every clime, and to every race of men; that they have each unfolded as much of truth and righteousness as human hearts were ready to receive.

This is a fine expression of the views and aims of those religious Spiritualists who believed that the old beliefs and forms of orthodox Christianity were narrow and outworn and who wished to see the establishment of a universal religion based on tolerance.

This has been a continuing and influential strain in Spiritualist thought, and formed the basis of attempts at unity in the movement. The conflict between Christian and non-Christian spiritualists did not come to a head until the years between the two world wars when the movement as a whole was booming. In 1925 the Christian spiritualists were again becoming a sufficiently important group to support their own paper appropriately entitled *The Christian Spiritualist*. The editor proceeded to attack the Spiritualist

[13] At this period the Christians had their own newspaper, the *Christian Spiritualist*.

National Union for being 'anti-Christian', and his comments on Maurice Barbanell, a prominent figure in the National movement were construed as an expression of anti-Semitism. Many Christian Spiritualist churches were formed in London and the south at this time and representatives of these churches met at 'Speers' Temple of Light' in 1928 to discuss unity, and as a result the Christian Spiritualist Federation was founded. They announced, 'The real object of this Federation shall be to secure for Christ due recognition in the Spiritualist movement' and held that 'The teaching of Jesus the Christ as the Master Psychic of all ages [was] to be adopted as the working basis of all instruction and lectures', to be held in their churches.

This move to establish a unified organization of Christian spiritualists followed an unsuccessful attempt to persuade the Spiritualist National Union to accept Christianity as a principle of their beliefs. This attempt was led by Sir Arthur Conan Doyle who moved a resolution asking that a new principle affirming, 'that we, in the Western world, acknowledge the original teaching and example of Jesus of Nazareth and look upon them as an ideal model for our own conduct'. Even such a moderate expression of Christian belief aroused considerable opposition within the National Union and a flood of correspondence appeared in the Spiritualist press. Doyle's motion was referred for consideration and finally rejected at the 1928 conference.

The first successful organization of Christian Spiritualists grew out of the Zodiac Mission which had its origins in the Home Circle of the medium Winifred Moyes. Winifred Moyes seems to have had a difficult and unhappy childhood. Even as a child she 'heard voices and saw visions' but she did not understand these as she 'knew nothing of clairvoyance or clairaudience and had never investigated Spiritualism', and she had felt it to be 'dangerous to meddle with evil spirits'. She says, however, that she associated her voices and visions with Christ. At Christmas 1917 Winifred and her friend Mrs Margaret Hoare bought planchettes, and Winifred soon discovered her mediumistic powers. She began to receive written messages from her guide Zodiac, and after some time Zodiac began to speak directly through her. Miss Moyes' Circle began to distribute duplicated copies of the messages given by Zodiac, and by 1928 it became necessary to start a weekly journal, *The Greater World*, in order that Zodiac's messages should reach a greater public. Zodiac claimed to be a teacher in the Temple in Jerusalem in the time of Jesus. He never disclosed his earth name but said that he was the scribe mentioned in St Mark XII 28–34, who asked Jesus, 'Which is the first commandment of all?' His teaching appealed to the many Spiritualists who also retained their belief in the teachings of Christianity, and in 1931 the Greater World Christian Spiritualist League was formed in order that Christian Spiritualist Churches should have the opportunity of associating together and of joining in the work of the Christ Mission of Zodiac. The League was an immediate success, and by 1935 had 580 affiliated churches and 20,000 individual members.

Spiritualism and Other Scientific Religions

It has been rare in history for a religious leader to claim that his religion could be proved experimentally, and only Spiritualism has claimed that the beliefs could be proved by the methods of modern science. The Buddha suggested that his methods of attaining salvation should be tried experimentally and not accepted on faith alone, but the only form of experiment possible in Buddhism is a subjective one of trying the method individually by the experimenter himself. The proof of the Buddha's claims cannot be demonstrated empirically, but only experienced individually.

Christian Science is a sect that at least by implication claims to be a science. Orthodox Christian opponents of the sect have sometimes stated that the name is a complete misnomer since it is, 'neither Christian nor a Science'. Leaving aside the question of how Christian the sect is, there is no apparent justification for its claim to be a science.

Christian Scientists do not appear to accept the experimental method as a suitable means of testing their beliefs. They accept the doctrine of their religion as uncritically as do the followers of most other religions.

The main emphasis of Christian Science is on healing, and this also forms an important element in Spiritualism. It is thus interesting to compare the attitudes of these two groups to healing. Christian Science is a monistic religion which denies the reality of the material world. Pain and suffering are illusions which can only be healed by religious or spiritual methods of healing.

The members of this body consequently reject medical aid and decry the science of medicine.[14]

Spiritualism is a dualism and accepts the reality of both the material and Spiritual orders, though emphasizing the importance of the Spiritual. Spiritualists believe that the two worlds are closely interconnected and that *causes* in the Spiritual world can produce results in the material world. They believe in the efficacy of spiritual methods of healing but they do not reject medical means of healing. Most Spiritualists see the two methods as complementary and would not hesitate to use both at the same time. They believe that God has provided both medical and spiritual methods of healing to alleviate human suffering.

Spiritualism appears to be much more scientific than Christian Science, since it accepts the methods of science and believes that its claims can be tested by these methods. Christian Science is much more firmly based in faith and does not submit its theories to empirical testing.

There are strong elements of faith in Spiritualism, but the movement certainly originated in the experimental investigation of psychic phenomena, whereas there is no evidence that Christian Science had any scientific origins.

H. J. Blackham argues that, 'Religious faith must include faith in scientific progress . . . the believer must have faith in science', in his analysis of the place of religion in contemporary society[15] and the many secularizing trends in the churches and in theology seem to be attempts to reconcile scientific theory with Christian faith, but in these cases there is no attempt to offer proof or evidence to support orthodox belief; there appears on the contrary to be a steady retreat of theologians before the advance of scientific ideas.[16]

Other Pseudo-Scientific Cults

There seems to be some parallel between the growth of Spiritualism and the growth of the Flying Saucer Movement; both originated in the study of phenomena unexplained and ignored

[14] W. I. Wardwell, 'Christian Science Healing', *Journal for the Scientific Study of Religion*, Vol. IV No. 2, April, 1965; *see* also B. Wilson, *Sects and Society*, Ch. 6, 1961.
[15] H. J. Blackham, *Religion in a Modern Society*, p. 161, 1966.
[16] *See* H. Cox, *The Secular City*, 1965; J. A. T. Robinson, *Honest to God*, 1963.

by science, and both movements developed from attempts to explain these phenomena.

Both movements started with attempts to use scientific methods of investigation and to develop theories which would explain the observed facts in terms compatible with the concepts of science. Scientific investigation of these types of phenomena continue to be made by psychic research societies and Flying Saucer Clubs.[17]

In both cases a religious cult based on a system of beliefs and practices grew up around and out of the study of the phenomena. These represent a particular theory of the nature of the phenomena. Spiritualists interpreted the messages received through mediums as coming from the Spirits and argued that this theory could be tested. In the case of Flying Saucer Cults, unidentified flying objects were identified as vehicles used by Space People who have superhuman if not supernatural powers, and leaders of such cults claimed to have made contact with these Space People either physically or in trance. The Space People are thought of as being wiser than man as are the Spirit Guides in Spiritualism and give inspiring and uplifting messages through the medium in group meetings.

The most important of these societies in Britain is the Atherius Society formed by George King in 1954. King claims to act as the medium for members of the 'Space Parliament' who wish to communicate with earth.[18]

New religions such as Spiritualism, Christian Science and the Atherius movement seem to emerge on the fringe of scientific advance, as investigations of areas which are 'not quite respectable', in the eye of many scientists who work in the older-established branches of science.

[17] The British Unidentified Objects Research Association.
[18] J. A. Jackson, 'Two Contemporary Cults', *The Advancement of Science*, June, 1966.

Chapter Nine

SPIRITUALISM IN
THE TWENTIETH CENTURY

Spiritualism and War

British spiritualists had been able to ignore the practical problem of war until 1914. During the later part of the nineteenth century the minor colonial wars in which this country had been engaged had not aroused much attention among spiritualists. Spiritualists were in theory against war and violence, as these were contrary to their belief in the brotherhood of man. Killing in any circumstances is murder in the view of Spiritualism, since it ends a man's earthly life prematurely. Killing the body cannot of course destroy the soul, but it is to be condemned for three reasons. In the first place the earth life is an important aspect of the whole life of spirit, a period in which the soul has important lessons to learn and consequently not a period of existence that should be cut short either by others or by the individual himself. Suicide is thus condemned as well as murder.

Further sudden death or death for which the individual is unprepared may temporarily harm the surviving personality; he may suffer from a psychic shock from which he will in time recover, but which should not be induced.

Finally, killing would be viewed by many Spiritualists as harmful to the spiritual development of the killer. Man is spiritually developed by feelings of love; these feelings and thoughts should be encouraged and the thought and emotions of hate should be rejected. There are obvious relations between hate and killing though there are also circumstances in which one may kill without hating, and indeed in 'mercy' killings one may be motivated to kill by love.

The outbreak of war in 1914 presented Spiritualists with a dilemma and from the first there were many arguments within the movement as to the attitude a Spiritualist should adopt to the war.

The majority of Spiritualists seem to have responded to the call of patriotism and to have supported the war effort, but a minority held to their belief that all war was inconsistent with Spiritualist teachings. The magazine *Two Worlds* regularly published a 'Roll of Honour' of the names of those who had joined the Forces. One pacifist spiritualist described this as a 'list of fighting Spiritualists, traitors to the principles they espouse'. It appears that many members of Lyceums refused to join the combatant forces for conscientious reasons, and the Lyceum Union gave these objectors support by giving them credentials. A controversy raged around the stand made by these 'non-combatant' Lyceumists, and this was reflected in the correspondence columns of *Two Worlds* during 1916, where the argument grew abusive on both sides. The editor was even described by a pacifist as 'a bloodthirsty Spiritualist who believes in and condones murder', because he allowed pro-combatant arguments to appear in the paper.

Most Spiritualists, including the many non-combatants, believed in the aims of the war and supported the war at least passively. In the Autumn of 1915, *Two Worlds* sponsored a 'Spiritualist Motor Ambulance Fund', which raised altogether over £900, with which six ambulances were bought and presented to the War Office.

During the inter-war years the majority of Spiritualists seem to have supported every effort to preserve the peace, and the literature of the Spiritualist movement frequently mentioned the activities of such bodies as the National Peace Council.

At the outbreak of the Second World War Spiritualists were again faced with making a difficult decision, and again the majority seem to have abandoned their pacifist principles and to have supported the war effort.

Again the movement was split by the controversy between supporters of the war and pacifists, and as in 1916, so in 1939, the controversy was reflected in the pages of *Two Worlds*. Many Spiritualists felt uncertain of their position, and to give them guidance the Council of the Spiritualist National Union issued a manifesto in which they declared that 'While recognizing the folly of war . . . it is the duty of spiritualists to serve the cause of liberty in any and every way which conscience dictates . . . by assisting the weak and oppressed'. The declaration did not come down firmly on one side or the other and left the individual to make his own decision in accordance with the dictates of his conscience.

The majority accepted that the choice was between two evils and that in order to defeat the evil of Nazism killing might be a necessity. The minority who became conscientious objectors seem to have become larger in the Second World War than it had been in the first.

Some spiritual platform workers claimed exemption from conscription and direction of labour on the ground that they were ministers of religion and in order to support the claims of such persons and also to provide credentials for Spiritualist workers who wished to visit churches in the Prohibited Zone that covered the south coast of England during the summer of 1940 when Britain faced imminent invasion, the Spiritualist National Union appointed a panel of Spiritualist ministers and issued a Spiritualist Minister's Identity Certificate which gave evidence of a platform worker's status when he was applying for permission to travel in the Prohibited Zone. Registered Spiritualist ministers were exempt from military service as were the ministers of other religious bodies, though there were few Spiritualist ministers; by July 1941 only sixty had been appointed.

The Effects of the Great War – War and Revival 1914–39

At the beginning of the war the work of many societies was affected by the absence of the men who joined the forces in large numbers, and a number of societies found themselves in difficulties; in Yorkshire, for example, at least nine societies were forced to close down.

Other consequences of war however furthered the growth of interest in Spiritualism. Britain became a nation of bereaved. There were thousands of persons who had lost relations and friends and who were attracted by the promise of a message from the departed. The Spiritualist churches grew but so did the fraudulent mediums; a host of these set up in business at home or in a hired hall in the back streets of the cities to cash in on the demand.

In such a time of uncertainty people also sought knowledge of the future, and the fortune tellers also flourished. The press and the courts were unable, and perhaps unwilling, to distinguish between the genuine and the fraudulent medium, between the 'spiritualist', who produced fake psychic phenomena solely for money and the Spiritualists, for whom phenomena were only an aspect of philosophy and religion.

In March 1916 a medium, Mrs Barnes, was convicted on a charge of fortune-telling for having acted as a medium at a service at the Spiritualist Hall, Longsight, Manchester, and two other persons, Mr and Mrs Chamberlain, were also convicted of aiding and abetting. The evidence had been obtained by police agents.

The Spiritualists felt this as a direct challenge to their rights to worship and decided to appeal, and 'The United Spiritualists' Defence Fund' was launched. The appeal, however, failed.

The only ultimate solution lay in amending the antiquated laws under which mediums were prosecuted, and in July 1916 the S.N.U. opened a fund for securing the amendment of the Witch-craft and Vagrancy Acts, but their efforts were doomed to failure for a very long time and it was not until the Second World War had ended that these Acts were in fact amended.

In August 1916 a paper called *The Umpire* published an article headed:

Women Duped at Fake Seances

How Soldiers' Wives are Preyed Upon

in which the author 'exposed' some of the practices at the dis-reputable 'spiritualist' meeting places which he claimed existed in our larger towns. He went on 'It is surely nothing less than criminal that these harpies of humanity should be permitted without prac-tical protest to trade upon the mental crucifixion of those whose loved ones have fallen to die upon the war-wasted fields of France and Flaunders'. The editor of *Two Worlds* protested strongly that this article misrepresented the Spiritualist movement. The tide of prejudice was rising and James Lawrence reported cases of Spiritualists who had been refused work because of their beliefs. The campaign against Spiritualism in press and pulpit intensified during 1917 and 1918 and continued after the war, but in spite of this, the movement grew rapidly. There were two main reasons for this; the most important we have already mentioned; this was the fact that thousands of people had been suddenly bereaved and the conventional churches were unable to provide the comfort and consolation these people needed. They turned to the Spiritualists who offered knowledge and not mere belief, and who claimed to provide them with communication with their dead.

The second was the effect of the conversion of several important people whose names gave weight to Spiritualist claims.

In 1916 Sir Oliver Lodge published a book called *Raymond: Or Life After Death*, in which he reported on messages received from his son who had been killed in France. Lodge had for many years been a psychic researcher, but now he proclaimed his complete conversion to Spiritualism. His book had a tremendous impact. The conversion of Sir Arthur Conan Doyle in 1917, followed by his book *New Revelation* in March 1918, made an even greater impact, for Conan Doyle immediately threw himself into the work of propaganda for the cause with tremendous ardour. Throughout 1919 he worked tirelessly, often conducting meetings at five different towns in a week. These tours were reported widely in the press and thus extensive publicity was given to the movement. Wherever he went the general public queued to attend his meetings and new societies grew up, and existing societies expanded rapidly in the wake of his missions. In 1914 there had been 320 societies in Britain, of which only 145 had been affiliated to the National Union. By 1919 309 Societies were affiliated to the S.N.U., and there were of course many unaffiliated societies in the country. The majority of S.N.U. societies were still in the north, in fact, there were only forty-six in the south (including South Wales); forty-five in the Midlands; five in Scotland; five overseas; and one in Ireland; all the rest were in the northern half of England. There was still considerable room for development and expansion by the Union in the southern half of the country where most of the societies were still unaffiliated.

The 1919 Conference of the S.N.U. approved New Memoranda and Articles of Association, the main points of which were that subscriptions of each Society were to be *per capita* of its members; thus every church member became a member of the Union. The Council was to consist of nineteen members including the President, Vice-President and Treasurer, elected by conference. The Secretary was to be appointed by the Council.

The growth of the movement in the south and London was largely outside the sphere of the Spiritualists' National Union and many new bodies sprang into existence in the years following the war. In 1919 a Jewish Spiritualist Society was established in the capital, thus clearly demonstrating that Spiritualism was not only a Christian movement nor even mainly derivative from that religion, but that it was at least compatible with other religions and even that (as many non-Christian spiritualists claimed) it might form the basis of all religions. An attempt to organize home circles was also made in 1919 when Thomas Pugh formed the International Home Circle Federation, with its headquarters at Furnival Street in London, but this failed as a result of dissensions among the leadership. It appears that Pugh attempted to dominate the Federation in ways that other members considered were undemocratic, and they deposed him from the office of chairman only a few weeks after the organization had been formed, whereupon Pugh formed a new organization having the same name with the added words 'as reconstituted July 28th 1919'. The existence of two organizations with the same name caused some confusion in the movement and towards the end of the year Pugh resigned from the chairmanship of this reconstituted society and retired from an active part of Spiritualism. A new chairman, H. J. Osborn, was appointed, and Pugh's society, which continued to do good work, changed its name to 'The Spiritual Rendezvous for Psychical Research'. In 1920 it changed its name again to 'The London Central Spiritualist Society'.

The original International Home Circles' Federation failed to recover and never had much influence on the movement.

A further attempt to organize home circles was made in the 'thirties. In 1931 N. Zerdin organized a conference which formed the 'Link' for home circles. Its objects were declared to be:

1. To establish psychical phenomena as a means of demonstrating survival, and to enhance the appreciation of the world as to the significance of those manifestations.

2. To assist members of 'The Link' to obtain results by the circulation of helpful suggestions as to the 'modus operandi'.

3. To enable members of a linked circle to visit other circles in the 'Link'.

A monthly magazine, *The Link*, was published for private circulation to members.

There were many home circles at this period and the 'Link' made an immediate appeal; by June 1933, 107 circles had joined the 'Link'. During the 'thirties the 'Link' continued to flourish, and conducted massed seances and investigated many mediums, but like many other organizations in London, its activities were severely curtailed by the Second World War. It was re-established after the war but was never again a success. It struggled on until 1960 when with only six circles remaining as members it was finally disbanded.

Sir Arthur Conan Doyle continued to work tirelessly for the cause, not only in Britain but in Australia and New Zealand, which he visited in 1920–21, and America in 1922 and 1923. During 1928 he visited South Africa and Northern Europe. He defended William Hope, the spirit photographer, when Hope was accused of fraud in 1922, and later led a mass resignation of eighty-four members of the Society for Psychic Research, when he came to believe that the Society was biased against the Spiritualist movement. In 1926 he published a lengthy *History of Spiritualism* and was president of the London Spiritualist Alliance. Only six days before his death in 1930 he led a deputation to the Home Secretary asking for the modification of the Fortune Telling Act. He was probably the greatest propagandist the Spiritualist movement ever had and a truly charismatic figure, who although not a medium attracted a considerable following, but he was not the only well known public figure who supported the movement in the inter-war period.

In 1924 Robert Blatchford, the famous socialist writer, who had for long been an agnostic, announced his conversion to Spiritualism, and in the following year he described the circumstances that led to this conversion in his book *More Things in Heaven and Earth*. Early in 1925 Hannen Swaffer, at that time the well known editor of *The People*, announced his conversion. Swaffer had decided to investigate Spiritualism for his paper. At that time he was an agnostic. He attended many seances, at some of which his 'chief', Lord Northcliffe, returned and communicated through the medium. Swaffer was convinced and organized a public meeting at Queens Hall to proclaim Northcliffe's return on 20th January 1925. Soon after he published an account of his experiences in *Northcliffe's Return*. For the remainder of his life Swaffer remained an active propagandist for the Spiritualist movement.[1]

---

[1] The charisma of figures such as Conan Doyle and Hannen Swaffer was never routinized. They worked outside the existing bodies and never became the focus of new organizations. Swaffer's home circle achieved fame as the place in which the guide Silver Birch gave his teaching.

During the early 'twenties the press as a whole was more favourable to Spiritualism than it had been in the past. In 1920 the *Weekly Despatch* published the Vale Owen scripts and followed this up with communications from W. T. Stead, and many other papers published ghost stories and accounts of psychic happenings.

Early in the 'twenties, the Rev. Charles Tweedale, the Anglican Vicar of Weston in Yorkshire, who was already well known as an advocate of Spiritualism and author of *Man's Survival of Death*, founded the Society of Communion as a society for Spiritualists of the Church of England. The society insisted on the acceptance of the doctrine of the divinity of Christ and existed mainly to encourage psychic study among Anglicans.

Mrs Dawson Scott founded 'The Survival League' in 1929 to unite the members of all religions who believe in human survival and to engage in psychic study. Its first chairman was H. Dennis Bradley and its official organ was the *Survival Magazine*, which, however, was not owned by the League but was an independent journal edited by Clifford W. Potter. Several attempts were made to encourage the unity and co-operation of Spiritualists in London. In 1924 six London churches formed the 'London Spiritualist Guild'.

Six years later, in 1930, Hannen Swaffer was instrumental in forming 'The Spiritualist Central Council', which aimed to improve co-operation between Steads Bureau, The British College of Psychic Science, The Spiritual Community, The Marylebone Spiritualist Association, and the London District Council of the S.N.U.

Most orthodox Christian churches were still opposed to Spiritualism, though Christian Spiritualism opened the way to a reconciliation between the two schools of belief.

A small group of Christian spiritualists, led by Mrs St Clair Stobart, felt that the ultimate aim should be to persuade the Christian churches of the essential Christianity of Spiritualism, and to show that the teachings of Spiritualism were in no way contrary to those of Christianity. They believed that the Christian churches should in effect absorb the Spiritualist movement, and in April 1935 an organization known as 'The Confraternity' was founded to propagate these ideas. For the next few years this organization conducted campaigns in the major towns of Britain to publicize their principles. They did not get very far towards the attainment of their ideals, but their meetings provided good propaganda for Spiritualism.

A Christian Spiritualist Church Union also existed in the 'thirties and was absorbed by the Christian Psychic Society in 1938. A year later this Society was reported to have fifty-nine affiliated or near affiliated churches.

The 'thirties were the high water mark of the Spiritualist Movement. An article in the magazine *Two Worlds* said that there were 'over' 2,000 properly constituted Spiritualist Societies in Britain in 1934. This was a reasonable estimate, though only just over half this number were recorded as being affiliated to either of the two major organizations; 562 being affiliated to the G.W.C.S.L. and 496 to the S.N.U. The number of unaffiliated churches can of course only be an estimate since many churches did not even advertise their existence.

Writing earlier in the same year, Maurice Barbanell estimated that there were 'at least 100,000 home circles' in England. This was an extremely optimistic estimate for, as H. A. Kerr writing in the same paper pointed out, if each circle had only ten members this would represent over one million Spiritualists in England – clearly a great over estimate, since the known churches affiliated to the G.W.C.S.L. and S.N.U. had a total membership of about 30,000. Even if one doubles this to include the unaffiliated churches and multiplies by four to include those who attended the properly constituted churches, one would only arrive at a figure of 240,000 Spiritualists.

Of course, in addition to the properly constituted churches, which we can take to mean those bodies having some sort of constitution and established for religious purposes, and not merely for private profit, there also existed a number of regularly constituted Spiritualist and psychic research societies that were not religious and were constituted to investigate and to study psychic phenomena in a scientific way. Such societies, however, had only a few thousand members at the outside, but there were also a large number of so-called churches, usually run by one person or a small group of persons for private profit. These places were neither religious nor scientific organizations, but provided their clients with fortune telling and displays of physical medium-ship which were usually fraudulent. These organizations flourished like weeds in the back streets of the industrial towns where they fattened on the insecurity of the working class in a period of great poverty and unemployment. They brought great disrepute upon the whole movement, and fortune-telling mediums and 'one man' churches were constantly condemned by the leaders of the Spiritualist Movement. Between 1934 and 1939 the movement continued to improve its position. By 1938, 539 churches were affiliated to the S.N.U.

Book Clubs were popular in the 'thirties as they provided their members with popular books at cheap rates. In 1938, three book clubs were founded that were aimed mainly at the Spiritualist market – these were the Occult Book Society, the Psychic Book Club and the Spiritualist Book Society.

War and Decline 1939–60

In the summer of 1939 the Spiritualist movement was still growing, new societies were being formed and new churches being opened. The outbreak of war in September hit Spiritualism with devastating force. At the beginning of the 1914–18 war the movement had at first been hit by the loss of its male members but, as we have seen, the ultimate result of that war was the expansion and popularization of the movement. The movement was affected far more seriously by the Second World War and, in fact, has never recovered fully from the blow, for at no time since the war has Spiritualism attained the popularity or membership it had in the 'thirties.

The first effect of the outbreak of war was to disillusion a section of the movement who had explicitly accepted certain predictions made by the spirits through their mediums about the possibility of war. For example, in August 1939, only two weeks before war broke out, a headline 'No World War' appeared in *Two Worlds*, and this referred to Spirit messages that predicted peace. Many such predictions were made during that anxious summer; even Estelle Roberts' guide, Red Cloud, predicted peace.

When these predictions were proved incorrect by the events, many spiritualists were bitterly disappointed, and C. S. Collen Smith, in a letter to *Two Worlds*, said that these false prophecies had dealt Spiritualism its greatest blow. His views were hotly contested at the time, but seem to have been borne out by subsequent events as the movement has never recovered its pre-war

Spiritualism in the Twentieth Century

position. These were typical examples of the result of the failure of charisma, which discredited the prophet, though, as we shall see, this failure of prophecy did not result in a permanent discrediting of either the particular prophets or of the movement.[2]

The failure of this prophecy unfortunately did not discourage further prophecies, and the consequent failure of prophecy continued during the war years. The Rosemary Records, published by Dr Wood in *Two Worlds* gave many further predictions during 1939–40, the majority of which were vague, but the few concrete predictions were doomed to be disproven. For example, in September 1939 two predictions were made referring to the war; it was said 'Nor will it take three years. There will be a sudden collapse.' The war of course lasted over five years. A further prediction was made that 'Italy will keep out' on 16th September 1939. Italy entered the war the following Spring.

Dr Wood confidently proclaimed that 'Hitler has a cancer of the throat and would die before the end of the war'. He also predicted 'there will be no Hitler to defeat when 1942 dawns'.

The failure of such predictions naturally cast doubt upon the claims of the Spiritualist movement, despite the fact that prophecy and fortune telling have always been condemned by reputable Spiritualists, who have taken care to point out that the 'departed' spirits cannot see the future but can only base their predictions on the same sort of evidence that is available to a 'living' person. Spirits therefore, have no advantage over the 'living' when it comes to foretelling the future.

Unfortunately many Spiritualists become so convinced of the infallibility of their Spirit guides that they are prepared to accept every message they receive from them as being unquestionable.

The failure of prophecy was, however, only one of the factors that led to the decline of the movement during the war years.

The blackout hit Spiritualist evening meetings, as indeed it did all social activities in the evenings. In the early part of the war people were reluctant to travel to meetings in the evening, and many societies had to abandon their evening activities. Some churches and societies found they were able to continue their evening meetings, but others were forced to restrict their activities

---

[2] L. Festinger, H. W. Riecken, and J. Schachter in *When Prophecy Fails*, Minneapolis University of Minnesota Press, 1956 discuss the consequences of such a failure in a millenarian movement in U.S.A.

to holding meetings on Sunday mornings and afternoons; while some found that they were unable to carry on and closed down 'for the duration'. The evacuation of children from London and other great cities had a disastrous effect upon the already declining Lyceum Movement, and the voluntary evacuation of some adult members also affected the movement in general. The activities of a few churches were curtailed when their premises were requisitioned by A.R.P. Committees (later Civil Defence) and for other war purposes. The 'blitz' on our great cities that started in the Autumn of 1940 also led to the closure of churches and the cessation of activities.

At the outbreak of the war over 500 churches had been affiliated to the S.N.U. with a total membership of 14,028. When the annual report was published in 1940 the number of affiliated churches had fallen to 361 and the number of members to 12,460.

In June 1940 the Spiritualist White Cross was formed for the purpose of training healers for national service and in an attempt to combine Spiritual healing with the more orthodox methods of first aid and ambulance work. It provided an outlet for the patriotic feelings of many Spiritualists and an opportunity for healers to assist in aiding the injured in the 'blitz'.

The movement continued to decline and reached a new low in 1941, when the interim report of the S.N.U. revealed that only 313 churches were then affiliated with a membership of 10,250. The West Midlands District Council had practically ceased to function earlier in the year, and the London District Council had found it so difficult to maintain contact with its affiliated churches that it had decided to subdivide its area into nine 'zones'. This proved to be a success and zone meetings of church representatives were held regularly to consider matters of common interest and maintain contact between churches. An appeal was launched for an Ambulance Fund, and in August the movement presented two Ambulances to the British Red Cross and St John's Society.

The British Spiritualists' Lyceum Union fell into financial difficulties in 1940, but when later in the year a plebiscite was held the members rejected a suggestion that the B.S.L.U. should amalgamate with the S.N.U. The Lyceum movement continued to decline, and there was little co-operation between the Lyceum Union and the National Union. The S.N.U. Conference at Derby in 1941 proposed the establishment of a new Youth Movement, and the Conference of 1942, which met at Coventry, launched the movement, but co-operation with the B.S.L.U. was urged. The breach between the two organizations continued to widen, and at its Conference in 1943 the S.N.U. carried a resolution that churches with Lyceums should end affiliation with the B.S.L.U. and register their Lyceums with the Union to be incorporated in the Unions Youth Movement. These two organizations had little association with each other until 1946, when the B.S.L.U. approached the S.N.U. to end the strained relations between the two bodies. A joint committee was set up to establish a basis for future co-operation. In January 1947 the joint committee recommended union between the two bodies, but that the B.S.L.U. should retain its own offices and executive council and hold its own conferences, and that the B.S.L.U. should administer the Youth Clubs and Lyceums. They also agreed on an experimental period of co-operation between their two organizations. Later in the year it was announced that the two unions were to merge from the 1st January 1948, and this was confirmed at the fifty-fifth conference of the B.S.L.U.

There was a slight revival of membership of the S.N.U. in 1942, and there was an increase of forty churches and some 1,000 members. But in that year a new campaign of police prosecutions started. On 27th September two police officers, disguised as sick soldiers in hospital blue, attended a seance conducted by Austin Hatcher and Emily Little. As a result Hatcher and Little were charged with 'pretending to hold communication with the spirits of deceased persons and deceive the public'. They appeared at Cardiff Magistrates Court and Hatcher was sentenced to three months' and Emily Little to one month's imprisonment; their appeal against convictions was dismissed by Cardiff Quarter Sessions. Soon after Mrs A. Townsend of South Harrow was visited by two disguised policewomen, and as a result of their visit was prosecuted and later fined £2 for fortune-telling. The Spiritualist movement became alarmed and a 'freedom fund' was set up to provide legal aid for mediums, healers and officials prosecuted for their activities in the movement. The S.N.U. became the trustee of the new fund. The Union at its Annual General Meeting in July protested at the 'continued persecution by the state against bona-fide and experienced mediums' and demanded 'freedom to worship'. The persecutions continued. In the same month another medium, Florence Camper, was fined at Southend for claiming to tell fortunes, and Miss Rhoda Wardle, a healer who claimed as such to be a minister of religion, was fined £5 for failing to comply with directions as to employment. This last case arose from the fact that the law did not recognize Spiritualist healers as ministers of religion. A deputation from the S.N.U. went to the Home Office to appeal for amendment of the Vagrancy Act of 1824. The Home Secretary, Herbert Morrison, later rejected this appeal. The prosecutions reached a climax in 1944. On 25th January the famous medium, Helen Duncan, was charged at Portsmouth Police Court 'with pretending to communicate with deceased persons, to deceive and impose on certain of H.M. subjects'. She was committed to the Old Bailey where, after a trial that obtained considerable publicity, she was found guilty and sentenced to nine months' imprisonment. Mrs Duncan's appeal against this sentence was dismissed. Later in the year the Witchcraft Act of 1735 was invoked against Mrs Jane Yorke when she was charged with pretending to exercise 'a kind of conjuration'. The same act was invoked against the President of Redhill Spiritualist Church. On 12th December 1944 the President, Mrs Emily Johnson, was visited by Police Officers who warned her that 'trance speaking, trance healing, clairvoyance and psychometry were offences, as they amounted to "conjuration", that if these activities continued she was liable under the Act' (1735). 'She was induced to give an undertaking that trance, clairvoyance, and psychometry would be discontinued' . . . 'The police insisted on a written undertaking'. The Redhill Church felt that under these conditions it would be impossible to carry on and the church had to be closed. This was probably the most blatant example of religious intimidation in Britain in the past hundred years and it called forth strong protests from the well known leaders of Spiritualism in the country, many of whom took part in a protest meeting organized at Redhill on 4th April, but it passed largely unnoticed by the general public.

A new church was formed at Redhill early in May, and this church was not interfered with in any way.

At about the same time the President of the Carlton Spiritualist Association in Glasgow was charged with having given psychometry. The S.N.U. Annual Meeting held at Paignton in July considered a report on the Duncan case and reached the conclusion that the only way to improve the position of Spiritualists was to get the Vagrancy and Witchcraft Acts amended. The fight for the amendment or supercession of the two antiquated Acts under which Spiritualists could be prosecuted for pursuing the normal practices of their religion, went on. At the Bournemouth conference in 1947 the Freedom Committee of the S.N.U. reported that they had made progress in their negotiations with the Home Secretary. Early in 1945 a further deputation went to the Home Office where it was received by Mr Chuter Ede. They asked for amendment of the Witchcraft Act. The Home Secretary promised to consider their views, and six months later his considered reply was published. In this letter he said 'Any relaxation of the law as it applies to such fraudulent activities would be especially dangerous at the present time, when there is such a wide field for the unscrupulous exploitation of personal loss and bereavement' . . . He went on to say that consequently . . . 'I cannot hold out any hope of legislation on this subject at the present time'.

The Freedom and Parliamentary Committee completed their draft of a new Bill which was presented to Parliament late in 1950. This passed through Parliament and received the Royal Assent as the Fraudulent Mediums Act in July 1951; under this Act the law recognized for the first time that genuine mediumship could occur and that not all mediums were either witches or attempting to deceive. This Act, which amended the Witchcraft Act 1735 and the Vagrancy Act 1824, in effect legalized the practice of mediumship in Spiritualist churches, and thus finally extended religious toleration to the Spiritualist movement.

Co-operation between Christian and non-Christian spiritualists improved during the war – at least in some areas. In 1943 the Essex Federation of Spiritualists was formed; its aim was to encourage co-operation between all Spiritualist churches in the County. The Federation consisted of churches belonging to the S.N.U. and the G.W.C.S.L. and some independent churches and proved a successful and useful organization.

After the war the movement recovered slowly, at least as reflected in the statistics of the S.N.U. until 1954. The G.W.C.S.L. does not publish figures of membership or church affiliation, and it is impossible to discover the exact number of membership of the independent churches, but there is no reason to assume that the trend in numbers and membership of Christian and Independent churches was very different from the trend as shown by the statistics of churches affiliated to the S.N.U.

The number of National Spiritualist Churches increased from 400 in 1944 to 498 in 1954, but since 1955 there has been a steady and continuous decline both in number of churches affiliated and membership. In 1962 the number of affiliated churches had fallen to 434 and the number of full members from a peak of 19,003 in 1950 to 15,497 in 1962. The number of church associated members fell in the same period from 2,496 in 1950 to 1,477 in 1962, but the number of Class B individual members of the Union remained comparatively stable over the same period.

Many Spiritualists in the early nineteen fifties were intrigued by the claim that an apparatus had been invented which would induce mediumship or provide a mechanical substitute for the physical medium. At the International Spiritualist Conference in London in 1948 this apparatus was demonstrated by its inventor, Mr N. Zwann. In 1949 Ernest Thompson, in association with Zwann, formed the 'Spirit Electronic Communication Society' to investigate Zwann's apparatus. Zwann claimed that his apparatus emitted radiation which became known as 'Super-rays', which could induce trance conditions and could also be used to cause or cure disease. These 'rays' appear to have been similar to the 'N-rays' which a French scientist Blondiot, claimed to have discovered in 1903. The 'Super-ray' craze flourished until 1952 when J. B. McIndoe, a Spiritualist with expert knowledge of electronics, attacked the claims made for 'Super-rays', in an article in *Two Worlds*. His article aroused the supporters of the Spirit Electronic Communication Society and a violent controversy raged in the columns of *Two Worlds*, who brought out a 'Super-ray' number devoted entirely to the subject. McIndoe replied to his critics by pointing out that the Zwann apparatus clearly could not work as claimed since there was no current flowing through the circuit, and that it consequently worked only by the power of suggestion.

Since the war there have been some attempts at unifying the Spiritualist movement, but these have only had a limited success and conflict has continued, mainly between the Christian Spiritualists as represented by the Greater World Christian Spiritualist League and non-Christian Spiritualists as represented by the Spiritualist National Union. A rally of delegates of the major London Spiritualist Organizations (British Spiritualist

Lyceum Union; London District of the Spiritualists National Union; Marylebone Spiritualist Association; London Spiritualist Alliance; Greater World Christian Spiritualists League; Union of Spiritualist Mediums; Essex Federation; Services Psychic League and Universal Brotherhood Federation), met at Kingsway Hall, London, in September 1948.

In 1948 the S.N.U. co-operated with the G.W.C.S.L. and M.S.A. in organizing the Centenary Celebrations of Spiritualism at the Royal Albert Hall, but in the following year a heated controversy broke out again between Christian and non-Christian Spiritualists, and at the 1950 Conference of the S.N.U. a resolution inviting 'Spiritualists and Spiritualist Organizations of all shades of theological opinion to join the Union', was amended to read, 'Spiritualists and Spiritualist Organizations who subscribe to the Seven Principles to join the Union'. The controversy, which was largely over the question of the recognition of Jesus Christ as the Son of God, died down during the next twelve months and a further attempt was made to unify all Spiritualists. In March 1957 the S.N.U., the G.W.C.S.L., and the M.S.A. agreed to set up the 'Spiritualist Council for Common Action', 'With a view to finding as wide a field of agreement as possible on the numerous questions that will beset the movement in the future'. The Council for Common Action existed for about seven years but did not achieve any very significant success in that period.

The success of the Essex Federation, formed during the war, in bringing together Spiritualists of all shades of opinion in that area led to the formation of other local federations. At a meeting held at Watford Christian Spiritualist Church on 17th March 1951, the 'Middlesex, Hertfordshire and Buckinghamshire Federation' was formed with two main aims:

> To co-ordinate the activities of the various churches and to form a pool of mediums and speakers for member churches to make use of in emergencies.
>
> To give advice and assist in every way possible, including financially, any church that was in need and was worthy of it.[3]

By April eight churches had affiliated to the new federation, including Watford C.S. Church, the Sanctuary of Truth and Light, Wealdstone; Garston Brotherhood of Spiritualists; St Albans C.S.

[3] *Two Worlds*, 29th May 1951.

Church; Welwyn Garden City Spiritualist Church; Manor Park C.S. Mission; and Northwood C.S. Church.

In 1955 controversy again flared up between the National Union and the Greater World C.S. League. H. Dawson at the S.N.U. Conference alleged that during its twenty-five years of existence the G.W.C.S.L. had disaffiliated 800 churches. He said that at one time the G.W.C.S.L. had 1,200 affiliated churches but that this number had now dropped to between 400–500. He implied that this was because a great number of Christian Spiritualist Churches were badly organized and run and consequently the League had expelled them. The League issued an official statement in which they denied that they had ever had as many as 1,000 affiliated churches. They admitted that many of their churches had closed over the previous twenty-five years, and listed three main causes of closure:

1. Illness or death of the pioneer who had founded the church and no suitable successor left to take over.
2. Halls sold by their owners leaving the church with no meeting place.
3. The consequences of the war.

They denied that any church had ever resigned because of prosecutions against mediums. The statement was signed by the founder of the League, Winifred Mayes, and by two other officials, F. N. Tolkin and W. S. Lawrence.

In 1956 the Union of Spiritualist Mediums was formed in London. Its existence was resented by the Spiritualists National Union, which soon described it as 'unnecessary and undesirable'. It was part of the National Union's endeavours to become representative of all Spiritualists and, in fact, to become the leader of the whole movement. In consequence they tended to resent the existence of other Spiritualist societies. In August 1957 the S.N.U. issued a statement of their position, in which they asked their affiliated churches to give priority to S.N.U. speakers when choosing platform workers for their churches, and asking S.N.U. mediums to give priority to S.N.U. churches. Mediums were asked not to 'serve any psychic organizations conducted for private gain and conducted without supervision of a constitution-ally elected committee'.[4] This last instruction was aimed mainly

[4] *Two Worlds*, 24th August 1957.

at the privately run spiritualist 'Churches' which, as we have previously seen, have often brought disrepute upon the movement by existing merely as money making institutions which guarantee to give the seeker a 'message' in return for payment. Many such 'churches' exist by the practice of fraudulent mediumship.

Two years later the S.N.U. launched a new attack on the Union of Spiritualist Mediums, and also upon the National Federation of Spiritual Healers which had been formed by Harry Edwards. In May 1959 the S.N.U. circularized its churches and members asking them not to support the U.S.M. or the N.F.S.H., and when this brought protests they followed up with a second circular in which they attempted to explain their attitude; they stated that the U.S.M. and N.F.S.H. were splinter movements that 'duplicate our work'. In reply Harry Edwards said that the National Federation of Healers had an important role to play because the S.N.U. did not promote healing effectively. He alleged that the S.N.U. did not insure healers against claims for compensation, and that they had failed to organize healing messages or to advise healing. The S.N.U. replied to Edwards by pointing out that the Union had, in fact, had insurance arrangements covering healers since 1952 and that it had organized healing meetings and issued advice to healers. Heat was added to the controversy by the allegation made by C. I. Quastel, President of the S.N.U., that absent healing was 'a very lucrative money making activity'. It was soon revealed that Edwards' healing sanctuary was running at a loss and that other healers were not 'making their fortunes', and Quastel thereupon issued an apology to Edwards.

The National Federation of Spiritual Healers soon proved its value to healers, when it obtained permission for its members to be allowed to visit patients in some London hospitals, and within a few weeks some 150 hospitals were admitting healers. By the following April, out of 435 hospital management committees that had been approached by the National Federation, 230 had agreed that accredited members of the National Federation would be permitted to visit in-patients at their own request. Only twenty-six management committees had refused permission. This development met with the opposition of the British Medical Association, which asked hospitals to ban spiritual healing and the British Medical Journal urged the Minister of Health to ban spiritual healers from hospital. They alleged that the National Federation had obtained permission by misrepresenting the views of the B.M.A. By July it was reported that only nine out of 273 hospital authorities which had by then agreed to admit healers withdrew their permission in response to the requests of the Medical Association.

This is a clear example of the way in which institutionalized science resists a challenge to its monopoly of a particular field of learning and the introduction of unorthodox methods within its field.

Chapter Ten

RECRUITMENT AND THE CHILD

The growth of interest in the religious instruction of the children of members of a religious body is one sign of the transition of a religious organization from being a sect to becoming a church.

The religious instruction of children in England first became institutionalized in the establishment of Sunday Schools. Robert Raikes (1735–1811) is usually credited with founding the first Sunday School, though there is some evidence that similar groups had been organized before Raikes established his first Sunday School in Gloucester in 1780. Raikes can at least be credited with popularizing the idea of Sunday Schools, and consequently he can be seen as the founder of the Sunday School Movement. By 1787 Sunday Schools had been established in several places, and Raikes claimed that they taught over a quarter of a million children.

From the first the movement was not restricted to any one denomination, and Sunday Schools were established both in Anglican Churches and Dissenting Chapels. The Sunday School Society, established in 1785 to promote Sunday Schools in all churches, was an early attempt at interdenominational unity which broke down because of suspicion between Anglicans and Dissenters. From the first John Wesley advocated Sunday Schools, and Methodist Societies took an active part in the establishment of Sunday Schools.

The Sunday School Union was founded in 1803 by a group of teachers in London with the three main aims of:

1. Stimulating the efforts of teachers.
2. Improving methods, and
3. Opening new schools.

This was for some years an interdenominational organization, but broke up in 1843 as a result of a dispute over the curriculum and methods of teaching, and the Sunday School Institute was formed to organize the activities of Church of England Sunday Schools.

In England at least, an interest in the formal religious training of children seems to have arisen in all types of religious organizations at about the same time, which suggests that by the beginning of the nineteenth century the old dissenting bodies such as Independents and Baptists were already some way along the line of development from sect to church. By the eighteen eighties the Sunday School was a popular institution, and it was customary for respectable persons of the lower middle and working classes to send their children to Sunday School. Spiritualists felt under some constraint to do the same. Many at first sent their children to Christian Sunday Schools, and it was to provide a specifically spiritualist form of Sunday School education for the children of members of Spiritualist bodies that the Lyceum movement was first established.

The Lyceum Movement

The Lyceum Movement was founded by the American seer, Andrew Jackson Davis. On 25th January 1863, Davis gave an address at Dodworth's Hall in New York, in which he described the methods used in the education of children in the Spirit World. Spiritualists believe that persons who die in childhood grow to maturity in the next world, and consequently that they have to be educated. Davis and many Spiritualists who succeeded him describe the Spirit World as the Summerland. The schools of Summerland were called Lyceums, said Davis, and were situated in beautiful halls surrounded by gardens, and here the Spirit Children were trained by their Leaders. Davis's audience at Dodworth's Hall were so impressed by his description of the Spirit Lyceums that they decided to form a Lyceum for the education of earth children in which the same methods could be used, and the first Lyceum was set up the same day at Dodworth's Hall.

The Lyceum movement owes its ideals and practices largely to Davis, and some consideration of his beliefs is therefore necessary. The focal point of Davis's teaching was that 'A child is the repository of infinite possibilities. Enfolded in the human infant is the beautiful "image" of an imperishable and perfect being'.

The theory that followed from these promises was the forerunner of much 'modern' educational theory. These assumptions meant that the methods used in education would be designed to draw out and develop the child's own potentialities rather than to cram in knowledge and to restrict the development of the personality of the child by moulding it in the image set by convention and society. Davis went on 'The divine image is within. It is the end of true education to develop that image, and so truly, too, that the child's individuality and constitutional type of mind shall not be impaired; but rather revealed in its own fullness and personal perfection'.

Davis pointed out that since children differed in their individual potentialities and needs they could not all be educated by the same methods. 'Different minds demand different methods', he said, and consequently he also believed that 'it is impossible for one teacher to quicken and instruct every type of character'.

He believed that conversation and discussion were the ideal methods of teaching, particularly where one was attempting to teach wisdom, since wisdom could best be produced by making the child think rather than by the more formal methods of teaching.

Davis suggested that a Lyceum should consist of twelve groups each containing twelve children. There should be a separate group for each year of age group, group 1 for four years old, group 2 for five years old and so on to group 12 for those of fifteen and over. This of course is only an ideal, and it is most unlikely that any Lyceum would have exactly this composition. Each group would have a leader (this title is used as being more appropriate than teacher), who would teach largely by conversation. Davis produced a *Lyceum Manual* in which he laid down a general scheme of group topics for discussion in each age group.

In addition to the group work the whole Lyceum met under the charge of the Conductor (who played the part of a Superintendent in a Christian Sunday School). The Conductor would suggest a topic for consideration of the entire school one week and the children would be asked to give their answers the following week. The children would also be taught by recitations in which the Conductor and the children repeated alternative lines of the verses or in which the children responded with an answer to a question recited by the Conductor. Music and physical exercises also played an important part in Davis's Lyceum.

In succeeding years the methods used in Lyceums have not changed greatly; they are still based on the ideals and methods laid down by Davis.

James Burns introduced a knowledge of the Lyceum movement into Britain when he published extracts from Davis's Manual, and the first Lyceum in Britain was established at Nottingham in June 1866. Unfortunately this Lyceum ceased to exist about 1871, although it was later revived. The founder of this Lyceum was a Mr J. J. Hitchcock. The movement grew slowly for the first twenty years. The second Lyceum was opened at Keighley in July 1870 and the third at Sowerby Bridge in October of the same year. The statistics collected by J. J. Morse for the conference held at Manchester in October 1880 show that in the intervening ten years little progress had been made and only four Lyceums were listed, at Keighley, Ashington, Glasgow and Sowerby Bridge.

It was during the later eighteen seventies that Alfred Kitson (who became known as the 'Father of British Lyceums') became interested in Lyceum work. Kitson had been born in 1855 at Gawthorpe in Yorkshire, where his father was a coal miner, and at the age of nine, started work in the pit himself. His father, who was a Primitive Methodist local preacher, brought him up in the 'fear of the Lord', until 1867, when his father attended a Spiritualist seance and was converted to Spiritualism.

The Spiritualists at Gawthorpe were persecuted with some violence by their neighbours but they prospered and succeeded in opening a meeting house. In the Summer of 1871 Kitson and other members of the Gawthorpe society visited Sowerby Bridge where the Lyceum was holding its first anniversary celebrations. They were all greatly impressed and an attempt was made to establish a Lyceum at Gawthorpe but this proved unsuccessful and, in fact, soon after the Gawthorpe Society fell apart as a result of a quarrel among the members.

Kitson's interest in Lyceum work continued and in April 1876 he organized evening classes for children in the house of a Mr Booth. In August of that year these classes were transferred to Ossett, where they became the Lyceum attached to the newly formed Spiritualist Society.

Kitson was largely self-educated as he had attended school for only one year. He worked hard to obtain the knowledge necessary to become a good Lyceum Conductor.

In 1882 Kitson joined the Batley Carr Society; he was soon asked to become President, and in May of that year he started a Lyceum at that society, which he conducted without any assistance for two years. The members of Spiritualist societies were slow to see the advantages of training their children in Spiritualist Sunday Schools, and in fact, many of them continued to send their children to Christian Sunday School, where they were taught beliefs inconsistent with Spiritualism. In an attempt to break down this indifference of Spiritualist parents and to spread a wider knowledge of Spiritualism, Kitson persuaded James Burns to insert a regular report of the activities of the Batley Carr Lyceum in *The Medium and Daybreak*, and also to publish two dialogues that he had written explaining the 'superiority of the Lyceum mode of tuition'; these attracted the attention of other Spiritualists.

Kitson appealed to the workers of the Yorkshire Committee assembled at Walton Street Spiritualist Church, Bradford, in September 1884, and he moved a resolution 'That all Workers in the Lyceums meet in Conference every year, to discuss the furtherance of the Lyceum Movement; and also for mutual encouragement in the work'. A Lyceum was formed at the Walton Street Church. The following year on Whit-Tuesday the children of the Sowerby Bridge and Batley Carr Lyceums gave an open air demonstration.

The marches and calisthenics that Kitson devised for the use of the Batley Carr Lyceum were published by James Burns in *The Medium and Daybreak* in 1885 and later appeared in the form of a pamphlet. Up to this time the Lyceums in England had had to rely for information entirely on the Manual produced in America by A. J. Davis.

When *Two Worlds* started publication in Manchester in 1887 Kitson reported the activities of the 'Batley Carr Children's Progressive Lyceum' in the paper. The report for Sunday, 27th November 1887 reads as follows:

Morning – present, six officers and twenty-four members.
Programme: musical reading; three silver chain recitations;

three select readings; one recitation; marching in all its phases; and calisthenics and lessons in the groups.

Afternoon – Programme: musical reading; three silver chain recitations; three select readings; four spiritual songs; and marching and calisthenics as in the morning.

A further meeting of Lyceum workers was held at Bradford on 28th March 1886, at which representatives were present from Batley Carr; Walton Street, Bradford; Otley Road, Bradford; Bingley; Keighley; Leeds; Sowerby Bridge; and Blackburn; and letters from Liverpool and Glasgow were read. The meeting saw the need for a comprehensive Lyceum Manual but were unable to proceed with the publication, for as Kitson said, 'We were all poor working men with small weekly wages which left no margin for printing a book for a new and unpopular cause'. The meeting agreed that it would be useful to hold an annual movable conference.

In September of 1888 Kitson was invited to open the Lyceum at Newcastle where he met Harry A. Kersey, the conductor of the new Lyceum, who had been introduced to the Lyceum work by Mrs Emma Hardinge Britten. While on a tour of U.S.A. Mrs Britten had been impressed by the part that Lyceums played in the American movement, and had collected items to form the basis of a Lyceum Manual; these she had given to Mr Kersey. Kitson persuaded Kersey to work on a Lyceum Manual and, together with Mrs Britten, they produced the first *English Lyceum Manual*, which Kersey had printed at his own expense by Mr S. Billows of Keighley.

It appeared on 31st March 1887. Its publication greatly offended James Burns, who had always supported the Lyceum movement and who had expected to have the publication of a manual when one was produced. He suspected Kitson of bad faith, and for some time attacked him and his work in *The Medium and Daybreak*.

On 26th March 1887, a Conference was held at the Psychological Hall, Liverpool, at which H. A. Kersey was elected President. The publication of the Manual stimulated the growth of the movement, and by the 1888 conference held at Halifax there were said to be forty Lyceums in Britain.

Early in 1889 Alfred Kitson wrote a book for the use of Lyceums, entitled 'Spiritualism for the Young', which was generally welcomed by the movement, though it did occasion another attack by James Burns on Kitson in his review of the book in *The Medium and Daybreak*.

The conference at Manchester in 1889 decided that the time had arrived when the Lyceums should join together to form a Union. There were by that time fifty-seven Lyceums with an estimated membership of 640 officers and 4,353 members. A committee was set up to draft a Constitution, which was submitted to a conference held at Oldham on 11th May 1890. The Constitution was adopted and the Spiritualist's Lyceum Union came into existence. The Rawtenstall Lyceum was the first to join the new Union. The movement felt the need for a magazine and in January 1890 the first copy of a monthly entitled *The Spiritualist's Lyceum Magazine* appeared. It was produced by W. H. Wheeler, Conductor of the Spiritual Temple Lyceum, Oldham.

Unfortunately this magazine soon ceased publication through lack of support, and in November 1890 it was replaced by *The Lyceum Banner*, edited and published by J. J. Morse in Liverpool. It was a more successful publication, and the Lyceum Union at its 1891 Conference at Sowerby Bridge decided to adopt it as the official journal. From 1892 the Union gave an annual donation to the paper. Morse continued to edit the *Lyceum Banner* until 1902 when he gave the paper to the Lyceum Union and Kitson was appointed editor.

Not all the existing Lyceums had joined the Union; by 1892 thirty-four had affiliated, and by the following year thirty-seven had joined, with a total of 2,600 members and 421 officers. At the Burnley Conference held in that year, the Union was subdivided into districts; the original districts were Leeds, Bradford, Halifax, Liverpool, Manchester, Rochdale, Burnley, North Lancaster, Midland, London, Tyneside, Teeside and Sheffield. The Lyceums were grouped into these districts and district visitors were appointed to look after the general welfare of the Lyceums in their district.

In 1894 the title of the Union was changed to the 'British Spiritualists' Lyceum Union'. At that time forty-three out of the sixty-six Lyceums in the country had joined the Union.

In 1896 Kitson, who had been the unpaid secretary of the Union, found that the work took so much of his time that he had little time to earn a living, and decided to resign, but he was persuaded to remain in office and was given a weekly salary of 5s., and in addition a subscription was raised on his behalf.

The fiftieth anniversary of modern Spiritualism was celebrated in 1898 and the Lyceum Union produced a 'Jubilee Medal' to commemorate the occasion. The movement continued to grow throughout the 'nineties and by 1900 there were 123 Lyceums in the country, of which 104 were affiliated to the Union; in consequence the work of the Union increased and need was felt for a full time Permanent Secretary. On 25th September 1901 Alfred Kitson was offered a full time appointment but since there was only a three months' notice required to terminate his secretaryship he declined to accept a full time secretaryship, preferring to continue to work part time in the pit. He continued as Secretary and was paid £1 a week for his part time services, until 1904 when the Union offered him a five years' contract as secretary at £2 a week.

A publishing fund had been inaugurated in 1892 to enable the Union to produce literature. In 1901 the copyrights of the *Lyceum Manual* and the *Spiritual Songster* (which he had also compiled with the aid of his sister) were presented to the Union by H. A. Kersey.

The British Lyceum Union in conference at Burnley in August 1901 discussed the relationship between societies and Lyceums. It appeared that in some cases there was little co-operation, and in a few cases actual antagonism between societies and Lyceums. Two views were voiced; the first was that Lyceums should be entirely self governing and the second that on the contrary they should form an integral part of the local society. A compromise resolution was passed which stated that 'Lyceums should be integral portions of their societies, and working in harmony with them, but if such was not possible in any case, the Union would not necessarily shut out such a Lyceum'.

It was also felt by some societies that a bridge of some sort was needed between the Lyceums and the societies along which members might be passed from one to the other. As with conventional Sunday schools and churches, children and adults were catered for but the teenager was neglected. To fill this gap the Lyceum Guild Movement was started, the first being opened at Sowerby Bridge in May 1900. Its objects were declared to be:

To provide rambles, literature, classes for debates, lectures, social evenings, gymnasium, games, and also to provide opportunities for enquiry into the phenomena of Spiritualism.

The movement had at this time made little progress in the south. The editor of *Light*, who visited a number of Lyceums in the north in 1904, gave a glowing description of their activities in his paper. He said that it was time the London societies woke up and encouraged Lyceums in the capital as they had been largely restricted to the north and the provinces. He particularly praised the singing, the rhythmical marching and the physical exercises carried out in union, and also thought highly of the Chain Recitation as a method of teaching the philosophy of the movement. The first Lyceum badge bearing a photograph of A. J. Davis was authorized in 1904.

The growth of the Lyceum movement went on during the early years of the twentieth century; in 1905 there were 140 affiliated to the Union; in 1908, 173; 1909, 183; and the following year the total reached 190. After this, progress slowed up. In 1912, twenty-eight Lyceums closed and only fourteen new ones were affiliated. At the Annual Conference held in June 1914 there were 186 Lyceums affiliated to the B.S.L.U., composed of 1,710 officers and 7,722 members. Writing in January 1915, James Lawrence pointed out that there were at least 155 societies which had no associated Lyceum and were doing nothing for their children. He stated that 185 Lyceums in Britain were affiliated to the Union and seventeen unaffiliated. Twelve foreign Lyceums were also affiliated to the Union at that time. The Union was organized in seventeen District Councils.

Study groups began to be formed at about this time with two main objects, the study of the facts of Spiritualism and of the questions of the day in relation to the movement. It was suggested that these should be co-ordinated by the S.N.U.

During and immediately after the war the Lyceum movement prospered, and at the conference in 1920, representatives were present from 240 Lyceums, who had a membership of nearly 11,000. In 1919 Alfred Kitson resigned from the secretaryship owing to ill-health. He was succeeded by James Tinker.

The Lyceum movement continued to grow during the great revival that followed the First World War. In 1922 there were

230 affiliated Lyceums with a total membership of 13,339 Lyceumists and two years later the movement reached its peak with 273 Lyceums and 16,252 members. The movement remained at slightly below these figures for another eight years, the membership dropping only slowly during this period.

The problem during this period was that although the total membership remained high, there was a constantly high turnover of membership. At the Union Conference held in 1930 it was reported that in the previous ten years 256 Lyceums had been admitted to membership, but during the same period 238 Lyceums had ceased to be affiliated. It is not known how many of these Lyceums ceased to exist, and some may have continued to work outside the Union.

This was the period in which the Christian Spiritualist movement developed, and Sunday Schools attached to these churches would not become affiliated to the Lyceum Union; in fact it was stated at the 1934 Conference of the Lyceum Union that Christian Spiritualist Lyceums would never be affiliated to the Union.

A sharp decline in the movement started early in the nineteen thirties. In 1931 there were 264 Lyceums with a membership of 13,018; in 1932, 257 Lyceums and 12,285 members. By 1934 there were only 230 Lyceums with 10,612 members. During this period there was growing co-operation between the Lyceum Union and the National Union. Joint meetings were held and Joint Committees set up, not only by the central organizations, but also by district councils. The Joint Education Committee devised an advanced education course, which was accepted by the A.G.M. of the National Union in 1925, and in the following year the Joint Committee set up the National Spiritualist College, which awarded degrees of Associate, Graduate, and Diplomatist to Spiritualists who had passed the approved examinations and had followed a three year course which was only open to those who had already passed the five grades of the Lyceum Union's examinations. It also granted Fellowships for distinguished service to the movement.

In the years immediately before the war, relations between the S.N.U. and the B.S.L.U. became increasingly strained. At the 1937 Conference of the S.N.U. a resolution to sever relations with the Lyceum Union was discussed.

Relations between the two organizations were not improved

by the strains of war, and in 1942 the National Union launched its own youth movement; the following year the S.N.U. passed a resolution that all member churches with Lyceums should end their affiliation with the Lyceum Union and register them with the National Union's Youth Movement.

In 1946 the Lyceum Union approached the National Union with the aim of healing the breach between them. As a result of the negotiations that followed, the two organizations decided to amalgamate, the Lyceum Union becoming the Lyceum and Youth Department of the National Union.

The Lyceum movement, however, has continued to decline. There were 105 Lyceums in 1950 but by 1962 the number had fallen to sixty-six.

The Spiritualist movement seems to have lost interest in young people and neglected to provide a suitable organization with a programme attractive to youth. But this development is paralleled in most Christian churches by a decline in the Sunday School Movement.

The Lyceum Today

A Lyceum is composed of members and officers. Membership is open to anyone who has attended at least four sessions in a period of five weeks but only members who have reached the age of twelve and been a member for at least three months have a vote.

The officers and committee are elected by the members, except that two members of the committee are appointed by the church. In addition to these two, the committee consists of three officers (Conductor, Treasurer and Secretary), Group Instructors of the Six Section Training Scheme, and other ordinary members. The election of the Conductor and Treasurer are subject to the approval of the Church Committee and the election of the Group Instructors is subject to confirmation by the Conductor.

The Conductor is the chief officer and his duties are to superintend the activities of the Lyceum.

Group Instructors are appointed to take charge of certain groups of studies. In 1944 the conference of the Union laid down 'that the Six Sections embodied in the Lyceum System of Training shall be paired off into the following three groups: Social and Physical; Mental and Moral; Psychical and Spiritual. Lyceums appoint three Group Instructors, each of whom takes charge of one of these groups of subjects, within the Lyceum. The Lyceum District Councils appoint Group Advisors, and the Union have National Liaison Officers to supervise this training scheme.

In addition to this scheme, the Lyceums are divided into groups based on age, as in Davis's original Lyceum, and each of these age groups is in the charge of a Group Leader who takes the place of a teacher.

Lyceums also appoint a Captain and Guards who take charge of the property of the Lyceum, give out banners, badges and books, arrange the seats and prepare the room for the Lyceum sessions. The actual conduct of a Lyceum naturally varies, but it is based on a programme laid down in the Lyceum Manual.

The Manual emphasizes that sessions should be carried out in an orderly manner. When the officers and members have assembled and taken their seats, the Conductor indicates that the session has commenced by ringing his bell. The Guards distribute the banners, badges and books, and then the whole company rises to sing a hymn. The Conductor then delivers an invocation at the conclusion of which the Lyceum sits. Next the roll of members is called and the registers or membership cards marked.

This is followed by a Silver Chain Recitation. These are poems of an instructive and devotional type and the lines or sentences are read alternatively by the conductor and the members of the Lyceum.

For example:

> *Conductor:* The seed which lies inert and cold
>   Will neither flower nor fruitage bear,
> *Lyceum:* Unless it struggles through the mould
>   For light and air.
> *Conductor:* The soul that seeks for Freedom's prize
>   Must Freedom's battle first begin –
> *Lyceum:* True effort never vainly dies
>   The Workers win, etc.

Following this there will be a musical reading which consists of a hymn; between the verses the Conductor reads a short commentary. Next there will be a Golden Chain Recitation; this is similar to the Silver Chain Recitation with the exception that it is usually on a spiritual or moral subject.

Recitations and songs by individual members of the Lyceum also form part of the programme, and some time is also given to learning and memorizing a hymn so that singing can accompany the marching.

Physical exercises have always formed a part of Lyceum training, and these consist of marching (including counter-marching and maze marching) and calisthenics, by which is meant rhythmical exercises.

The Lyceum then divides up into groups for lessons conducted by the Leaders. At the end of these lessons the entire Lyceum reassembles for the closing hymn, which is followed by the Benediction. The Guards collect the badges, banners and books and finally the Lyceum is dismissed.

Lyceums that are affiliated to the National Union are also affiliated to the appropriate District Council. The District Councils also accept Associate Members from Lyceumists or sympathizers with the movement.

These district councils are governed by executive committees elected by the delegates of societies and associate members.

The Committee includes four offices, the President, Treasurer, Secretary and District Visitor.

The Spiritualist's Lyceum Union has since 1948 been a branch of the Spiritualists' National Union and is in fact now the Lyceum Department of the S.N.U. The Lyceum Union consists of affiliated Lyceums, Associate Members, District Councils and other Spiritualist organizations having similar objects.

The activities and functions of the Union are defined in its Constitution as:

A. The holding of an Annual Lyceum Conference and such other conferences and meetings as may from time to time be deemed expedient.

B. The guiding of Lyceums in the training of their members in matters social, physical, mental, moral, psychical and spiritual.

C. The design of apparatus, the preparation of books, pamphlets, and other literature, and the issue of badges and other things needful or useful for the work of Lyceums.

D. The institution of courses of study, summer schools and

the like, either for young people or for leaders, teachers, organizers and other Lyceum workers.

E. The Conduct of appropriate examinations.

The affairs of the S.L.U. are conducted by the Central Committee composed of the Officers (President, Vice-President, Secretary, Editor of the Official Journal, and the President of the S.N.U.); two members nominated by the Council of the S.N.U., four members elected by conference; and not more than two members co-opted to serve until the close of the Annual Conference following their co-option.

The President and Vice-President are elected by conference but the Secretary and Editor are appointed by the Central Committee.

The democratic nature of the Union is emphasized by the fact that an Associate member only has one-fifth of a vote. It is true that this might not prevent the associate members from out-voting the delegates of affiliated bodies but it does in fact make this much less likely. The existence of individual members in an organization that exists primarily to serve the interests of affiliated bodies always presents a problem, since the interests of individuals may not always coincide with those of the constituent organizations; however, the Union appears to maintain the balance here very well.

The apparent lack of concern of Spiritualists for the religious education of their children is difficult to understand, except that it is perhaps more apparent than real. The child of active Spiritualists will be brought up with a familiarity with Spiritualist beliefs and practices, and if he has any psychic gifts these will be encouraged. Some Spiritualists take quite young children to services and meetings, but there are differences of opinion as to whether young children should be permitted to take part in seances. Some people believe that too early psychic development could be dangerous for the child.

The Lyceum movement originated as a counter influence to the Sunday School movement and both movements have tended to decline in strength since the nineteen thirties. In the Victorian period it was customary to send one's child to Sunday School, and Spiritualist parents felt impelled by social pressure to also send their children to a Sunday School. Many Spiritualists objected to the official Christian teachings and did not wish to have their children taught Christian dogma. They therefore established Lyceums to provide Spiritualist education for their children.

Since the nineteen thirties there has been a general decline in Sunday School attendance, and parents no longer feel obligated to send their children for religious education on Sundays. Spiritualists have therefore no longer felt it necessary to react to social pressure by supporting their own version of the Sunday School.

The child of Spiritualist parents cannot however avoid being influenced by his home environment, and the proportion of young people attending Spiritualist services has not been observed to be noticeably lower than the proportion attending services in the major Nonconformist denominations which have organized Sunday Schools.

Lyceum Union
Growth and Decline

1888 – 38	1914 – 186
1889 – 37	1915 – 200
1892 – 34	1922 – 230
1893 – 37	1928 – 271
1899 – 120	1929 – 271
1900 – 104	1931 – 264
1902 – 116 (estimated 126 in country)	1932 – 262
1904 – 122	1933 – 217
1905 – 140	1950 – 105
1907 – 166	1951 – 113
1908 – 173	1952 – 119
1909 – 183	1954 – 98
1910 – 190	1962 – 66
1912 – 194	1964 – 64

Chapter Eleven

SPIRITUALISM TODAY

The Spiritualist movement today can be divided in three ways. The first of these is according to beliefs. In this respect Spiritualists may be divided into Christian Spiritualists, Secular and non-Christian Spiritualists. This division does not correspond exactly with the existing organizational divisions except for the fact that all members of churches affiliated to the Greater World Christian Spiritualist League are Christians. The other major national Organization, the Spiritualist National Union, includes Spiritualists who are Christian as well as those who are non-Christian. Most Spiritualists today appear to accept some Christian beliefs and few are completely anti-Christian, but Spiritualists may be arranged along a continuum from the completely orthodox Christian to the anti-Christian, though those at the later polar extreme form a much smaller group than in the nineteenth century.

The second way is to classify them according to practice. In this way they can be subdivided into religious Spiritualists who are organized into churches and include worship in their activities; and scientific Spiritualists who are organized mainly into psychic research groups and who are mainly occupied in investigation.

Finally the movement may be subdivided on the basis of organization. In this case we find that there are several types of organization.

1. National organizations composed of affiliated or member churches and individuals, such as the Spiritualist National Union or the Greater World Christian Spiritualist League.

2. National bodies catering for the needs of particular sections of the movement, such as the Union of Spiritualist Mediums, the National Federation of Healers and the Society for Psychic Research.

188

3. National bodies having local branches – such as White Eagle Lodge.
4. Local independent churches. and societies

In 1964 the Spiritualists National Union reported a total of 464 affiliated societies and nine kindred bodies. A year earlier the Greater World Christian Spiritualist League issued a list of 215 affiliated churches. The Commonwealth of the Spiritualist Association of Great Britain had seventeen member societies, but all except two of these were also affiliated to the S.N.U. or the G.W.C.S.L.

There were also many societies unaffiliated to the major national bodies and it has not been possible to obtain a complete list of independent societies. It has been possible to list 160 societies who have advertised in the Spiritualist press between 1961–64, but this certainly only represents a small proportion of independent societies, mainly situated in London and the south east.

If the situation of the known societies is plotted on a map, certain important facts regarding the geographical distribution of Spiritualists emerge. The areas of concentration of Spiritualist societies coincide with the areas of greatest density of population; while this is a natural and expected result, it demonstrates that Spiritualism is an urban religion. Few societies exist outside large towns except in the mining and industrial villages of the Tees–Tyne area and South Wales, and these villages are of course urban in character. The majority of societies are found in areas in which the density of population exceeds 512 inhabitants per square mile.

The majority of societies are in industrial areas except for the concentration of societies along the south and south west coasts. These are in areas in which there is a high proportion of elderly retired persons, who naturally tend to become interested in the spirit world.

In the Greater London conurbation there were at least 140 societies with a further 120 societies in the commuter country of the home counties and the south-east coast.

There were sixty-four societies in the heavily industrialized Tees–Tyne district on the coast strips about fifty miles long.

In the south east Lancashire area based on Manchester there were fifty churches, a further nineteen in east central Lancashire, and in the adjoining Bradford, Halifax and Leeds areas of Yorkshire an additional thirty-five societies.

In the south Yorkshire area around Sheffield there were thirty societies.

In the West Midlands conurbation around Birmingham there were thirty-eight churches, and in North Staffordshire a group of twelve churches in the potteries around Stoke-on-Trent.

There were fifty-five churches in South Wales. With the exception of two in Pembroke these were concentrated in the industrial areas of Glamorgan and Monmouthshire. Of the Scottish churches, twenty-nine are in the industrial strip between the Clyde and the Forth.

Within these areas of dense population, churches are found in comparatively small communities, whereas much larger towns situated in areas having a generally low density of population may have no society, though there are few towns in England with a population of more than 30,000 that do not support at least one church.

There are many local anomalies that can only be explained by reference to local social and religious factors and to the accidents of history. An interesting comparison can be made for example between Manchester, with some fifteen societies and Liverpool, where there are only four. The density of population in these two towns is comparable, as is also the population of the towns. A possible explanation may be sought in terms of the social and religious situation. About one third of the population of Liverpool are Roman Catholic,[1] largely as a result of the influx of Irish settlers. The Roman Catholic church is strongly opposed to Spiritualism. There are also many Irish Protestants in Liverpool and conflict was rife between Protestants and Catholics particularly in the nineteenth and early twentieth centuries. Such conflict tended to maintain the loyalty to their own group of Protestants as well as Catholics. In such an environment Spiritualism would find few recruits.

There are also a few cases of small towns situated in areas of low population density in which Spiritualism has become firmly established. The most outstanding example is that of Wisbech in Cambridgeshire, an isolated urban area of some 17,000 inhabitants

[1] *Encyclopaedia Brittanica*, 1963 says one third of school children in Liverpool are Roman Catholic.

situated in a sparsely populated agricultural district. There have been Spiritualist groups in the town since 1879 and for some years there were two active societies. A comparison may be most directly made with the nearby town of Kings Lynn, a somewhat larger town, with a population of 26,000, which has never supported any successful Spiritualist activities. There are no simple or obvious socio-religious explanations for this case and detailed historical research would be necessary to elucidate this problem.

After taking these exceptions into consideration there remains a clear correlation between density of population and the concentration of Spiritualist societies, and this also indicates a relationship between industrial urbanism and Spiritualism.

Spiritualism took root in the expanding urban-industrial areas of Britain in the eighteen fifties and 'sixties because it was in such areas that the masses were most alienated from the religious traditions of Christianity; it is in such areas that the movement has continued to survive, and in recent years when the movement as a whole has been at a standstill or even slightly declining, expansion has continued in areas of new urban-industrial development. In particular it is notable that such expansion has mainly occurred in the London area and the south-east, whereas some decline has taken place in the old industrial regions of the Lancashire–Yorkshire area and the north-east.

The regional distribution of S.N.U. churches show a significant pattern when compared with the distribution of G.W.C.S.L. churches and independent societies. In the London district of the S.N.U. (which includes the south east and East Anglia) there were ninety-four churches in 1964. In the same area the latest statistics (1962) show ninety-two G.W.C.S.L. churches and 112 independent churches. In other words under a third of the churches are affiliated to the S.N.U. and over a third are not affiliated to any national body.

In the north on the other hand the great majority of societies are members of the S.N.U. There are few G.W.C.S.L. or independent churches. For example, in the northern district of S.N.U. (Tees–Tyne) there were fifty-one S.N.U. churches, only eight G.W.C.S.L. and three independent churches.

It is only the S.N.U. that supplies any detailed statistics, and if we compare their statistics for 1951 with those for 1964 some important trends in the distribution of Spiritualists are revealed. Only two districts show an increase in both churches and membership, the London and West Midlands districts, both rapidly expanding areas economically and industrially. There are no comparable figures for G.W.C.S.L. and independent churches.

Modern Organizations

The S.N.U.—The history of the Spiritualists' National Union has already been considered in previous chapters. It was incorporated in 1901 as a company limited by guarantee, and succeeded the old National Federation of Spiritualists which had been formed in 1890.

The S.N.U. Limited is a Union of individuals and not a Union or federation of churches or societies as such. Churches or societies may become affiliated to the Union. The members of the Union are divided into three classes:

A. Class A members are the accredited representatives elected by affiliated churches.
B. Individual members are known as Class B members.
C. Class C members are the accredited representatives elected by kindred bodies.

The Union may also appoint honorary officers and honorary members; and young people between fourteen and eighteen may become Junior Associates.

Any Spiritualist Church or Society may become affiliated to the Union, provided they are established to promote Spiritualism and have a constitution or set of rules that complies with the conditions laid down by the bye-laws of the Union. There are three types of affiliated bodies: Churches, Mission Churches and Kindred Bodies.

In order to be affiliated as a church the organization must have a membership of at least twelve full members. There must be two classes of membership, full and associate; a record of membership must be kept and all full members must adhere to the Seven Principles laid down by the Union. The church must be controlled democratically by a committee elected by the full members and an Annual Meeting must be held at which an audited statement of accounts is presented. In the case of a Mission Church or Kindred

Body all persons who take part in management or have a vote must be required to adhere to the Seven Principles.

There were in 1964, 473 churches and other organizations affiliated to the Union, and these organizations had a total full membership of approximately 17,000. These churches are grouped together into eight Electoral Areas and these are sub-divided into thirteen District Councils.

These District Councils act as the local administrative branch of the Union.

The objects of the S.N.U. are laid down in its Memorandum of Association as amended on 11th March, 1950. These define Spiritualism as a religion and philosophy that recognizes certain principles, the Seven Principles to which all members of the Union must subscribe, though they are given freedom to interpret these principles in their own way. The principles are vague and open to a wide variety of interpretation, thus enabling people of widely differing views to become members of the Union.

The Seven Principles are:

1. The fatherhood of God.
2. The brotherhood of Man.
3. The Communion of Spirits and the Ministry of Angels.
4. The continuous existence of the human soul.
5. Personal responsibility.
6. Compensation and retribution hereafter for all the good and evil deeds done on earth.
7. Eternal progress open to every human soul.

The Spiritualists' National Union is a democratic organization in that it is administered by a Council elected by the members of the Union.

At General Meetings of the Union every member of the Union has one vote, but members of the Council, of a Branch or District Council, have an additional vote. When a vote is taken by a show of hands no person may vote under more than one qualification, but in a ballot or postal vote a person who is both a Class B member and an accredited representative may vote under both qualifications.

So far it would seem that democratic rights are somewhat overridden in that a Class B (individual) member has as much power as a Class A member, who may be representing a church

consisting of up to seventy-five full church members. The balance
is restored to some extent by the provision that: 'In a ballot at a
meeting, and in a postal vote on a resolution or for the election
of the President or Vice-President, every complete five (or part
of five) votes cast by Class B members (in that capacity) shall be
calculated as one vote.' Thus in these cases making the vote of
one accredited representative equal to the votes of five individual
members.

A further article that limits the powers of individual members
and strengthens that of the church representatives lays down that:
'The Chairman of a general meeting may, at the instance of not
less than ten Class A members, declare that any particular resolution to be put to the meeting is one which concerns Churches
only, and upon such declaration being made only Class A
members shall be entitled to vote upon the resolution'.

As we have already mentioned, only democratically organized
and controlled churches are eligible to become affiliated to the
S.N.U., and such affiliated churches elect representatives in proportion to the number of their full members. If a Class A member
is unable to represent his church at a meeting he is allowed to
appoint a proxy to attend in his place. The Union lays down in
detail in its bye-laws the 'Conditions for Affiliation of Churches',
and also publishes Model Rules and Constitution for churches,
which may be adopted by churches affiliating to the Union.

An affiliated church undertakes to make returns of membership,
supply a copy of the audited accounts and supply any other
information required by the Council of the Union. The Union has
the right (when requested by not less than three members of a
church) to inspect the accounts of the church. Under the Model
Rules the S.N.U. or the District Council may appoint a representative to attend the A.G.M. of an affiliated church. Each affiliated
church is required to pay a subscription based on the number of
full members. When a church becomes affiliated to the National
Union it also becomes a member of the appropriate District
Council and the Class A members it elects as representatives
on the National Union also act as delegates to the District
Council.

The Constitution of District Councils is laid down in the
bye-laws of the Union. These bye-laws leave each district council
free to determine the number of its officers and members of its

executive committee, except that they must include a president,
a treasurer and a secretary. The officers may be either elected
directly or appointed by the executive committee from among
themselves. The district council may also decide to allow certain
classes of members to elect particular members of the executive
committee.

A district council may establish a class of associate (individual)
members or it may accept Class B members as associate members.
It is entitled to raise funds by subscription from associate
members, by donations, collections and 'other lawful methods',
and it also receives one quarter of the subscriptions received by
the Union from the churches in its district. The actual work
carried out by District Councils varies from district to district.

The Greater World Christian Spiritualist League.—Many of those
churches and societies which have explicit Christian beliefs are
associated with the Greater World Christian Spiritualist League.
The League originated from the Home Circle of the medium,
Winifred Moyes, and in 1963 had about 220 affiliated churches
and over 20,000 members.

Miss Moyes became the president of the League and together
with a small group of self appointed leaders effectively led and
controlled the League until her death in 1957. Mr F. N. Tolkin
was elected president and remained in office until 1963, when he
was succeeded in that office by Mrs Margaret Hoare.

The League continues to be organized on an autocratic rather
than democratic system. It is administered by a Council of not less
than five members who are described in the official literature as
'Christian Spiritualists of experience'. There is no means for the
representation of affiliated churches, and member churches have
no method of controlling the actions of the Council of the
League. On the other hand the 'Council does not interfere with
the internal management of Churches provided the Constitutions
remain satisfactory'. The League also makes no condition that
its churches should themselves be democratically organized and
is prepared to accept member churches that are controlled by
individuals and have no elected committee. Further it is not
necessary for churches to have voting and subscribing members.
If they prefer, churches may operate a scheme of voluntary financial support instead of having subscribing members. Affiliated

churches pay a minimum annual subscription of £1 10s. 0d. and individual members pay 2s. 6d. per year.

The League has drawn up standard rules for the administration of churches which, however, churches are not required, but only recommended, to adopt. Two versions of these standard rules are produced, a version bound in blue covers 'which provide for the permanent management of the church by the Founders', and a version in green covers, 'for churches that are subject to an annual election of officers'. There is thus a great variety of organization within the churches affiliated to the League.

Beliefs are more nearly uniform, for members of the League subscribe to the following beliefs and are required to make a pledge.

The beliefs are:

1. I believe in one God who is Love.

2. I accept the leadership of Jesus Christ.

3. I believe that God manifests through the illimitable power of the Holy Spirit.

4. I believe in the survival of the human soul and its individuality after physical death.

5. I believe in the communion with God, with his Angelic Ministers, and with the Soul's functioning in conditions other than the Earth life.

6. I believe that all forms of Life created by God intermingle, are interdependent, and evolve until perfection is attained.

7. I believe in the Perfect Justice of the Divine Laws governing all Life.

8. I believe that sins committed can only be rectified by the sinner himself or herself, through the redemptive power of Jesus Christ, by repentance and service to others.

The pledge states: 'I will at all times endeavour to be guided in my thoughts, words and deeds by the teaching and example of Jesus Christ.'

The League recommends that the Authorized Version of the Bible should be used in Christian Spiritualist Churches. The League also produces its own Hymn Book and Orders of Services for Holy Communion, Healing, Baptism, Marriage, Burial and for Good Friday. Some C.S. Churches have Sunday Schools which are generally closer in organization, in practice and beliefs to other Christian Sunday Schools than they are to Spiritualist Lyceums.

The business of the League is conducted through the Greater World Association Trust, which is managed by a management committee of fifteen members. The League has a Board of Literature which is responsible for the official publications of the League and a Board of Arbitration which deals with claims or disputes arising out of League matters which are referred to it for ruling.

The League may award the G.W. Diploma to public workers, 'who, as the result of careful inquiry, are found to qualify for it'. A list of Diploma holders is circulated to churches who find it useful in their choice of speakers. Healing has always played an important part in the work of the League, but it was not until 1960 that the G.W. Healing Fellowship was founded. In 1961 it became affiliated to the National Federation of Spiritual Healers.

The Greater World C.S. League has from its earliest days carried out philanthropic work. On 21st January 1933, a Free Night Shelter was opened for homeless women in Lambeth, and a second Night Shelter was opened in Leeds in 1935. These shelters did excellent work and were open to people irrespective of their beliefs. The Lambeth shelter was destroyed by enemy action during the war but the work continued in private homes until a new Shelter and Rest Home was opened at Deptford in 1948. This carried on its work for five and a half years until a new bye-law was enforced which made it an offence for any woman to be found on the streets at night without a lodging. The Police were given instructions to direct such women to hostels or to lodge them at a police station. Philanthropic work in London continues to be organized from the League headquarters. The Leeds Shelter continues its work as a Home for Women and Children. Since 1937 the League has supported a Convalescent Home for elderly women at Leigh-on-Sea and in recent years a Rest Home has been opened at Bridlington.

The Spiritualist Association of Great Britain.—In February 1960 the Marylebone Spiritualist Association changed its name to the Spiritualist Association of Great Britain. The change of name was a recognition of the fact that the Association was no longer restricted to members from London, let alone from Marylebone. The Association is the oldest existing Spiritualist organization in London, having been founded in 1872. The Association became limited by guarantee under the Companies Act in 1905, and it is a recognized charity.

It is the largest unitary Spiritualist association in the world with a membership of about 7,000. There are no branches, and all the activities of the Association are carried on at the premises at 33 Belgrave Square.

The Association is governed by a Council of fifteen members. A third of the Council retires each year and council members are elected by the Annual General Meeting. The President is elected by the Council from its own members for a period of a year, but no member may serve as President for more than three consecutive years. The Council also elects a Treasurer from among themselves, and may also elect two Vice-Presidents, also from the members of the Council. They also have powers to appoint a paid Secretary and Assistant Secretary and any such other officers as may be required at any time.

The Association does not lay down any creed or require its members to subscribe to any articles of belief. While it holds regular Sunday services in the chapel at headquarters it is mainly concerned with providing facilities for investigation. The facilities include group seances which are held daily (except Sundays). These are limited to five people and are concerned with experiments in clairvoyance, clairaudience and psychometry.

Demonstrations of clairvoyance and clairaudience to larger audiences are also given daily as also are demonstrations of psychometry. There are also lectures on Spiritualism and allied subjects every day. Trance lectures are frequently given and a discussion group meets weekly. Meetings for Spiritual healing are held daily and arrangements are also made for absent healing. Classes for psychic development are held every evening and a class for esoteric thought meets weekly.

In 1961 the Spiritualist Association of Great Britain decided to invite a select number of the major Spiritualist organizations in the country to join it in forming a loose federation called the Commonwealth of the Spiritualist Association of Great Britain. This Commonwealth has no formal organization; each member organization is completely autonomous and free of all central control. The aim of the Commonwealth seems to have been to associate together those organizations which the Council of the S.A.G.B. considered to be the best organized and most respectable. The only apparent advantage to be gained from the Commonwealth is that the members of a 'Member Organization' are welcome to attend the activities of any other 'Member Organization'.

The Commonwealth grew slowly. In 1961 it consisted of eleven member organizations; by 1963 there were seventeen; most of these were also members of the S.N.U., two were members of the Greater World C.S. League and only two were unaffiliated to other organizations.

The Union of Spiritualist Mediums.—This organization was established in June 1956 to advance and protect the interests of mediums, to present the philosophy of Spiritualism and demonstrate psychic gifts to the public.

The 'aims and objects' of the Union as set out in the Constitution read:

The Union shall be an Association of Spiritualist mediums, demonstrating psychic gifts, spiritual healers, and public speakers presenting Spiritualist theory and philosophy, and other persons who are in agreement with and support the Aims and Objects of the Union. The Union shall not be affiliated to any other Spiritualist organization and shall be entirely non-political.

The objects are declared to be:

1. The advancement of the religion and religious philosophy of Spiritualism.
2. The training of prospective workers – young and old – in the principles of religion and religious philosophy of Spiritualism.
3. Such other charitable objects as may be decided upon from time to time by special Resolution of all the full members in General Meeting.

The membership is divided into two classes. Full members, who must be either mediums, public speakers for Spiritualism or

Spiritual healers; and associate members. Any adult sympathizer may become an associate member.

The official journal *The Medium* listed 673 full members of the Union in June 1963. The total membership was over 900. *The Medium* is published quarterly. The Union has a Benevolent Fund which helps needy mediums and other spiritualists. They plan to open a Home for Elderly Spiritualists and the Secretary states 'In the meantime, we help, where we can, to alleviate the loneliness of these elderly Mediums and Spiritualists, help in a financial way where we can, and send comforts to them when necessary'.

The Union is a voluntary organization and charges no fees for its help. The Union supplies churches with mediums and does particularly good work in providing a medium at short notice, when a church has been let down by a medium already booked. The Union also attempts to ensure that mediums get a 'square deal' from the churches. It protects their interests and settles disputes.

The Union has its headquarters in London at which demonstrations are given. This enables new mediums to have the opportunity of platform work and provincial mediums to appear in London. The work of the Union is confined very largely to London and the South-east and the great majority of its members reside in this area.

National Federation of Spiritual Healers.—Healing by spiritual means has formed a part of the Spiritualist Movement since its early days, and Spiritual healing is part of the work of nearly all Spiritualist churches and organizations today. Certain mediums appear to be endowed with the power of healing and in most churches healing services and healing circles are held.

There have been famous healers throughout the history of Spiritualism; probably the best known healer at the present time is Harry Edwards, who operates from a headquarters at Shere in Surrey. Edwards is the founder president of the National Federation of Spiritual Healers, and also publishes a monthly magazine entitled *The Spiritual Healer*.

The object of the National Federation is laid down as 'the due promotion and encouragement of the study and practice of the art and science of Spiritual healing', and Spiritual healing is defined by the Federation as 'all forms of healing of the sick in body, mind or spirit, by means of prayer, meditation, laying on of hands, manipulation and otherwise, whether or not in the actual presence of the patient'.

The Federation aims at:

A. Uniting healers for the protection both of healers and of patients.
B. Raising the standard and status of healing and healers.
C. Giving recognition to healers of sufficient standards of competence; and
D. Acting as a representative body for healers in all matters appertaining to healing.

The Federation is not incorporated and consists of regional or other associations of healers and individual members. The Federation has a membership of over 2,500, and is organized and controlled entirely by healers whose interest it represents, though sympathizers may become Associate Members. Members are insured against 'negligence' and the Federation also provides legal services. It provides an advisory service for enquirers, patients and healers, referring patients to healers and putting healers in touch with fellow healers whose aid and co-operation they require. Lectures and demonstrations are organized in many parts of the country as part of the Federation's educational services.

There has been an increasing interest in Spiritual healing in recent years and even some National Health Service hospitals have permitted Healers to visit their patients, but generally the medical profession remains suspicious of Spiritual healing.

Other National Bodies

It would be impossible within the limits of this study to examine the beliefs and organization of all the independent churches and societies in Britain, but it will be useful to consider briefly some of the more important of these bodies. One of the most important of these is the White Eagle Lodges.

The first White Eagle Lodge was opened on 22nd February 1936, at Pembroke Hall, Kensington, by Mrs Grace Cooke under the inspiration of 'White Eagle', her spirit guide.

Mrs Cooke had been a Spiritualist medium since 1913. At first she concentrated on giving evidence of survival. She gradually became convinced, under the influence of White Eagle, that the philosophical aspect of Spiritualism was more important, and together with a small group of followers she formed a church in Middlesex which was intended to be an example to the movement for its treatment of mediums and for the quality of its teaching.

Mrs Cooke worked at this church for some years, but eventually broke with the church when the Committee wanted to concentrate upon the proof of survival. In the early nineteen thirties Mrs Cooke worked with Steads Library and the Marylebone Spiritualist Association, and was also taking meetings in other parts of the country.

The next move that Mrs Cooke and her family made was to lease Burstow Manor in Surrey where the White Eagle Brotherhood was founded. When the lease of Burstow Manor expired the Cookes set up White Eagle Lodge at Pembroke Hall. The new organization was entirely under the direction of Mr and Mrs Cooke so that there should be no possibility of interference with the teachings of White Eagle by a democratic committee. White Eagle apparently believes in the importance of a family atmosphere and in the importance of harmonious conditions.

The war temporarily set back the work of the Lodge. White Eagle had insisted on working for peace and many of his followers were disillusioned when war broke out; furthermore the Lodge headquarters were destroyed early in the 'blitz' in 1940.

Early in 1941 the Lodge acquired new premises at 9 St Mary Abbot's Place; in the meantime the work was carried on at the daughter Lodge which had by then been established in Edinburgh. At the end of the war, in 1945, the Cookes acquired new premises, 'New Lands', at Liss in Hampshire, which was opened as a Retreat and Training Centre. In 1948 and 1950 two Trust Deeds were drawn up under which the administration of the London premises were handed over to a Trust, and in 1953 New Lands was also taken over by a Trust. In 1953 The White Eagle Publishing Trust was also formed. The Council of the three Trusts consists of Mr and Mrs Cooke, their two daughters and their husbands, so the Lodge remains very much a family affair.

The work of the Lodge has continued to prosper, and by 1962 there were also branches in Edinburgh, Bournemouth, Plymouth, Worthing and Reading; and at New Jersey in the U.S.A.

The teaching of White Eagle is summed up in the principles of the Lodge.

1. The Father–Motherhood of God.
2. That Christ, the Son of the Father–Mother God, is the light which shines through Wisdom and Love in the human heart; and that by reason of this Divine Sonship all are brothers and sisters regardless of race, class or creed; and that this brotherhood and sisterhood embraces life visible and invisible.
3. The expression of these principles in daily life through service.
4. The awareness of the invisible world which bridges separation and death and reveals the eternal unity of life.
5. That life is governed by five cosmic laws: Reincarnation; Cause and Effect; Opportunity; Correspondence (as above, so below); Equilibrium (the law of Compensation).
6. That the ultimate goal of mankind is the blooming of the Rose at the Heart of the Cross; the realization of the Christ-consciousness as exemplified by the Master; the reunion of the Holy Family.

The Lodge has a symbol which consists of 'The Cross within the Circle with the Six-pointed Star at its heart'. The literature of the Lodge carries a six-pointed star with the Tudor Rose at its centre.

These symbols together with the principles indicate clearly that the Lodge derives its teachings at least in part from the Rosi-crucian Brotherhood, and in fact White Eagle is claimed as a messenger from the White Brotherhood which all Occult groups claim exist both in the Spirit and Earth Worlds as wise guides of the human race.

The work of the Lodges consists of conducting public services, meditation groups and lectures, and with providing 'inner teaching for students of the deeper truths of life'. An important part of the work consists of Spiritual healing and trained healers are available. The Publishing Trust, in addition to books and pamphlets, produces a magazine, *Stella Polaris*.

In April 1957 a new occult-spiritualist society was formed in London with the aim of propagating the teachings of Melio-Archanoplues, a spirit guide claiming to have lived in the lost continent of Atlantis. The Society teaches a philosophy based on that accepted by the ancient Atlanteans. They believe that certain 'Spirits from the Planet Venus incarnated into Earth bodies to assist the evolutionary strain of the Earth'. These people founded the Atlantean civilization which the 'Atlanteans' believe to have been the forerunner of all subsequent civilizations.

It is only one of several societies that exist on the fringe of Spiritualism. These societies are concerned with occult teachings rather than contact with the dead but their teachings are said to be given by elevated Spirits through a medium who is the leader of the group.

Another of these societies is the School of Universal Philosophy and Healing of whom the founder and present leader is Mrs Grace Spearman-Cook, who is the medium for the spirit guide Ra-Men-Ra. The School publishes a monthly journal, *The Occult Gazette*.

The Theosophical Society is yet another occult society. It has branches throughout the country and is probably the major society of its type in the country. The Theosophical Society today has little connection with Spiritualism, but it was, in fact, founded by Madam Blavatski, a medium who had great psychic powers.

Finally there are many local churches not affiliated to any national body. While many of these are perfectly respectable religious bodies usually run by their founders, there is no doubt that some of these 'one-man' churches are run only for personal profit and that some are indeed bogus churches run by fraudulent mediums.

Chapter Twelve

BELIEFS AND PRACTICES

The Spiritualist system of beliefs is extremely complex and varied. Spiritualism is far from being a homogeneous religion, and there are many 'schools' of thought within the movement. There are numerous groups, each with its own beliefs, which differ in some degree from those of all other groups in the movement. Spiritualism in its belief structure is a very individualistic religion and many of these groups are small and tend to cluster around an individual, usually a medium, with distinctive teachings. The lack of cohesion within the movement as a whole, the existence of many groups and societies, is directly attributable to the lack of a consistent body of teachings accepted by all Spiritualists. Spiritualism has no creed, no dogma. There is no formulation of belief nor any 'Scriptures' that would be accepted without question by all those who might be defined, or would call themselves Spiritualists.

There are only two propositions to which all Spiritualists would assent. And these are the two basic definitions of Spiritualism.

All Spiritualists believe that:

1. The human personality, in some form, survives the death of the body.

2. That it is possible to communicate, in some way, with the 'spirits' of the dead.

The first of these propositions is accepted by many persons who are not spiritualists, it forms an element in the teaching of the Christian churches and of most of the other major religions. There is, however, an important difference between the way in which a Christian and a Spiritualist accepts a belief in human 'survival'.

The Christian accepts 'survival' as a matter of faith; he accepts because he has been told that it is so, he accepts because the founder of his religion and most of the greatest exponents have taught it as a fact and because it has become accepted as a dogma of the church. He accepts it on authority.

The Spiritualist believes in survival because of the evidence of his senses and of what he has experienced at Spiritualist meetings. He believes because he has received a communication from the dead or experienced some other form of psychic phenomena. Of course his experience may be the result of an illusion, but this does not invalidate his claim that he believes in 'survival' as a fact because of his experience and not as an article of faith as in the case of the Christian. Spiritualism thus claims to be based upon fact and not upon faith, upon evidence and not upon authority. There are a few Spiritualists who accept because of what they have read and been told by others, but the great majority believe in survival because of their own experiences in Spiritualist circles, where they have had some evidence strong enough to convince them of the truth of the basic Spiritualist beliefs.

Spiritualists also claim that there is the same sort of evidence for psychic phenomena as for any natural phenomena investigated by science, and that consequently their claims are susceptible of proof by anyone who cares to test them, as are the claims of physical science, that one can prove survival by tests carried out under suitable conditions in the same sort of way that the proposition that water boils at 100°C can also be proved under standardized conditions. Survival to the Spiritualist is not a matter of 'faith' but an established fact of the natural universe.

It is the second of our propositions that is unique to Spiritualism, the belief in the possibility of regular communication between the living and the dead. Many religions believe that their founder and a few 'saints' and holy men have had on occasion the ability to communicate with the spirits and there are many accounts of such communications in the religious literature of the world, but only Spiritualism has put communication with the spirits at the centre of its practices and made it the basis of its beliefs. It is through the practice of communication with the spirits that the Spiritualists derive the evidence for their belief in 'human survival'. It is thus easy to see that there is a close connection between practices and beliefs in the Spiritualist movement. The Spiritualist derives his beliefs from the evidence produced by his practices and his practices give support to his beliefs. This is not a rephrasing of the old problem of which came first, the chicken or the egg, for it is clear that in Spiritualism at least the practice came first in a historical sense and that it generally comes first in the experience of an individual Spiritualist.

All the subsidiary beliefs of Spiritualism also stem from the practices, since these beliefs, varied, complex and contradictory as they are, are usually derived from the messages received from the 'spirits' through various mediums, or deduced from the type of phenomena that manifests at Spiritualist seances.

We have thus two sources from which beliefs are derived, the teachings of the spirits and the evidence of psychic phenomena; we shall consider these in turn.

The majority of the messages that come through from the 'dead' are not concerned with theological or philosophical matters but are apparently trivial little messages designed only to prove to their friends that it is really the 'dead' person communicating. The triviality of the messages at a typical Spiritualist meeting has caused many people to abandon Spiritualism after their first experience, but on the other hand a message which is apparently trivial to an outsider can be highly convincing to the person to whom it is addressed if it contains detailed personal evidence probably known only to him. Messages of an apparently trivial nature but which contained evidence of the survival of personality have been responsible for the conversion of many people to Spiritualism. In fact it is usually as a result of obtaining a message of this sort that a person becomes a Spiritualist. The great majority of Spiritualists are converted as a result of receiving a trivial message; very few have been converted by an elevating moral discourse from the 'Spirit World'. A small number of people become Spiritualists as a result of experiencing the 'physical' phenomena of Spiritualism apart from any message that may have been received. There are many recorded cases of conversion as a result of a personal message.[1]

The teachings that come from the 'Spirits' through a medium differ greatly both in quality and in content. Some are highly conventional 'sermons' while others are original in thought and expression. At one extreme they may be rambling and almost

[1] R. Blatchford, *More Things in Heaven and Earth*, 1925; Arthur Findley, *Looking Back*, 1955; *On the Edge of the Etheric*, 1931.

incoherent while at the other extreme one gets highly fluent and erudite discourses.

The opinions of the spirits are as diverse and varied as are those of the living, except that naturally one never hears from a spirit who is a materialist, though one does occasionally hear of a materialist, since survival is believed to be an automatic and universal fact of nature and consequently not dependent upon belief. The convinced materialist survives equally with the convinced Spiritualist but if he communicates, tends to be converted, since it would be difficult to deny 'survival' if one has 'survived'. There have been many claims that noted sceptics and materialists have returned and admitted their errors.

Some authorities hold that those who do not believe in 'survival' remain in an unconscious state after death and by a process of auto-hypnosis fulfil their own beliefs[2] but even these spirits eventually wake from their spiritual 'suspended animation' to realize that they have survived.

The Spiritualists have a simple explanation for the great variety of religious beliefs that are taught by the spirits. Spiritualists say that when an individual dies he does not suddenly become an all wise, all good angel. He takes with him the preconceptions, ideas and beliefs he has had in life; he also takes with him his moral characteristics. The man who believed in God continues to believe in God in the spirit world, for there appears to be no more direct evidence for the existence of God at least in the lowest levels of the spirit world than on earth. On the other hand the atheist continues to hold to his beliefs for the same reason. The Christian remains a Christian, the Jew remains a Jew. Only as they develop in the Spirit world, do they learn more and evolve spiritually; by that time it appears it is more difficult for them to communicate with 'earth people'. A further explanation appeared in *The Spiritualist* as long ago as 1875, when the editor attempted to explain the wide variety of teachings held by spiritualists as resulting from the ideas of the Spirits becoming 'coloured in the vital telegraphic process through which they reach the external world'.

The thoughts of mortals have had a considerable influence in moulding the religious ideas now prevalent in Spiritualism.

[2] Lord Dowding, *The Dark Star*, p. 22, 1951.

. . . This is how one set of religious teachings will be found among one set of Spiritualists and a different set of religious teachings among another detachment and why the said teachings usually bear a distinct relation to the opinions of those who promulgate them. There are certain points of agreement running through all the spirit messages. . . . All the spirits are agreed that there is no eternal punishment, and that the state of life after bodily death is one of progression.

It is said that some highly advanced spirits voluntarily retard their translation to the higher levels of the spirit world in order to help those still on earth. It is these advanced spirits that are claimed as the source of the more elevated types of religious teaching that comes through Spiritualist 'mediums', but even these more advanced spirits do not agree in the teachings they give.

The physical phenomena of Spiritualism includes psychometry, healing, materialization, ('direct-voice') messages, levitation and spirit photography. The experience of such phenomena reinforces belief in the spirit teachings and contributes to the formation of beliefs about the nature of the world and Ultimate Reality.

In view of the diversity of phenomena and beliefs there is not and cannot be any generally agreed body of beliefs amongst spiritualists. The nearest we can get to this is probably contained in a book called *Spirit Teachings* by the Rev. W. Stainton Moses. This book was produced by Stainton Moses as the result of communications he received through automatic writing. It has been described as the 'bible' of Spiritualism.

A further summary of Spiritualist beliefs was given by the spirits through Emma Hardinge Britten.

In reply to queries as to what Spiritualism has taught and what good it has done for humanity, she said:

1. It proves Man's Immortality, and the Existence of a Spiritual Universe.

2. It destroys all fear of Death, annihilates the doctrine of eternal punishment, and substitutes the cheering assurance of eternal progress.

3. It sweeps away the idea of a personal Devil, and locates the sources of evil in man's own imperfections.

4. It denies the immoral and soul corrupting doctrine of any

vicarious atonements for sin, and on the testimony of millions of immortal spirits, solemnly affirms that every guilty soul must arise and become its own Saviour.

5. It ignores the degrading conception of a partial and vindictive God, and substitutes the worship of an Infinite Eternal and all perfect Spirit, an Alpha and Omega, all Love Wisdom and Law.

6. It demolishes the absurd and materialistic conception of the theological heaven and hell, making each a state of happiness or misery dependent on the good or evil within the soul itself.

7. It is the death blow to superstition, sectarianism, and religious persecution, but the friend and prompter of all reforms that tend to elevate and benefit humanity.

8. Whilst Spiritualism proclaims that there is a Standard of Truth in everything, it acknowledges man's incapacity to discover all truth, and therefore it fetters no one's opinions, and teaches, but never forces its beliefs on anyone.

9. Concerning all Spiritual life, state and being, Spiritualism accepts no theories that are not sustained by proven facts and corroborative testimony.

10. Its phenomena – being all based upon immutable principles of law – open up endless arenas of new research for science, and its consensus of revelations being founded upon facts, tend to place true religion on the basis of science, and vitalize science with all that is true and practical in religion.

11. Spiritualism is a ceaseless incentive to practise good; it reunites the friends separated by death; strengthens the weak and desolate by the presence of angel guidance and protection; cheers the afflicted with the certainty of another and better world, where justice will be done and every wrong will be righted. It is terrible only to the guilty, proving that spirit eyes can and do read every secret crime and that all crimes must be abandoned and atoned for by personal suffering and personal compensation before any guilty soul can attain happiness hereafter.

12. Spiritualists have no creed, but may all unite in the following simple summary:

'I believe in the Fatherhood of God,
The Brotherhood of Man,

The Immortality of the Soul,

Personal Responsibility,

Compensation and Retribution hereafter for all the good or evil deeds done here.

And a path of eternal progress open to every human soul that wills to tread it by the path of eternal good.'

These beliefs formed the principles of the Spiritualists' National Federation and remain the basis of the Seven Principles of the Spiritualists' National Union.

These Seven Principles are discussed in the section on National organizations. The principles of the Greater World Christian Spiritualist League are also derived from messages from the Spirit World given through Winifred Moyes.

The White Eagle Lodge, the other organization of national importance that has clearly defined principles, base these on messages received from the spirits.

Internal Structure of Churches

In such a diverse and divided movement as Spiritualism, there is naturally a wide variety of type of internal structure and organization within the churches. These vary from organizations in which the power and authority are vested in one man to those in which the church is controlled democratically and run by elected officials.

All churches affiliated to the Spiritualists' National Union are organized on democratic lines. It is a condition of affiliation to the S.N.U. that a 'church must be controlled on a democratic basis by the full members through an elected committee', and that 'There must be annually a meeting of full members at which an audited statement of accounts is presented'.

The National Union issues Model Rules and Constitution for the use of their affiliated churches.

In the democratically organized churches there is nothing resembling the priesthood of the Catholic, Anglican or Episcopal churches. The organization resembles most nearly the pattern of Congregational churches.

The S.N.U. indeed appoints ministers and individual churches may appoint a resident minister but these ministers have no pastoral authority or hierarchical power over the members of a urches resemble the ...he Congregational or ...hes do not appoint a ...t of services and meet-... f the church, who is an

...es are served by different exponents each week. These exponents are mediums having various psychic gifts who assist in the conduct of services and meetings. In some cases they may conduct the entire proceedings under the chairmanship of the president of the church they are visiting, but in many cases the worship is led by the president who leads in prayer and gives the readings, while the visiting medium gives a trance or normal address, and demonstrates some form of mediumship during or at the conclusion of the service.

The member churches of the S.N.U. are free to book the services of mediums of their choice, but the Union has compiled a register of exponents whom it recognizes as suitable and proficient.

In any church there will probably be several members who have psychic gifts of various sorts which they have developed to varying degrees, and these mediums will play their appropriate part in the activities of the church.

Psychic gifts are at the centre of all Spiritualist organizations, and while many Spiritualists claim such gifts, it is those who are well endowed with such gifts who tend to be at the centre of a Spiritualist church.

Of course, psychic powers are not necessary for the exercise of the organizational offices within the churches, such as secretary, treasurer or president, but such is the prestige that the possession of such powers confers, that mediums of all types tend to exert considerable influence within the churches.

Mediums are held in respect not so much because they possess special powers but because they are instruments through which the Spirit World may communicate. The great medium is generally honoured as the mouthpiece of a wise spirit guide.

Mediumship takes many forms but these are all attributed to the work of the spirit world. Mediumship however has to be developed by the efforts of the individual. Some people appear to be spontaneously endowed with psychic powers but even these can usually be improved with training and practice. Most people at first appear to have no psychic abilities, but many Spiritualists claim that all people have latent psychic abilities and that they may develop these abilities.

Consequently many Spiritualist Churches have development circles in which aspiring mediums may sit to develop their powers. A development circle consists of a comparatively small group that meets regularly and as far as possible is composed of the same individuals over a comparatively long period.

The development circle is only one of the many types of groups that arise within the Spiritualist movement. The home circle still remains an important factor within the movement. Within the churches Open Circles are formed to give seekers the opportunity to experience psychic phenomena.

Special healing circles are also formed in many churches, and meetings or services, for healing, are a feature of the whole movement. Lectures, classes, discussion groups and demonstrations also form part of the activities of the churches and societies.

It would be difficult (for the reasons already mentioned) to give an adequate description of a typical Spiritualist service, but perhaps a broad description should be ventured. Many Spiritualist Churches meet in hired rooms forming part of a building devoted to other uses, some meet in halls which are used by other organizations during the week, and only a minority have their own church buildings. In such circumstances the appearance of the churches will obviously vary widely. The Spiritualist church is generally rather austere in appearance, resembling most nearly a Nonconformist chapel. The form of service generally follows a pattern similar to that of a Nonconformist church.

The service opens with a prayer of invocation followed by a hymn. Then there is usually a reading and even in non-Christian churches this is often from the Bible. A second hymn may be followed by informal and impromptu prayers led by the chairman or speaker. A collection or offering will be taken probably during the singing of a third hymn, and in Christian churches a prayer of offering may be said. The address is normally given by the visiting speaker, this may be a normal sermon or it may be a trance address in which the medium's Control speaks through her/him to the congregation. The service concludes with a hymn and prayer of blessing. The service is usually followed immediately by a demonstration of mediumship in which the medium gives messages from the spirits to members of the audience.

This, of course, is a very brief and inadequate description of a Spiritualist Service, but the details vary greatly, so that a more detailed description of a particular service could in no way be taken as representative of the whole movement.

A study of Spiritualism demonstrates that belief tends to arise as a result of experience and that the organizational structure of the movement is determined by the pattern of beliefs.

In order to contain within it a diversity of beliefs and practices the movement must remain tolerant. Intolerance would drive the majority out of the movement and into the formation of their own separate cults. The same factor, a need for tolerance and the inclusion of many beliefs and practices, means that the movement remains a loose association of local groups which are themselves largely democratic in structure.

Part Three

SOCIOLOGY AND SPIRITUALISM

Chapter Thirteen

CHURCH, SECT AND CULT

In the course of the study of the origins and development of the Spiritualist movement certain trends in the origin and organization of spiritualist groups become apparent. We have examined in terms of sociological theory the origins of Spiritualism but have so far not considered sociologically the development of organization within the Spiritualist movement. In the following chapters we shall apply sociological theories which we have developed largely from the theories of Max Weber to the analysis of the movement in an attempt to explain the way in which Spiritualism has developed in Britain.

One of the most interesting tools for the analysis of religious groups is the Sect–Church typology. The concepts of Sects and Churches as distinct types of religious bodies are derived originally, at least as sociological terms from the work of Max Weber, but it was left to his friend Ernst Troeltsch to formulate and expand this typology. Since Troeltsch's great work, *The Social Teaching of the Christian Churches* was published, a considerable literature has grown up devoted to the study of the typological analysis of religious organizations.

In his study of Christianity, Troeltsch traced the existence of three basic types of organization which he named as Church, Sect and Mysticism. All three types, he argued, have co-existed throughout the history of Christianity. The Church is an institution endowed with grace which it administers to the world through the priesthood. It is universalistic and seeks to include everyone, in consequence of which it tends to relax its moral demands. The Church adjusts itself to the world, it supports the existing authorities and the social order, and is thus closely connected with and dependent upon the upper classes. Members are normally 'born into' the Church, and it does not actively seek adult converts. The Church emphasizes the importance of doctrine and sacraments, and while its discipline is comparatively lax on moral questions, it is much more strict on questions of faith.

The Sect is a voluntary society of strict believers who are bound together by a common religious experience. They reject any compromise with the world and form small separate groups who stress the virtue of individual perfection and asceticism. They are either hostile or indifferent to the state and the existing social and ecclesiastical order and look forward to the coming kingdom of God.

Mysticism arises when ideas which have hardened into formal worship and doctrine are transformed into purely personal and inward experience. This gives rise to the formation of groups on a purely personal basis, and having no permanent form or organization, they give little importance to forms of worship, doctrine or to historical factors, but emphasize individual religious experience, the freedom of the individual, the liberty of conscience and thus they encourage religious toleration.

The development of Troeltsch's 'Ideal' typology has concentrated on an expansion of his concepts of Church and Sect and subsequent students have largely ignored his third major concept of Mysticism. This has had an unfortunate effect on later typological analysis, and as we hope to demonstrate, his concept of Mysticism has important implications for the analysis of movements such as Spiritualism.

Let us first examine more closely the development of the Church–Sect typology and trace its relevance to the development of the Spiritualist movement. The ideal typology of Troeltsch was found to be inadequate to explain and classify certain types of religious organization, in particular the type commonly known as the denomination which appeared to be somewhere between the Sect and the Church in its characteristics, and which seemed to many investigators to be the 'ideal type' that approaches most nearly to the form of church organization and structure in the U.S.A. As a result of his studies of American denominations, R. H. Niebuhr introduced a dynamic element into the analysis by arguing that there was an inevitable process whereby a Sect developed into a Church.

Howard Becker in his adaptation of the work of Leopold Von Wiese[1] developed a four-fold classification, which was later used

[1] H. Becker, *Systematic Sociology on the basis of the Beziehungslehre and Gebildelhre of Leopold Von Wiese*, pp. 624–8, New York, 1932.

as the basis of his six-fold typology by Milton Yinger.[2] Yinger's types are:

1. The Universal Church, which he suggests is the most successful in supporting the integration of society and satisfies most of the personality needs of individuals in all strata of society. The best example of a Universal Church would be the Catholic Church in Mediaeval Europe.

2. The Ecclesia is less successful in incorporating sect tendencies, and while it is adjusted to the needs of the dominant strata in society, it tends to frustrate the needs of the lower strata. A good example would be the Church of England.

3. The Denomination or Class Church is in Yinger's typology limited either in class or racial membership or in regional distribution. It is in substantial harmony with the existing social order. It is conventional and respectable in its outlook and has often developed from a middle class sect. The Congregational and to some extent the Methodist Churches fit into this category.

4. The Established Sect is a sect which has resisted development towards a denomination and is usually one which had originally been concerned mainly with the evils of society. An example of the Established sect is the Quakers.

5. Sects were divided by Yinger into three types according to their responses to and means of dealing with the undesired situation which had given them birth.

A. Acceptance. Sects arising from this response are basically middle class organizations. The middle classes tend to accept the social pattern. Their difficulties arise from lack of faith, selfishness, isolation and other personality problems, not from the evils of society. An example of this type of sect would be Moral Rearmament or Christian Science.

The underprivileged may react to the evils of their situation by aggression or avoidance, and consequently two types of sect may result.

B. Aggression. In the type of sect arising from aggressive feelings the teachings of Jesus are interpreted in radical–ethical terms and the efforts of the members are directed towards obtaining social reform.

[2] J. Milton Yinger, *Religion Society and the Individual*, pp. 142–55, New York, 1957.

C. Avoidance. In sects arising from avoidance the hopes for a better life are projected into the supernatural world or into Chiliastic hopes for the early establishment of the kingdom of God.

6. The Cult. Yinger suggested that this is normally a small short lived group, often local, which develops round the personality of a charismatic leader. Its beliefs differ widely from those generally accepted in the society concerned and it is basically concerned with the problems of individuals. Yinger pointed out that the best examples of this type are Spiritualist groups.[3]

Spiritualism in Britain does not fit completely into Yinger's Cult type since it has survived as a movement for over a century and has developed a form of organization that has enabled even local groups to survive the passing of Charismatic leaders. Yinger's suggestion has however led us to expand his concept of the Cult in an attempt to classify and explain the organization and development of Spiritualism.

Much time has been devoted to the study of the sect since Richard Niebuhr suggested that sects arose as protest movements of the disinherited and developed into denominations or churches of the middle class.[4] Most of the work has been carried out in America and may not be entirely applicable in countries where the cultural pattern differs.

Liston Pope, in his brilliant study of the religious organization of Gaston County, North Carolina, evolved a useful scale for the measurement of the position of religious organization along the Sect–Church continuum.[5] The criteria that Liston Pope laid down may be used to analyse the Spiritualist movement.

Criterion One: 'Development proceeds from membership composed chiefly of the property–less to membership composed of property owners.'

It is difficult to trace any movement in this direction. From the first the movement has been composed of the members of all social classes. Spiritualism was never a sect of the socially dis-

[3] J. M. Yinger, op. cit., p. 155.
[4] H. Richard Niebuhr, 'The Social Sources of Denominationalism', particularly pp. 19–21, New York, 1929.
[5] L. Pope, *Millhands and Preachers*, pp. 122–4, New Haven, 1942.

inherited. The motives for membership were other than social dispossession or poverty and they were and remain mainly three: the desire of the bereaved for comfort and reassurance; curiosity about the after life; and the need of many people for an assurance of their personal survival. These three motives are not class determined and consequently the movement has consistently recruited members from all social classes. It is true that observation indicates that the present membership of the movement is largely composed of members of the upper working and lower middle classes, but this is probably not statistically significant since these classes taken together comprise about half of the total population.

Criterion Two: 'From economic poverty to economic wealth as disclosed especially in the value of church property and the salary paid to ministers.'

In the early days of the movement most groups met in the homes of believers and public meetings were held in hired premises, whereas at present many churches meet in their own places of worship, but of course many (probably the majority of) churches today still meet in hired premises and few, if any, Spiritualist Churches have acquired wealth. Circles meeting in the homes of believers also continue to play an important part in the life of the movement. Salaries are paid today to some officials, mainly of national bodies, and some churches have full-time ministers, but the great majority of churches are still run as voluntary bodies dependent on the unpaid services of their officers. Professional mediums exist and have increased in numbers, and the semi-professional or non-professional mediums who serve the churches are usually paid their expenses or a small fee for their services. The Spiritualist movement in general remains a poor movement and throughout its history one reads of complaints that church members are reluctant to give financial support to the movement. It remains dependent for its organization very largely on the voluntary work of its members.

Criterion Three: 'From the cultural periphery towards the cultural centre of the community.'

In spite of its popularity in Britain in the nineteen twenties to 'thirties, when it was claimed that some two million people were interested in the movement, it has never moved towards becoming the cultural centre of any community. Spiritualism is not a communal movement. It is associational in its nature, a Gesell-schaft not a Gemeinschaft. Members join voluntarily to satisfy their own needs and interests, and while the movement develops and calls forth loyalty from its members it does not give rise to a closed communal feeling.

Criterion Four: 'From renunciation of prevailing culture and social organization or indifference to it to affirmation of pre-vailing culture and social organization.'

Many Spiritualists have rejected and sought to reform the social order, rather than renouncing or being indifferent to it. Robert Owen, the Socialist pioneer, was one of the founders of Spiritualism in Britain and there has always been sympathy between the Spiritualist movement and movements for social reform. Towards the end of the nineteenth century and during the early years of the twentieth, the Spiritualist press frequently discussed the question of whether one could be a Spiritualist without also being a Socialist, and letters on this subject still occasionally appear in Spiritualist publications The connection is perhaps less close today than in the past, but one could hardly claim that the movement had reached the point of affirming the existing social order. If anything the movement has become more indifferent.

Criterion Five: 'From a Self-centred (personal) religion to a culture-centred religion, from "experience" to a social institu-tion.'

Spiritualism has made no advance along this dimension. It remains mainly a personal religion based on the experience of its members and existing primarily to satisfy their individual needs. Spiritualist churches and societies play only a marginal part in the social life of the culture group or community.

Criterion Six: 'From non co-operation or positive ridicule towards established religious institutions to co-operation with the established churches of the community.'

The relationship between Spiritualism and orthodox religious bodies has always been complex and rather one sided. Spiritualism has always been a tolerant movement and has generally sought peaceful co-existence with other bodies, though it has sometimes ridiculed the beliefs of others. Generally it has been the orthodox religious bodies that have refused to have any relationship with spiritualists and have poured ridicule on Spiritualist beliefs and practices. Very little change has occurred in the feelings of Spiritualists towards members of orthodox religious bodies, while on the other hand orthodox religious bodies have tended to become increasingly tolerant towards Spiritualists.

Criterion Seven: 'From suspicion of rival sects to disdain or pity for all sects.'

As mentioned in the comment on criterion six, Spiritualists have always tended to be tolerant of those with other beliefs, and this has applied to members of its nearest rival sects, for example the Swedenborgians, the Christian Scientists, and the Theosophists, all of which were founded by mediums,[6] but which have become antagonistic to Spiritualism. The attitude towards these sects remains one of rather amused tolerance.

Criterion Eight: 'From a moral community excluding unworthy members to a social institution embracing all who are socially comparable with it.'

Spiritualism has never been a 'moral community' with exclusive membership, and when branches of the movement have become sufficiently well organized to expel members this power has seldom been exercised. The movement as a whole has been far too loosely organized to maintain any effective control over its mediums. The movement as a whole has always welcomed any interested person and been very tolerant of his beliefs. There has been little attempt to force conformity upon individual members, and any member who found himself uncomfortable in one branch of the movement could usually find a home in some other church or society whose beliefs were nearer to his own. It is true that a few individual churches have had strict rules of membership and have expelled members for non-conformity, but these expelled persons could usually find another church where their beliefs were tolerated, so that such persons were not lost to the movement.

Criterion Nine: 'From an unspecialized, unprofessional part time ministry to a specialized, professional, full time ministry.'

Here again there has been little change. It is true that the Spiritualist National Union has established a registered ministry and that since the eighteen eighties a few churches have had a

---

[6] E. Swedenborg. *See* A. C. Doyle, *History of Spiritualism*, Ch. 1, Madame Blavatski was an extremely powerful Spiritualist medium. *See* F. Podmore, *Modern Spiritualism*, Ch. 10.

full time paid minister. The S.N.U. ministers are not generally attached to any one church. In most churches the 'ministry' remains unspecialized, unprofessional and part time. Its functions are divided between the chairman, the secretary and the officials of the church and the mediums. Services are usually conducted by visiting mediums. There has certainly been an increase in the number of professional mediums, but these are often in 'private practice' and not attached to a particular church. There is still no ministry within Spiritualism comparable to the ministry in any established denomination.

Criterion Ten: 'From the psychology of persecution to a psychology of success and dominance.'

The Spiritualist movement has certainly had a psychology of persecution and with justifiable cause. Until 1951 Spiritualists were always liable to be arrested for carrying out the practices of mediumship which formed an essential part of their religious services. As late as 1945 a Spiritualist Church was forced to close as a result of the threat of police action.

Criterion Eleven: 'From voluntary confessional basis of membership to ritual or social prerequisites only.'

The membership of Spiritualist societies has always been and remains voluntary confessional.

Criterion Twelve: 'From a principal concern with adult membership to equal concern for the children of members.'

The Spiritualist movement was at first an entirely adult movement, but gradually a concern for children and young people developed, and the Lyceum movement came into existence. This movement, which was the equivalent of the Sunday school movement in the orthodox churches, reached its peak in the nineteen thirties, but since then it has rapidly declined, and few S.N.U. churches now make provision for the religious education of members' children. Among the Christian Spiritualist Churches Sunday Schools on more orthodox lines exist but even among these churches a concern for children is by no means universal. Interest in the children of members has thus fluctuated in the Spiritualist movement and has not followed a clear line of development.

Criterion Thirteen: 'From emphasis on evangelism and conversion to emphasis on religious education.'

The techniques of evangelism and conversion have rarely been used by Spiritualists. They have used rational rather than emotional methods of spreading their beliefs, and have sought to convince the public of the truth of their claims by persuasion and by offering proof based on personal experience of the phenomena of mediumship.

Criterion Fourteen: 'From stress on a future in the next world to primary interest in a future in this world – a future for the institution, for its members, and for their children: from emphasis on death to emphasis on successful earthly life.'

In a sense the Spiritualist movement is inseparably involved in an interest in death and the next world, and to change would be to abandon their central beliefs and thus cease to be Spiritualists. At the centre of Spiritualism remains the belief that the personal survival of the personality of man can be demonstrated and that the dead can communicate with the living. It is true that some sections of the movement have concentrated on the philosophical and religious aspects of their beliefs, and have played down the investigation and demonstration of psychic phenomena. However, Spiritualism has never been exclusively concerned with the next world. There has always been a strong element of socialist and social reformist thought within the movement. In this case political radicalism is linked with radicalism in religion.

Criterion Fifteen: 'From adherence to strict Biblical standards . . . to acceptance of general cultural standards as a practical definition of religious obligations.'

As only part of the movement has claimed to be specifically Christian, this criterion can hardly be said to apply. Even the specifically Christian sections of the movement have never been fundamentalist or adhered to strict biblical standards, neither have any sections of the movement completely accepted cultural standards. The Spiritualist has his own standards based fundamentally on the Bible in so far as that book reflects the common basis of all religions and moral codes, but based also on reason and on the messages from the spirits.

Criterion Sixteen: 'From a high degree of congregational participation in the services and administration of the religious group to delegation of responsibility to a comparatively small percentage of membership.'

There has always been a high degree of membership participation in the activities of Spiritualist societies and this remains the case. This is particularly true in the case of churches having a democratic constitution, but the very nature of Spiritualist practices makes for a high degree of participation. The giving of clairvoyant messages involves participation, the conduct of seances implies that all those present are taking an active part in the proceedings.

Criterion Seventeen: 'From fervour in worship to restraint: from positive action to passive listening.'

In the early stages of the movement there was little sign of any religious fervour, for religious practices played little part in the activities of the movement. From the first development of religious services the practices and worship have been orderly and restrained. On the other hand the movement has always been more concerned with positive action than with passive listening.

Criterion Eighteen: 'From a comparatively large number of special services to a programme of regular services. . . .'

In the early period meetings were held irregularly in private houses or public halls, but soon the meetings began to be held regularly. From the beginnings of organized societies, meetings tended to be held regularly with occasional propaganda meetings and special events. Even in the case of home circles, which play an important part in the totality of the movement, meetings are held regularly because, it is argued, only in this way can those relations be built up between members which are essential if spirit communication is to be successfully carried out.

Criterion Nineteen: 'From reliance on spontaneous "leadings of the spirit" in religious services and administration to a fixed order of worship and of administration.'

In the early days of organized worship mediumistic activities tended to dominate the whole meeting. Today it is usual for the demonstration of mediumship to be given at the end of the service, but this concentration of mediumship is modified by the fact that the address may be given 'in trance' when a spirit guide speaks through the medium. The inspiration of the 'spirits' as distinct from the orthodox Christian concepts of the 'leading of the Spirit' forms an essential part of the beliefs of spiritualists, so that while a Spiritualist service follows a fixed order similar to that followed by many Nonconformist churches, a very real belief in spirit inspiration continues as the whole basis of the Spiritualist movement. Services for worship only form a small part of the activities of most Spiritualist churches much time being taken up by seances and circles of various kinds. These are conducted in an orderly way, but the order is flexible and may be imposed by the 'spirits' rather than upon them.

Criterion Twenty: 'From the use of hymns resembling contemporary folk music to the use of slower more stately hymns coming out of more remote liturgical tradition.'

The Spiritualists adopted and adapted orthodox Victorian hymn tunes as they also adopted and modified the words of orthodox Christian hymns. There are of course a large number of original Spiritualist hymns and some new tunes, but the Spiritualist music tends to follow the type of nineteenth century church hymn tunes, and there has been no trend towards the adoption of a liturgical form. Prayers also continue to be spontaneously led and there is no trend towards a set form.

Criterion Twenty-one: 'From emphasis on religion in the home to delegation of responsibility for religion to church officials and organizations.'

The Spiritualist movement started in home circles for the study and demonstration of psychic phenomena, and even after the establishment of societies and churches the home circle has remained a most important part of the movement. There has however been a tendency for Spiritualist activities to become centred in the churches and the organization of activities to be undertaken by church officials.

This analysis makes it clear that the Spiritualist movement does not fit the Sect–Church continuum as this typology is used by Pope.

Denomination and Cult

In its attitudes to the world and in its belief system Spiritualism has something in common with the denomination as described by D. A. Martin.[7] It does not, for example, damn all those outside its own membership, though it may consider them to be ignorant of the facts. It would no more condemn them morally or spiritually than would a scientist condemn those unaware of the conclusions reached within his branch of science. Like many English denominations the Spiritualist movement has not changed

[7] D. A. Martin, 'The Denomination', *British Journal of Sociology*, March, 1962.

radically in its structure since its inception; there has been no trend from sect towards denomination or church. On the other hand, unlike the typical denomination, Spiritualism from the first discarded the traditional eschatology and substituted a new revelation of the nature of the spiritual and material worlds. Martin gives a clue to the typological nature of Spiritualism in his brief comments on the 'cult', when he points out that 'any attempt to define the meaning of cult only points to its marginally Christian character', and that 'its peculiar characteristics do not merely separate it from other forms of Christianity but from Christianity as such'. He goes on to point out, 'The cult does not embody the tension with "the world" underlying the symbol of "judgment", and does not point towards the "Reign of God".' This final statement is true of Spiritualism where there is no concept of 'judgment' or of an earthly 'Reign of God'.

Before we consider Spiritualism as a cult we must give some further consideration to Troeltsch's typology.

As Moberg points out in his discussion of the criticisms of the Church–Sect typologies, these typologies although derived largely from Troeltsch's concepts have omitted his concept of mysticism.[8] This would appear to be a serious defect of all such typologies, since the inclusion of 'Mysticism' would convert a bi-polar continuum and two dimensional analysis into a tri-polar continuum and necessitates three dimensional analysis. It would appear that these three concepts treated as 'ideal types' should be placed at the points of a triangle and not represented as lying along a unilinear continuum.

Church

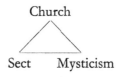

Sect   Mysticism

The representation of these concepts in this form does not imply that the Sect or Mysticism are in any way inferior to the church because the church is represented at the apex of the triangle; any of these types could be represented at any point of the triangle. The figure is intended to emphasize that there is no

---

[8] D. O. Moberg, 'Potential Uses of Church–Sect Typology in Comparative Religious Research', *International Journal of Comparative Sociology*, 1961.

necessary unilinear connection between these types. The Church may include within it (as indeed the Catholic church did in Mediaeval Europe), both Sects and groups of mystics.

As Troeltsch says, Mysticism is based on 'Purely personal and inward experience', which, 'Leads to the formation of groups on a purely personal basis, with no permanent form, which also tend to weaken the significance of forms of worship, doctrine and the historical element'.[9] He goes on to assert, 'Mysticism has an affinity with the autonomy of science, and it forms a refuge for the religious life of the cultured classes; in sections of the population which are untouched by science it leads to extravagant and emotional forms of piety'. In Troeltsch's definition of Mysticism we may find a clear indication of the position of the Spiritualist movement as a religious organization. Spiritualism appears to fit very well into the category of mysticism. It is based on personal experience, and at least initially the groups arose on a purely personal basis and had no permanent form. There has been no significant concern with forms of worship, no rigid doctrine and little emphasis on any historical elements. Spiritualism is also a basically tolerant faith.

It is also interesting to note that Spiritualism has no class basis, but that the membership can be divided between the 'intellectuals' who are interested in the scientific and philosophical aspects of the movement, and the majority who are attracted for emotional reasons, mainly in the form of reassurance in the face of bereavement or the fear of death.

Although Troeltsch was concerned mainly with Mysticism as a form of religious expression within the Christian tradition, it is a type which may be applied universally to the analysis of religions and not only to those within the Judaeo–Christian–Islamic tradition. In this respect it falls within a different category from the Church and Sect analysis which can only be applied within that tradition, and it might form the basis for the development of a universally applicable classificatory system of religious groups.

We must make it clear at this point that we are only considering 'Mysticism' as a form of organization. Only in this sense is Spiritualism a form of Mysticism. Clearly the Spiritualist experience differs from that of the mystic if we use that term in the

[9] E. Troeltsch, *The Social Teaching of the Christian Churches*, p. 993, Trans. O. Wyon, 1931.

narrow theological way, but it is of course possible to extend the definition of Mysticism to include all forms of psychic experience. To avoid confusions of meaning we shall in future include both mystical experiences and other psychic experiences within a general category of Shamanism. [10] Also to avoid any terminological confusion, it is preferable to substitute the concept of cult for that of Mysticism when referring to a type of organization based on personal and inward experiences of all kinds which we have incorporated in our category of Shamanism.

Finally we must consider the contention that the Church–Sect typology can only apply within the Judaeo–Christian–Islamic tradition.

Benton Johnson argues that the reason why the Church–Sect typology can only be applied within the Judaeo–Christian–Islamic tradition derives from a basic difference in the charismatic origins of these religions as compared with the religions of eastern Asia. Religions in the western tradition are based upon the emissary prophet whereas the religions of eastern Asia are based upon the exemplary type of prophet. [11, 12]

The emissary prophet is the agent of a personal God who makes ethical demands on men whereas the exemplary prophet is one who shows how men may attain individual perfection by following an impersonal law of nature. Johnson argues that it is the ethical demands of the Judaeo–Christian–Islamic tradition which results in its organizational structure fitting into a Church–Sect typology and he formulates a definition of church and sect in terms of a single variable.

A church is a religious group that accepts the social environment in which it exists. A sect is a religious group that rejects the social environment in which it exists.

[10] The term Shamanism has been selected as an omnibus term covering all forms of psychic and mystical experience because in primitive societies Shamanism does in fact cover this wide range of experiences of the 'sacred the 'numinous' and the holy. Shamans have experiences that vary from the mediumistic to the mystical.

As I hope to make clear later the category of Shamanism is useful in drawing a distinction between those religious practitioners whose authority is based on a direct contact with the sacred who are Shamans, and Priests whose authority is derived from other sources.

[11] B. Johnson on Church and Sect. *American Sociological Review*, August, 1963.

[12] M. Weber, *Sociology of Religion*, Ch. 4, Trans. E. Fishoff, 1965. (Johnson's concept of emissary and exemplary prophet are derived from Weber whose concept of ethical prophet is identical with Johnson's emissary prophet.)

While this is a useful re-definition having the virtues of clarity, it is not very revealing when applied to the classification of Spiritualism. It might be argued that the typology cannot be applied to Spiritualism since the movement does not fall within the main Christian tradition, but there are serious difficulties here. Most Spiritualists would feel that they are successors to the Christian tradition, and many would argue that since communication with the spirits was practised by the early Christian church they are in fact returning to an earlier and purer practice than that of the orthodox churches today. This is not an uncommon plea of Christian reformers. This is certainly the position of the Christian Spiritualists whose position might be said to rest largely on the emissary prophecy of Jesus somewhat modified by the exemplary prophecy of mediumship. This is a very qualified form of exemplary prophecy since for Christian Spiritualists the spirit world is subject to the laws of a personal God.

Non-Christian spiritualists in Britain tend also to accept the idea of a personal God who however is not a saviour in the Christian tradition. They emphasize the importance of personal responsibility for one's spiritual condition and thus emphasize the element of exemplary prophecy.

Spiritualism is not a unitary movement and we are therefore faced with the problem that whereas the Christian branch may be fitted (at least in theory) into the Church–Sect continuum it is impossible to fit the non-Christian spiritualists into the typology.

If Spiritualism is to be treated as a single movement it is necessary to extend and elaborate the concept of cults so that all religious elements of the movement may be fitted into a single typological continuum. The purely scientific investigation of psychic phenomena must be left outside this classification in spite of the fact that the movement had its origins in the non-religious investigation of such phenomena.

The Concept of Cult

David Martin in a brief but perceptive discussion of cults describes them as essentially individualistic and points out that in such groups, 'The highest level of interpersonal action is a 'parallelism of spontaneities', more particularly of the kind involved in the common pursuit of psychological techniques or therapeutic discussion'.[13]

It is necessary to develop further the concept of cult because of certain inadequacies of Troeltsch's and Yinger's definitions. These inadequacies arise out of Troeltsch's description of cults as having no permanent form and organization and Yinger's similar definition of cults as short lived groups. It is true that in many cases cults are short lived and do not develop a permanent organization, but there are exceptions, and the tendency for cults to have an extended life through the development of permanent organizations has been particularly observed in the Spiritualist movement.

There are three features of a cult that distinguish it from other types of religious groups.

1. They are groups that emphasize the importance of their members having a personal religious experience of a type which would be defined as mystical or ecstatic.

2. Cults represent a fundamental break with the religious traditions of the society in which they arise.[14]

3. They are concerned with the problems of individuals rather than social groups.

The suggestion that cults are also distinguished by a lesser degree of organization is not true of all groups that make a fundamental break with religious tradition, and is consequently not a useful definition. Using our first criterion we may clearly classify the Theosophical Society and the Kosmon Church as cults, but both are highly organized and clearly would not come within Yinger's definition of a cult; neither would many occult societies such as the Atlanteans, the Rosicrucians and the

[13] D. A. Martin, *Pacifism*, pp. 193–7, 1965.

[14] The cult as a type is universal and not restricted to the Judaeo-Christian-Islamic tradition. Buddhism started as a Hindu cult. The numerous new religions of Japan are Buddhist or Shinto cults. The successful cult tends to evolve into a new religion. Christianity was a Jewish cult, Bahai an Islamic cult. The point of transition from cult to new religion is difficult to determine and a cult can only progress in this direction if it progressively discards ties with the parent faith. In Christianity this happened decisively when Paul opened up a mission to the gentiles.

There were indications that this might have occurred in Spiritualism but there has been no decisive break. On the contrary the development of a Christian spiritualist element in the movement is an indication of a relapse from a cult type. The Christian spiritualist churches have developed many of the characteristics of a Christian denomination.

Aetherius Society. In that case we should need a new category to include highly organized groups that have made a break with religious tradition.

The Classification of Cults

Cults may be classified into three main types: cult movements, local cults and centralized cults.

(a) Cult movements, which are united only in holding common basic beliefs, which have a minimum of organizational unity and which may contain within them highly organized groups.

(b) Local cults – local groups which may be associated with national bodies or may be entirely independent and which may vary widely in type of organization. All types of cults start as local cults; they may remain as purely local groups having no relationship with any other groups or they may develop in one of two ways, (i) the original group may establish branch groups which usually remain subject to some extent to the founding group; (ii) in the second case the beliefs of the original group may spread by a process of diffusion and new groups holding beliefs similar to those of the original group may form spontaneously without the direct initiative of the original group playing any part. Spiritualism is a good example of the second process of development. This process gives rise to a cult movement.

(c) The centralized cult consists of a central organization (regional, national or international) composed of a number of local groups. This type of cult may arise in one of two ways (i) it may come into existence as a result of the first process mentioned in the paragraph on local cults. In this method the original local cult forms branches. An example of this type of cult within Spiritualism is White Eagle Lodge; (ii) a centralized cult may arise as the result of spontaneously formed local cults creating a central organization for their mutual benefit. In this way the whole of a cult movement could become organizationally unified as a centralized cult.[15] In the case of Spiritualism two main centralized cults have developed within the movement around slightly different belief patterns (the Christian and non-

[15] Although it is a Christian sect or denomination and not a cult the Independent Church movement developed into the Congregational Union in this way.

Christian patterns). Both cults within the movement continue to share common basic beliefs.

Spiritualism then is a cult movement containing within it centralized cults and a large number of independent local cults. Other examples of cult movements are the occult movement and the flying saucer movement,[16] both of which contain centralized and local cults and as with Spiritualism also groups of scientific investigators, although scientific groups are not an essential feature of cults.

The original local cult and other spontaneously arising cult groups have their origins as groups that gather around a charismatic leader. The group is dependent upon charismatic leadership for its existence and seeks to perpetuate its existence. The group may seek new charismatic or quasi-charismatic leaders to succeed the original leader, as does the Spiritualist movement through the institution of mediumship, or it may routinize charisma by putting it on a traditional or legal-rational basis.

Occult groups for example develop into occult orders in which the charisma of the founder is transmitted through the development of a hierarchical structure. In this way authority is vested in those members who have acquired high rank in the order by passing the appropriate tests and acquiring knowledge of the secret inner teachings. The Rosicrucians and the Freemasons are examples of this type of development. Occult orders may thus be classified as unitary centralized cults.

The Witchcraft and Spiritualist movements represent a very different form of development. Both of the movements have their origins in local charismatic leadership and are based on the primacy of the local group. Witchcraft groups are entirely independent, and it is only in recent years that any attempt has been made to co-ordinate witchcraft at a national level.[17]

Spiritualist local groups have also largely maintained their independence, though, as we have seen, regional and national organization has developed. Spiritualism has however never become a single unified cult, but has remained a movement. Within the movement local groups have come together to form regional and national organizations. These have been of two types, those

[16] H. T. Buckner, 'Flying Saucerians Linger on', *New Society*, 9th September 1965.
[17] The Witchcraft Research Association, founded 1964.

with a democratic and those with a modified form of autocratic structure. The democratic centralized cult is typified by the Spiritualist National Union in which the local groups *must* have a democratic constitution and in which these local groups are federated into a national and regional organization. The national

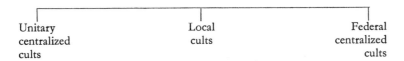

Cult Movements

Common basic beliefs

Unitary centralized cults	Local cults	Federal centralized cults

Development of Local Cult

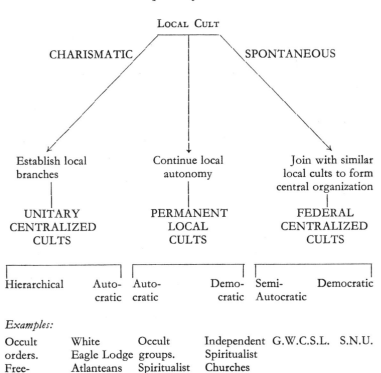

LOCAL CULT

CHARISMATIC   SPONTANEOUS

Establish local branches	Continue local autonomy	Join with similar local cults to form central organization
UNITARY CENTRALIZED CULTS	PERMANENT LOCAL CULTS	FEDERAL CENTRALIZED CULTS

Hierarchical	Auto-cratic	Auto-cratic	Demo-cratic	Semi-Autocratic	Democratic

Examples:

Occult orders. Free-masons	White Eagle Lodge Atlanteans Scientology	Occult groups. Spiritualist groups	Independent Spiritualist Churches	G.W.C.S.L.	S.N.U.

organization has no powers of coercion over member churches, except that it can exclude from membership a church which does not conform to the standard of democratic government laid down in the bye-laws of the Union. The National Union exists as a co-ordinating and advisory body which can speak nationally on behalf of Spiritualists. A closly comparable organization within the Christian churches is the Congregational Union, which stands in a similar position with regard to the local Congregational churches to that in which the S.N.U. stands in respect to the local Spiritualist churches.[1]

The nearest example of a semi-autocratic cult within Spiritualism is the Greater World Christian Spiritualist League. The central organization of this League is autocratic, the members of its national governing body being self appointed or co-opted and not elected, but their powers over local churches are limited in practice. The League is in fact also a federation; the local churches are free to adopt any form of constitution they choose. In consequence, while some G.W.C.S.L. churches have a democratic constitution others are autocratically ruled.

Both major national Spiritualist bodies are thus federations of local churches, and so too is the Commonwealth of the Spiritualist Association of Great Britain. The bulk of the remainder of Spiritualist societies are entirely independent. Spiritualists are thus either not organized at all beyond the local level, or have a form of federal organization which allows considerable freedom to the local churches.

The few groups which have a highly centralized organization with power resting at the centre, such as the Atlanteans, White Eagle Lodge and a number of other groups, are on the fringe between the Spiritualist and the Occult movements.

We have not considered the place of scientific groups within the movement, but these exist in the form of societies for psychical research. These groups cannot be defined as cults, since they do not share the religious attitude to the subject found in Spiritualist churches; though composed of scientific investigators and sceptics they can be included within the movement as a whole since they are interested in phenomena that form the basic stimulus of spiritualist activity.

[18] The Congregational Union has now been reconstituted as the Congregational Church.

The Spiritualist religion has evolved from a non-religious interest in psychic phenomena, and we have traced the development of worship within Spiritualism in the first sections of this work. Spiritualism differs from other religions in that it claims that its basic beliefs are of the same general nature as scientific theories, that is, that they are susceptible of proof. They claim that they have demonstrated their theories to be true, and that only the weight of prejudice has prevented their recognition by the scientific world. Spiritualists would claim to have demonstrated the survival of human personality beyond death at least in so far as this is the only way to account for some psychic phenomena; that they have demonstrated the effectiveness of healing without the use of normal medical techniques, and that they have demonstrated the powers of clairvoyants to obtain information which is not available to them through their normal senses. The Spiritualists extend the spirit hypothesis to the explanation of healing and clairvoyant perception, which is a matter of belief derived from their claim to demonstrate spirit survival. Their acceptance of spirit teachings give a religious aspect to the movement, since such teachings are not only concerned with the nature of the immediate after life but also beliefs about the nature of ultimate reality and the conduct of the good life.

The only other religion which could claim to be based on demonstrable facts is Buddhism.

Chapter Fourteen

AUTHORITY, LEADERSHIP AND ORGANIZATION

Spiritualism throughout its development has remained a cult, since it has retained the three characteristics of the cult as a type of religious institution. It emphasizes the importance of personal experience of psychic and mystical phenomena, it still represents a break with the traditional religion of the Christian West, and it represents even more a sort of resistance movement to the major ideological basis of our society, namely materialism (both in the sense of a belief that only the material world is real and in the sense of an exclusive concern with material values). It has also retained its concern with the problems of individuals, both in connection with healing and with the relief of those distressed by the death of relatives and friends.

The sociologist is also interested in the location of authority and leadership in the movement and in the relationship between beliefs, leadership and the organizational structure of Spiritualism. The unique role of the medium as a link between 'two worlds' and the emphasis on the need for freedom to express one's spontaneous psychic experiences have both had important effects on the development of the organization of the movement.

Resistance to Organization

The process of routinization of charisma is a somewhat neglected aspect of studies of Sect–Church development patterns, but one which nevertheless plays a vital part in the analysis of the causes of changes that take place in the structure of religious organizations.

A religious movement typically comes into existence as the result of the work of an inspired leader with charismatic powers. Such a leader attracts to him a group of enthusiastic followers and during the life-time of the leader little formal organization may exist. The leader often selects a small group of apostles who are particularly in his confidence, and who on the leader's death succeed to leadership of the movement. In some cases one of these is singled out by the leader as his successor. In some cases religious movements cease to exist on the death of their founders, but if he has made a good choice in selecting his successors the movement may continue to develop.

When a charismatic founder dies the future of his movement usually rests in the hands of a group of men who may have few powers of charismatic leadership and whose authority derives from the fact of their having been the chosen friends and successors of the founder. They are respected not for any powers they may have but for the powers they have been invested with by the founder. These powers they will seek to transmit to their chosen successors in turn, and in this way what was spontaneous becomes institutionalized, and leadership passes from those who hold it in virtue of special spiritual gifts to those who hold it as the result of induction into an official position.

This process does not seem to have taken place in the Spiritualist movement. The Spiritualist movement has very largely failed to transform itself into an organization, and has remained a movement. Charisma has not been routinized in the Spiritualist movement but has remained spontaneous.

The concept of charisma is derived from Max Weber, who described natural leaders as 'holders of specific gifts of the body and spirit; and these gifts have been believed to be supernatural, not accessible to everybody'.[1] This definition would apply at least partly to the Spiritualist medium, with the exception that mediumistic powers are believed (at least in theory) to be available to all. Weber goes on to describe charisma. 'It knows no regulated "career", "advancement", "salary" or regulated and expert training . . . It knows no agency of control or appeal, no local bailiwicks or exclusive functional jurisdictions, nor does it embrace permanent institutions like our "bureaucratic departments" which are independent of persons and of purely personal charisma'. 'Charisma knows only inner determination and inner restraint. The holder of charisma seizes the task that is adequate for him and demands obedience and a following by virtue of his

[1] H. W. Gerth and C. Wright Mills, from *Max Weber*, p. 245, 1947.

mission'.[2] Weber seems to have recognized that mediumship, at least in its primitive form of Shamanism, is charismatic, since he says, 'Shamanistic ecstasy is linked to constitutional epilepsy, the possession and testing of which represents a charismatic qualification'. We may however agree with Eliade in holding that Shamanistic ecstasy differs from mental disease in that the Shaman is always in control and can direct his powers, whereas the insane have no control over their seizures.[3]

Weber believed that charisma became routinized in one of two ways. In the first place it could be transmitted by traditional ascription, and typically to a successor in a hereditary line, as is commonly the case in the establishment and transmission of kingship. In the second place charisma becomes attached to an office and not to a person. This form of routinization leads to the establishment of a bureaucracy.

Weber seems to have failed to see that in certain limited cases a permanent movement might be carried on by a succession of charismatic leaders, and this in spite of the fact that he was aware of the central importance of shamanism as a form of charismatic leadership in the religion of many primitive peoples.[4] It would appear that where the gifts required of a charismatic leader are not uncommon there need be no shortage of such leaders, and a movement even on the level of local organization will always be able to find several such leaders. The major difficulty is containing charisma in such a way that it is prevented from proliferating a multiplicity of competing groups. In this respect the Spiritualist movement has been successful; few groups have broken away entirely, although some mediums have used their gifts to claim exclusive rights of religious leadership. Madame Blavatski, the founder of Theosophy, and Mrs Baker Eddy, who founded Christian Science, were mediums who used their charismatic powers to establish cults outside the Spiritualist movement. There have been few breakaways from Spiritualism because it is essentially a movement and not a centralized organization. There is thus complete freedom of belief and practice within the movement, which is limited only by the fact that unless one believes in the existence of spirits and in the possibility of communication

[2] H. W. Gerth and C. Wright Mills, from *Max Weber*, p. 246.
[3] M. Eliade, *Shamanism*, pp. 23–32, 1964.
[4] H. W. Gerth and C. Wright Mills, op. cit., p. 246.

with them one can hardly be classified as a Spiritualist. Given these two basic beliefs, mediums are free to proclaim any additional teachings they are 'given' by the spirits.

The position of charismatic leadership within the Spiritualist movement is complex. In the first place, unlike most religious movements Spiritualism did not originate in the work of any one charismatic leader. Andrew Jackson Davis was indeed a man with great personal charisma who had considerable influence on the rise of the movement in America, but he did not found the movement. He was however responsible for the establishment of the first children's Lyceum and was looked upon as the founder of the Lyceum movement. Davis's 'Harmonial Philosophy' formed the basis of the philosophy of Spiritualism for the first twenty or thirty years, and has had a continuing influence on the thought of the movement. There were in America in the early days of the movement several other leaders, including Mrs Hardinge–Britten, whose personal charisma played an important part in the growth of Spiritualism.

In Britain also charismatic leadership at the national level has not been lacking, but it has seldom led to the establishment of a permanent organization. D. D. Home, the most impressive medium of the nineteenth century, founded no groups of disciples, and left neither a successor nor an organization behind him. James Burns, who ran an organization in London for many years, left no group of disciples to continue his work, and neither have the majority of great mediums whose personal charisma has attracted many recruits to the movement.

Charisma has often appeared outside the national organizations, and where it has appeared within them it has not played an essential part in their establishment and growth. Emma Hardinge–Britten came to Britain and played a part in the establishment of the Spiritualist National Federation, but many other persons also played an important part in the foundation of that association, and it would be a great exaggeration to suggest that the organization was founded by Mrs Britten.

The great charismatic figures in the national field in the nineteen twenties and 'thirties such as Conan Doyle and Hannen Swaffer, were not the mouthpieces of any organization, and themselves founded no permanent organizations.

There is one major exception to the theory that national

Spiritualist organizations in Britain have not been founded on or grown out of the work of a charismatic leader, and that is the case of the Greater World Christian Spiritualist League, which was founded by Winifred Moyes, a leader with considerable personal charisma, who retained control of the movement until her death, when control passed to a group of her disciples.

It is at the local level that charismatic leadership has played a vital part in the structure of the movement. The local group, society or church has always been founded and based on the charisma of a medium. In the early period Spiritualist circles were usually temporary, meeting only on a few occasions to test the powers of mediumship of an individual who believed himself to have such powers, or of a group of individuals who hoped that they (or one of their number) possessed such powers.

When it was found that one member possessed psychic powers a more continuing circle tended to form around that person, who became the medium; this person became the focus of authority in the group. Many of these home circles were only temporary groups which broke up when the medium died or lost her powers, or when the members discovered a more attractive or powerful medium. But some such groups developed a more formal structure, and a permanent organization grew up, though in this the medium often played only an insignificant part. This does not however minimize the importance of the medium but shows that his charismatic authority was often exercised informally.

The importance of the medium in Spiritualism has been generally recognized, and historians of the movement such as Sir Arthur Conan Doyle and Joseph McCabe have considered the story of the lives and exploits of the great mediums to be synonomous with the history of the movement. This is true in the sense that without mediums there could be no Spiritualist movement, and the success or decline of the movement during the past century has coincided with the existence of good mediums. The so called 'Golden Age' of the eighteen sixties and 'seventies was a period in which many gifted mediums were working. In the 'eighties and early 'nineties there was a decline in the movement at least in so far as the public work and public interest was concerned and this was even at the time attributed to a dearth of good mediums. The movement revived between 1895 and 1905. The great revival that lasted from 1915 to 1939 again coincided with a period in which many public mediums flourished. Since 1950 the decline of the movement has been marked by a shortage of good mediums.

For the movement to exist at all, it is clear that there must be sufficient mediums available to meet the demands of existing Spiritualist groups, that is to say at least one medium for each active group. Normally there will be more than one medium in each group, for Spiritualists claim that all have the ability to develop psychic powers. Most members of any Spiritualist group will probably have not developed these abilities to any great extent as this often involves a lengthy period of training. It is therefore clear that such groups tend to centre round one or more active mediums.

While there is a great deal of formal organization today as compared with a century ago, a great deal of Spiritualist activity continues to take place informally. There are numerous 'Home circles' and informal groups often unconnected with any national or local organization. Some of these circles continue to function regularly for years; others die after a few meetings.

Organization within Spiritualism tends to cut across the charismatic leadership of mediums. The mediums have considerable prestige within the movement, but the organization of the churches and national bodies is not necessarily in the hands of the leading mediums. In the democratic organizations mediums may not always be elected to official posts. In the more autocratic type of organizations the leadership is more frequently in the hands of a medium. For this reason there has always been a considerable number of churches having a very short life, the life of the charismatic powers of their founders. In some cases the founders have trained mediums and leaders to succeed them, but in many cases such founding leaders are jealous of their own position and discourage the development of mediumistic powers among their members. The type of church based entirely on the claims and powers of one autocratic individual has constantly been condemned as 'one man shows' by organized Spiritualists, and indeed fraud seems to occur more frequently in such a situation, or in any situation where the medium depends for his livelihood on the exercise of mediumistic powers.

In fact the majority of Spiritualist organizations, and in

particular those affiliated to the S.N.U., are democratically organized. This would appear to contradict the idea that Spiritualism is based on charisma, but in fact it does nothing of the sort. Spiritualists believe that all persons are potential mediums and most of the active members of a Spiritualist church will have made some efforts to develop these powers. Since all members are mediums or potential mediums all have actual or potential charisma. The most powerful and impressive mediums will naturally tend to have the greatest charisma, but in organizations that are based on the belief in the universality of psychic abilities the claims to exclusive revelation (and powers based on such a claim) are checked by a democratic structure. Strictly speaking it is not the medium who possess charisma but the spirit guide who uses him. Some of this charisma tends to 'rub off' or be displaced on to the medium, but all Spiritualists recognize that mediums are only the instruments used by the spirits to communicate with people on the 'earth plane'. Most mediums are careful to point out that credit should be given to the 'spirit guides' and not to themselves. The medium is thus an ambiguous figure in the movement, a mouthpiece for beings greater than himself and yet having certain charismatic powers at least in respect to the non-mediums within the movement (the members of the congregation who are less active in the organizational councils of the movement) and the general public.

The fact that it is the spirit guides and not the mediums who are the ultimate holders of charisma means that charismatic leadership within the Spiritualist movement is not challenged by human frailty. The failure of a medium to live up to the precepts of his guides is not felt to be a condemnation of the message or teaching of the guides, as might well be the case if the teaching came from a purely human source. The failure of a message to predict future events or to be accurate when tested against facts can always be explained by the suggestion that the human channel through which it has passed was inadequate and has failed to transmit or interpret it correctly. The medium may lose his prestige but the spirits do not lose theirs. This may be compared to the self-validating claims of magic. In this sense the Spiritualist movement is based on the continuing charisma of the spirits. To some extent all charismatic leaders project their charisma unto its supposed supernatural source, but the charisma of the supernatural sources are seldom so clearly distinguished from that of their human agent as in Spiritualism where the spirit guide sometimes becomes better known than the human medium.[5] In fact the same spirit guide may manifest himself and give messages through more than one medium.

The churches have an active membership largely composed of mediums at various stages of development, and since these are all equal in the sense that they are all instruments used by the Spirits an ethos of democratic equality emerges. Many churches exist independently of national organizations, in which the powers are concentrated in the hands of a single dominant medium. These organizations tend to be short-lived as they are based on true or pure charisma. If they fail to develop a democratic structure, or, more rarely, to find a charismatic successor to the founder, they cease to exist on the death of the founder, or when he loses his powers.

As mediums are believed to be instruments of the spirits, they must have freedom. This freedom can best be found in a loose democratic organization, in which local groups are largely self governing and come together at regional, national or international level only for specific purposes. Outside the Spiritualist movement this type of democracy, linked with a loose form of national federal organization, exists in other religious movements which place a high value on spontaneity and freedom. The most notable example is the Congregational church, where the organizational practice derived from the doctrine of the priesthood of all believers and that all men have access to communion with God without the necessity of a priest as an intermediary. These principles are also found in the Society of Friends and the Baptist Churches.

In all these cases the belief system has moulded the shape of the organization. A belief system based on a non-authoritian view of the nature of the supernatural or of ultimate reality, and on a belief in the ability of the individual to contact the supernatural personally and without intermediaries, has led to a democratic structure within these religious organizations. There is thus a close association between belief and organization, and a change

---

[5] Silver Birch, the spirit guide of Hannen Swaffer's home circle was for long far more widely known than his medium who was later revealed to be M. Barbarnel.

R

in one would indicate a change in the other or lead to such a change taking place.

The importance of a belief system as a determinant of organizational form has been greatly underestimated, and it has certainly played a primary role in determining the organizational structure of Spiritualism.

Finally, in sociological terms, the democratic form of government within Spiritualist churches is legitimated by the charisma of the spirits acting through their human mediums.

Shamans and Priests

One of the major distinctions in the study of religious leadership has been between prophet and priest.[6] This distinction becomes clearer and more useful if we widen the category of prophet to include all those religious leaders who have mystical abilities or psychic powers. This inclusive category of leaders with psychic and mystical powers can conveniently be equated with the concept of Shaman. An analysis of the distinction between Shaman and priest forms a vital part of any assessment of the role of the medium in the Spiritualist movement and of the reluctance of Spiritualists to accept organization or to permit the development of priestly roles within the movement.

Lessa and Vogt describe a Shaman as 'a ceremonial practitioner whose powers come from direct contact with the supernatural, by divine stroke, rather than from inheritance or memorized ritual', and they contrast this with a priest at the opposite pole, who 'is a ceremonial practitioner who often inherits his position and who learns a body of codified and standardized ritual knowledge from older priests and later transmits it to successors'.[7]

There is frequently conflict between the roles of Shamans and priests, and we shall examine some of the causes and consequences of such conflict as it has been expressed within the Spiritualist movement.

Shamans are in a sense primitive mediums, but we shall use the term Shaman in a wider sense as a generic term covering a

[6] Max Weber, *Sociology of Religion*, 1965.

[7] Lessa and Vogt, *Reader in Comparative Religion*, p. 410, 1st Ed., Evanston, Illinois, 1958. The use of the concept of Shaman may be compared to Max Weber's use of the term Magician. I use the term Shaman as this is less value-ridden than the word magician.

number of distinct types of religious roles of which mediumship is one, but also including all types of practitioners who derive their position and their authority from the possession of natural Spiritual powers or gifts. These powers are usually interpreted as gifts of the gods or spirits. The powers of leadership of Shamans depend upon the possession of personal charisma.

The above figure presents a simple classification of the major forms of Shamanship, and shows that Shamans may be divided into Mystics, Prophets, Mediums, Healers and Sorcerers. Each of these has contact at a different level with the supernatural world. The distinctions between these types are not always clear, and any one individual may display more than one of these different forms of Shamanship. It is however possible to distinguish these as ideal types. The Mystic is one who reaches contact with 'God' or 'Ultimate Reality' at the highest level of experience. The Prophet is one through whom this 'Ultimate Reality' speaks or discloses itself at the human level. The Medium is one through whom spirits or the subordinate levels of Spiritual reality can be contacted in a general capacity. Whereas the Healer is one in whom this contact is specifically restricted to the sphere of dealing with human problems of health.

Finally the Sorcerer is one who is able to use supernatural forces (at the low level of magic) to obtain physical and psychological effects. In all these cases the Shaman derives his position from his personal experience based upon the development and use of natural abilities, and his authority is based upon and legitimated by his personal contact with the sacred. He is a truly charismatic personality.

A revealing analysis of the differences between the prophetic and mystic experience is made by Isidor Thorner.[8] He says that the mystic 'is convinced that the non-empirical referent of his perception is imminent in nature as a whole and that he has been in some sense, "altogether one with it", whereas the prophet,

[8] I. Thorner, 'Prophetic and Mystic Experience. Comparison and Consequence', *Journal for the Scientific Study of Religion*, pp. 82–96, Fall 1965.

TABLE 1

The following table, which is based on Thorner's ideal typology of prophetic and mystical experiences, reveals the necessity for a third 'ideal type', mediumistic experience which appears to cut across the other types.

	Prophetic experience	Mystic experience	Mediumistic experience
1. Preconditions	Other-orientation ethical-emotional conflict	Self-orientation serenity based on achieved affective and moral neutrality	Other orientation
2. Onset	Unexpected, sudden while active	Deliberately induced in a passive state	Spontaneous or deliberately induced in a passive state
3. Technique	None	Sensory deprivation via relaxation, immobility, breath control, withdrawal of attention from external and internal environments	Sensory deprivation (as for mystic experience)
4. Physiological aspect	Unknown but with the possibility of psychomatic disturbance	Hypotension, physiological hibernation	Unknown
5. Subjective experience	Conflict coupled with tension relief: Hallucinations with auditory and visual content having cognitive meaning: possible psychopathologies	Descent into infrapersonality depths. Hallucinations without meaning: coloured lights: intensely enjoyable: 'oceanic feeling': white light fusion of knower and known: contentless comprehension: timeless eternity of being	Hallucinations with auditory and visual content having cognitive meaning Also lights and objects having symbolic meaning

	Prophetic experience	Mystic experience	Mediumistic experience
6. Subjective interpretation	Anthropomorphic transcendental deity demanding obligatory action according to ethical-political message	Impersonal, imminent divine force with which ego 'fuses': subject as 'vessel': no ethical-political message, no obligatory activity for the subject	No direct contact with deity or impersonal reality, but with sub-divine supernatural beings from whom ethical personal messages transmitted through medium who is an instrument. Service demanded of mediums
7. Consequences	Orientation to others, desanctification of at least part of the traditional social order; its alteration by subjects activity despite opposition	Self-orientation: acceptance and support of the traditional social order: passive exemplar of ideal behaviour: emotional and moral neutrality combined with mild generalized compassion	Other orientation, moral and emotional commitment to social improvement and to active personal help for others. The medium as a passive instrument of the supernatural is not of necessity involved in personal moral action

This demonstrates clearly that mediumship is a distinct type of experience. It shares certain factors with mysticism (2 and 3), others with the prophetic experience 1 and part of 4, but in other respects it differs from both of the other types.

"understands the non-empirical referent to be wholly beyond nature and he has only been in communication with it".'

The mediumistic experience does not appear to fit either of Thorner's ideal types, but to constitute a distinct type of religious experience.[9] That it does constitute a form of religious experience is clear if one accepts Thorner's description of these elements of the religious experience that are common to both the prophet and the mystic. Thorner argues that 'The subject of a religious experience believes not only that (i) his perceptions are extraordinary and constitute a sharp break with the world of everyday experience, but that (ii) they are far more important than ordinary perceptions and unlike the latter, (iii) their objective referents are not to be found in 'discrete aspects of the empirical world order'. This definition clearly includes the mediumistic experience.

Priests occupy their positions not by virtue of any specific natural abilities they possess (though by chance some priests may possess natural psychic powers), but because they have either inherited the position or been appointed or elected to it. Any charisma they display is derived from the office they hold and not based on personal qualities. though some priests may also possess personal charisma.

The priest indeed usually has to undergo training to fit him for his role and to pass through rites of initiation and dedication in which he is brought into symbolic contact with the 'sacred', so that his authority is based upon and legitimated by a symbolic rather than a personal contact with the holy. The mystic in Christian tradition experiences at-one-ness with God, but the priest is ordained by the symbolic laying on of hands whereby the sacred is transmitted to him through a human agency. The mystic's experience is subjective, the priest's objective.[10]

The priesthood then tends to develop a bureaucratic structure, either traditional as in the case of a hereditary priesthood, or legal-rational as in the case of an appointed priesthood, such as the priesthood of the Roman Catholic church.

A different type of religious functionary having a closer affinity to the priest than the Shaman is the Minister, who has less power

[9] *See* Table 1.

[10] W. Mouston, 'The Mystical Consciousness and World Understanding', *Journal for the Scientific Study of Religion*, Spring, 1965 emphasizes the importance of the immediate religious experience and comparative neglect of this in Western religions.

than a priest and does not act in the same way as an intermediary between man and the supernatural world, but who is appointed to hold a particular position in the religious group. Finally there is a group of religious officials who may be described as Elders. These people play various roles within the group and differ widely in the amount of power they wield, but they are distinguished by the fact that they are elected by the general body of the group. The most typical examples of this type of religious leadership are the elected officials of a Spiritualist or a Congregationalist church.

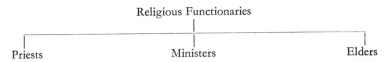

Religious Functionaries

Priests	Ministers	Elders

There is considerable antagonism between priests and Shamans, arising from role conflict.[11] The priest having no psychic powers fears and is envious of the possessor of such powers. He fears that his authority which is based partly on tradition, inheritance or appointment and on training will be threatened by one whose authority is directly derived from contact with spiritual powers. This is illustrated in the life of Jesus, who is described as 'Speaking with authority and not as the Scribes and Pharisees'. The conflict between Jesus and the priestly bureaucracy is an archetype of the universal conflict between the charismatic leader and the bureaucratic official.

The Shaman tends to ignore the priest, to express spontaneously his religious experience which is often at cross purposes with the religious authority of the priest. The freshness and directness of his experience presents a challenge to the priest to attempt to control and regulate the expression of religious experience.

Priesthood arises out of an attempt to regulate the potentially disruptive activities of Shamans as well as in the process of routinization of charisma described by Weber.[12] Once a priesthood has become established it perceives the Shaman as a danger to existing religious institutions and attempts to deal with Shamanism either by the suppression or devaluation of Shamanship or by institutionalizing its expression.

11 J. Wach, *Sociology of Religion*, pp. 360, 368, University of Chicago, 1947.

12 M. Weber, *The Theory of Social and Economic Organisation*, pp. 363–73, Glencoe, Ill., 1964.

Attempts at suppression are always ultimately unsuccessful, and Shamanship continues to exist in all forms of society. Attempts to devalue Shamanship are more successful as in the case of the Puritan influence in the seventeenth century, or the influence of scientific materialism and of Marxism in the nineteenth and twentieth centuries. The effects of such movements are to create an atmosphere within society which is unfavourable to the spontaneous expression of psychic powers. Puritanism viewed such powers as evil and an expression of the work of the devil. In consequence, Shamanism only continued to find expression in a non-Christian or anti-Christian form. It is in this period that we find a great increase in public interest in witchcraft. In this period witchcraft becomes seen as a direct challenge to the church and extreme means are taken to effect its suppression.

In a scientific or Marxist culture psychic phenomena are derided as 'unreal' in some sense, and in particular as compared with physical phenomena which alone are considered to be 'real'. Psychic phenomena are described as the result of an illusion or an hallucination, and the Shaman is in danger of being classified as insane and finding himself incarcerated in a hospital or receiving psychiatric treatment. In such circumstances the layman considers the expression of psychic powers as symptoms of insanity, and many incipient Shamans consider their own experiences of psychic phenomena as signs of mental disease and seek psychiatric treatment. In the climate of scientific opinion of today it is likely that the great religious figures of the past, including Jesus, would have great difficulty in obtaining a hearing in the western world, since they would be suspected of insanity.

In such circumstances Shamans tend to form small groups outside the official religious organizations. In a situation where the climate of opinion is that of scientific materialism but in which there is no suppression of religious institutions, shamanism manifests itself primarily in two directions. In a new form of religious cult (Spiritualism), and in the scientific study of psychic phenomena.

The Spiritualist movement arose at a time when the predominant puritan ethos and its devaluation of the supernatural was being replaced by the growth of scientific materialism.[13] In

[13] It has been argued that both eighteenth century rationalism and modern science had their origins in puritan thought.

consequence of this the first manifestation of Spiritualism took the form of an investigation of psychic phenomena along scientific or pseudo-scientific lines. The early Spiritualists tended to see science as an ally against the attacks of the priesthood and of the attempts of the religious establishment to devalue the movement by attributing psychic manifestations to the works of the devil.

When Spiritualists found that the ethos of scientific materialism was also opposed to the acceptance of psychic phenomena, and also resulted in the devaluation of shamanism, the majority of the movement turned to a religious interpretation of the phenomena and to a religious expression of their beliefs. A small group, the psychic research movement continued to investigate on a scientific basis and has had considerable success in establishing the existence of certain psychic phenomena, notably those phenomena now usually described as Extra-Sensory Perception, or Psi Phenomena.[14]

The institutionalization of the expression of shamanism within existing religious organizations takes several forms. In Christianity we find that Shamanism becomes institutionalized in the form of the acceptance of miracles, the recognition of mysticism and the organization of ascetics, within the Catholic and Orthodox traditions. In Protestantism there is some scope for the expression of Shamanism in the concept of a divine calling to the ministry. But it was mainly manifest in the proliferation of cults and sects based on the psychic revelations given to charismatic leaders. In most cases the charismatic and shamanistic powers of the founder were looked on as unique and not to be copied or sought by the followers, and consequently in the absence of adequate institutionalization these sects often fragmented on (or even before) the death of the founder as new charismatic leaders emerged. One early sect which found an answer to this was the Quaker movement, which evolved methods of institutionalizing the expression of mystical gifts.

Not only Puritanism but all branches of the Christian church

R. Merton, *Social Theory and Social Structure*, pp. 574–606, New York, 1965; H. F. Kearney, 'Puritanism Capitalism and the Scientific Revolution' in *Past and Present*, July, 1964; S. A. Burrell (Ed.), *The Role of Religion in Modern European History*, New York, 1964.

[14] G. N. M. Tyrrell, *The Personality of Man*, 1946; D. J. West, *Psychical Research Today*, 1962.

have been suspicious of the more extreme expressions of Shaman-ism. The Churches have seen shamanism as a threat to the unique revelation given to Jesus and to the approved fathers, saints and founders of their particular branch of the faith. Extreme Shamans who were not amenable to the discipline of the church have there-fore been persecuted and excommunicated by the churches. Some of them have been merely eccentric Christians such as the Albigenses and the Cathars, others have reacted to the constraints of a bureaucratic church by rejecting Christianity in favour of anti-Christian practices such as Black Magic or Satanism or by reverting to an older faith such as witchcraft.[15] Spiritualism in France under Alan Kardec may be one manifestation of a revolt against Catholicism. In America and Britain a major element in the origin of Spiritualism is to be found in a rebellion against the constraints of nineteenth century Christianity.

In recent years the Protestant churches in Britain have made some attempts to institutionalize Shamanism through the estab-lishment of the Churches Fellowship for Psychic Study, and the Anglican church contains within it the Guild of St Raphael, which is concerned with faith healing.

On the whole Shamanism finds its outlet in Britain in the Spiritualist movement, though there has also been a considerable expansion of Occultism and witchcraft in the past twenty years.

Psychic and mystical experiences are closely related to religious experiences, and indeed form the basis of those religious experi-ences which are not merely emotional. It is on this foundation of religious experience that the superstructure of theological specu-lation and religious organization is erected.

The conflict between Shamanism and religious bureaucracy, which is a universal situation, finds its expression in the conflict between the Spiritualist movement and the churches. At a deeper level this conflict forms the basis of the Spiritualist's rejection of organization. The expression of a fear of organization and of the development of priestly authority has been endemic in the history of the movement. It is clear that the restraints of institutionaliza-tion would in fact destroy the spontaneity of the Shamanistic expression which is central to mediumship and to the movement. Spiritualism is dependent upon mediumship and Shamanship and

[15] M. A. Murray, *The Witch-Cult in Western Europe*, 1962; J. Michelet, *Satanism and Witchcraft*, 1965.

consequently takes the form of a movement rather than an organization, a movement dependent upon the renewal of charismatic leadership, which would be stifled by the growth of routinization.

Chapter Fifteen

SOCIAL SOURCES OF SPIRITUALISM

In what sort of social conditions does Spiritualism arise? And what sort of people are attracted to the movement?

In the first part of this book, I have analysed the origins of Modern Spiritualism in America. In that section I traced the social origins of Spiritualism to the conditions of anomie brought about by the changes in life conditions and expectations among people whose whole pattern of life had been disrupted by the effects of migration.

These people had been uprooted (often as a direct result of the pressure of social and economic forces), from the traditional patterns of culture in their homelands and thrown into contact with people of widely differing cultures who were also cut off from their traditional roots. In these circumstances traditional culture patterns break down and old beliefs are no longer accepted without question. Spiritualism was born in an area of America, upper New York State, that was on the direct route of the new migrants in their progress westward. The area had been partly settled earlier, but the developing traditions of the settlers were disrupted by the flood of new ideas that came in with the new migrants. Social life was also disrupted by the newcomers. Doubt was thrown on traditional religious beliefs in several ways. In the first place rationalist ideas popular among the intelligentsia in the eighteenth century, and which to a large extent determined the secular orientation of the American constitution, were being widely diffused among the middle and working classes in so far as such classes could be distinguished in America at that time. The American people had achieved a high degree of literacy, and this made possible the wide spread of rationalist ideas among all sections of society. It is interesting to note that many of the known members of the Spiritualist movement at that time had been atheists, agnostics or rationalists before they were introduced to Spiritualism.

In the second place the sudden influx of migrants with widely differing religious beliefs, and the contact between such people and a community that was already pluralist and tolerant towards all varieties of belief, led to a dilution of beliefs. In an atmosphere of free thought many people came to question their previously held beliefs. Beliefs accepted in the 'old country', for reasons of tradition began to be modified or discarded when they came into competition with other belief patterns either religious or secular.

In these circumstances the traditional answers to fundamental problems of life and death are no longer felt to be adequate by many people, and consciously or unconsciously such people seek new beliefs that will satisfy their needs for knowledge and emotional security.

One of the fundamental human problems has always been the problem of death, and all religions offer some solution to this problem. Death presents not only an emotional and intellectual problem, but is also the potential source of disruption within the social group concerned. One of the functions of religion has always been to provide an answer to both the individual and social distress caused by death.

In the social conditions of mid-nineteenth century America, people were unable to accept the traditional religious answers to the problems of death, because their whole faith in the religious order of Christianity had been brought into question. These people had rejected (or at least felt serious doubt about) the whole religious tradition of their fathers. When faced with bereavement or with the imminence of death, people who had recently lost faith in the traditional explanations of religion often also found the explanations of their new rationalism inadequate. They were no longer able to fall back for comfort and consolation on the Christian hope of immortality and neither were they attracted to the great number of fundamentalist and millenarian sects that were springing up in America at that time, for these also demanded a faith that could no longer be given by men who were able to accept only that for which there was evidence.

The psychic phenomena of Spiritualism offered proof of the survival of human personality beyond death, proof based on evidence which was open to personal investigation. This at least was the claim made by Spiritualists, and indeed most early converts were convinced by their personal experiences at seances and not by philosophical arguments.

Not all early Spiritualists were attracted to the movement as a result of the experience of bereavement or the fear of death. A number were attracted by a scientific interest in psychic phenomena and their desire to investigate a subject on the expanding frontiers of science. Their inner motivation for investigating psychic phenomena may well have been connected with unconscious fears and desires, but it was at least controlled and directed along rational lines.

Psychic phenomena have been a familiar feature of the legends and folk tales of the human race and are clearly based on certain personal experiences. The explanations of such experiences have varied with the ethos of the place and time and with the orientation of the culture in question. In a predominantly settled religious situation these experiences tend to become assimilated to the religious beliefs of the society. In mediaeval Europe they tended to be interpreted as the result of the visitation of angels or devils and there are numerous accounts of the encounter of saints and holy men with such beings. The Roman Catholic church continues to view psychic experiences in this way.

On the other hand a secularized and scientifically based society such as the western world in the later nineteenth and twentieth centuries tends to reject such experiences as 'unreal', to view them as the result of illusion or hallucination, and to seek for explanations at the material level in the psychological and biological structure of man.

In the mid-nineteenth century Britain and the U.S.A. were in a period of transition between a religiously and a materialistically oriented culture, and men were consequently free to interpret psychic phenomena in terms of either, or a combination of both these orientations. In fact the phenomena were accepted very much more at their face value than they would have been in a society in which basic attitudes were determined either by a religious or materialistic world view. The triumph of a materialistic world view is illustrated in the case of the Soviet Union. A recent visitor to Russia who discussed parapsychological research with the Russian research teams investigating E.S.P. was informed that there were now no ghosts in Russia.

Spiritualists seem to have treated the evidence impartially

without a bias imposed by the previous acceptance of either general theoretical background, both of which they criticized. Spiritualists were attacked continually from both sides, by the churches and by the scientists, because they rejected the interpretations of both these world views and treated the problem of the explanation of psychic phenomena empirically. We are speaking here of the early Spiritualists and of a continuing element within the movement which maintains critical standards of assessing the evidence. It is true that as the movement developed it attracted many uncritical believers who would accept any 'wonder' unquestioningly. The existence of such a body of uncritical believers gave rise to many abuses, and no Spiritualist would deny that the movement has almost from its inception been plagued with frauds. It is comparatively easy to produce fraudulent phenomena which are a sufficiently good imitation to deceive the uncritical, and consequently the genuine Spiritualists have always emphasized that investigators must be critical and use care in selecting the mediums with whom to work, and that they should make every effort to test evidence.

To return to the analysis of the social conditions that gave rise to Spiritualism, we have seen that such movements arise in anomic conditions. In America during the eighteen fifties and 'sixties anomic social conditions were widespread and Spiritualism flourished. At one time it was said to have had over two million members.

In Britain the movement has grown slowly and always remained on a comparatively small scale. The only period when it showed signs of becoming a mass movement was in the period following the First World War, when it grew rapidly and attracted perhaps half a million supporters. This was a period when old values were being questioned and a traditional way of life breaking down as the result of the disruption of war. There was a much less pronounced expansion of the movement in the years following the 1939–45 war when occult movements also attracted much attention. This was also a period of rapid cultural and social change in which old values were challenged.

In the nineteenth century British society was much more stable than American society. Anomic social conditions were far less widespread than in the U.S.A. and the lower level of literacy in Britain tended to restrict the spread of rationalist ideas. These ideas therefore presented less of a challenge to traditional values in the lower strata of society. On the other hand the working class saw their economic situation in capitalist society as the major problem and, faced this by collective action through the formation of trades unions and political groups, rather than by individual action, as was the more common response in America. America was flooded at that time with immigrants who had left their native lands because they rejected the traditional pattern of life. Such people were clearly individualists.

Those who were extreme individualists left the old countries for the new, leaving behind those who were more conformist and those who believed in a collective solution.[1] Within Britain the individualists and non-conformists would on this argument also be more mobile (geographically and perhaps socially) and tend to leave the rural for the urban environment.

Spiritualism as an Urban Religion

Spiritualism in Britain is an urban religion. The expanding industrial towns of the mid-nineteenth century provided Britain's nearest equivalent to the frontier environment of America at the same period. These towns were growing rapidly and traditional ways of life were being superseded by a new urban pattern of life. In the transitional period an anomic situation arose. It was in the industrial towns of Lancashire and Yorkshire, the north-east and in London that Spiritualism took root in the eighteen fifties. It was to these areas that the rural workers were flocking to work in the developing industries. These new town dwellers were cut off from their traditional roots in the country, they were free from the restraints imposed by the forces of social control within the narrow confines of a rural community. Many found the Christian faith unsatisfactory in the new conditions of life; they tended to become secularized. As K. S. Inglis has pointed out,[2] the urban working class of Victorian England was largely divorced from religion. In the course of their migration from the village to the town these people became detached from the church of their ancestors and the majority of them never returned to an association with the Anglican church. The old dissenting denominations,

---

[1] Some collectivists emigrated and formed communities in the U.S.A.
[2] K. S. Inglis. *The Churches and the Victorian Working Class*, 1963.

Congregationalists, Baptists and Quakers also, never gained a working class membership in the towns and remained largely middle class.

In the early period of industrialization the Methodists attracted elements of the working classes. The majority of the working class remained unattached to any church even at the height of the Victorian religious advance. General William Booth, founder of the Salvation Army, was shocked into social as well as religious action by the irreligious attitudes of the urban working class in 'darkest England' in the eighteen eighties.[3]

It was not until the inter-war period that Spiritualism spread widely beyond the industrial cities of the North, the Midlands and London. As late as 1908 there were only twenty-seven societies in London and only three in the Home Counties, whereas there were eighty-eight in Lancashire and sixty-two in Yorkshire. No complete national statistics are available for later periods, but some indication may be obtained from the statistics of distribution of their churches, published by the Spiritualist National Union. These are somewhat difficult to interpret, since the district covering the rural south-east, eastern counties and Home Counties is the London District which also include the Metropolitan area. The Southern District which covered the south coast and originally the South-west was later divided into Southern and South-western Districts. In 1940 there were fifty-three societies in the London District and thirty in the Southern compared with sixty-seven in Lancashire (divided between the Manchester, South West Lancashire and North Lancashire Districts) and fifty-six in the Yorkshire District. By 1951 the London District had increased to seventy-four societies and the Southern and South-western to a total of fifty-four. The Lancashire area had increased to ninety but Yorkshire had declined to thirty-nine. Thirteen years later in 1964 there had been an increase in the London District to ninety-four, the Southern and South-west had remained steady at fifty-three but the Lancashire area had declined to eighty-one and Yorkshire to thirty-one societies.

The only area apart from London which has shown consistent growth since 1940 has been the West Midlands.

The Spiritualist National Union statistics do not represent a

---

[3] W. Booth, *In Darkest England and the Way Out*, 1890; *see also* David Martin, *A Sociology of English Religion*, 1967.

S

complete picture but this may be improved by taking into consideration the churches belonging to the Greater World Christian Spiritualist League and Independent Churches. The statistics relating to the G.W.C.S.L. are not published, but a typescript list of their churches was made available to the author in 1962. This showed that there were ninety-two churches belonging to the League in the area covered by the S.N.U. London District, and twenty in the Southern and South-western areas, whereas there were only eighteen societies listed in the Lancashire area and sixteen in Yorkshire. The distribution of independent churches is impossible to state accurately, since the numbers can only be arrived at by an analysis of those churches that advertise in the Spiritualist press; this is not of course a representative sample. There were, in 1961–62, 112 independent societies in the London area who advertised in the press, whereas there were only six such societies in Lancashire and few in Yorkshire. This however probably reflects the fact that Spiritualists' publications are published in London.

Nevertheless it seems clear that the centre of interest and activity in the Spiritualist movement has moved from the north to the London and south-east and that a growing centre appears to exist in the West Midlands.

This trend coincides with the movement of population to the south-east and the Midlands, which has been a prominent feature of post-war development.

The movement arose in the industrial towns of the North and in London, and has only spread to those residential areas which are inhabited by urban workers or by retired persons. The movement has proliferated along the south coast in resorts largely occupied by old people.

The spread to the south, the appearance of Spiritualist societies in small towns and residential areas has followed the conversion of Britain into an urban society. Since 1920 there has been a steady spread of urban influences from the cities into the country, until by the 'sixties it is possible to argue that with the exception of remote communities in Scotland the whole of Britain has become urbanized, that the countryman no less than the city dweller has come to accept most urban values and to adopt urban attitudes. As the acceptance of urban values has spread so has the acceptance of Spiritualism.

Spiritualism arose and had its first successes in urban areas for a variety of reasons. In the first place Spiritualism arose as a result of the challenge of science to religion. The urban population, being on the whole better educated in the nineteenth century than the rural, was more aware of the tension between science and religion, and was consequently more active in seeking a solution.

The second factor arises from the differences in the quality of life in urban as compared with rural areas.

The anonymity of urban life makes it much easier for the individual to deviate from the normal social behaviour. Conformity is a feature of the rural community, men are more easily influenced by the opinion of the group in the village than they are by the opinion of others in the urban environment. New ideas consequently tend to arise and achieve popularity in urban areas. Spiritualism was a new and revolutionary idea which conflicted with the official pattern of religious belief, and consequently it had little influence in the rural situation where the Christian pattern was almost unchallenged. Those elements of rural belief patterns that appear to be most closely consistent with Spiritualist ideas were an obstacle rather than an aid to the spread of Spiritualism. The belief in ghosts and in the powers of witchcraft were still very influential in the rural England of the second half of the nineteenth century,[4] but these ideas were not only opposed by the churches as being anti-Christian, but were derided by the progressives as being contrary to the concepts of modern science. They were survivals of magic and not the result of a synthesis of science and religion, as was Spiritualism. The man who lives in the mythopoeic world of magic and primitive Spiritualism has no need for modern Spiritualism, with its emphasis on proof: for him a simple faith is enough.

The magical world view of the nineteenth century countryman living close to the rhythms of nature and still largely dependent upon her unpredictable moods for his livelihood has now almost entirely disappeared. The agriculturalist is today much more in control of his environment, agriculture has become highly mechanized, and the farmer tends to become much more ready to accept urban values and the rational world view of modern science.

[4] *See* A. Jessopp, *Arcady: For Better For Worse*, (No date *c*. 1886) for an account of the religious beliefs and practices of rural workers in the 1880s.

The growth of mass communications has also spread the urban way of life into the rural areas, and a general growth in the accessibility of the products of an industrial system has led to a situation in which it is increasingly difficult to distinguish between the rural and urban patterns of life. This urbanization of the countryside has led to the spread of Spiritualism into small towns and rural areas.

The urban way of life has also been characterized as 'anomic', as lacking in consistent norms, and this has been seen as producing a situation in which men seek for a new 'norm', and for a group to which they can give their allegiance. This process has been used as an explanation for the rise of many social and religious movements, and is partly an explanation of the attraction of Spiritualist Churches.

Finally, Spiritualism is an urban religion because it arose not only out of the conflicts of science and religion but also out of the needs of many urbanites to replace the magical or mythopoeic world view of the rural dweller with a substitute world view which is more significant and satisfactory than the rationalist world view.

Not only did Spiritualism arise in urban areas, but it grew most rapidly in certain types of towns – the rapidly growing industrial cities – and was least successful in the old traditional and largely pre-industrial towns that survived at least until the end of the nineteenth century.[5] It is industrialization rather than urbanization that is responsible for the breakdown of the traditional pattern of life and gives rise to an attitude of doubt in the sphere of religion. It is an industrial urban society that gives rise in an acute form to those problems of individualism that follow the collapse of social and cultural norms and gives rise to the search for a new basis for personal and social integration.

Spiritualism and Social Class

Spiritualism, unlike revivalist and extremist sects, did not appeal only to the working class. Its appeal was to all classes in society, and in particular to individuals who had become detached from conventional Christianity as a result of dissatisfaction with the teachings and practices of the churches.

[5] This distinction between industrial and pre-industrial cities is based on the work of G. Sjoberg in his book *The Pre-Industrial City*, New York, 1965.

In the south the London movement included the aristocrats who patronized D. D. Home, the intellectuals who were concerned mainly with the scientific investigation of the phenomena and who later formed the Society for Psychic Research, and the middle classes who formed the membership of the majority of the societies. The membership of the National Association of Spiritualists was certainly largely composed of wealthy members of the upper middle class in the eighteen seventies, for Harrison writing in 1875 observes that 'Now that the dark evenings are returning and Spiritualists are finding their way back to town, the monthly soirees of the National Association will be resumed'. The only class that could afford to be away from London for extended holidays during the summer were the wealthy upper class. To spend the summer season in London was considered very unfashionable in upper class society, therefore since the activities of the National Association were curtailed by the absence of its members in the summer we must conclude that this society was largely composed of members of the upper classes.

In the provinces the movement was at first largely lower middle and working class. A London Spiritualist who travelled in the north of England in 1878 commented on two differences which he noticed between Spiritualists in the north and in London. He said that in the north, 'In many instances I have found the circles to consist of persons utterly illiterate to an astounding degree'. He also noticed another important difference, this time in the outlook and attitude, of Spiritualists in the north. 'In most cases,' he said, 'they regard Spiritualism as a religion and practice it strictly as such'. In the north they were beginning to hold regular religious services in addition to meetings for the study and production of phenomena, whereas in London in the 'seventies the approach was more scientific, and it was not until much later that the religious approach became popular in the south.

The editor of *The Spiritual Reporter*, writing in 1879, claimed that 'Spiritualism sinks all differences of caste, position and wealth', and interest in psychic phenomena certainly knew no class boundaries in Victorian England, members of all classes from the Queen to the poorest labourers showed interest in the subject.

In 1846 a medium, Georgiana Eagle, demonstrated clairvoyance to the Queen at Osborne House and was presented with a gold watch for her services, Queen Victoria's interest in the psychic continued, and it has been claimed that the Queen's personal servant and confidant, John Brown, was a medium. It is also known that H. J. Lees, the medium, gave seances for the Queen.[6]

Social Class and Deprivation

Charles Y. Glock's theory of the role of deprivation in the origin and evolution of religious groups[7] provides a useful clue to the origin and development of the Spiritualist movement.

Glock has attempted to expand the concept of deprivation to provide a general explanation of the origin of all social movements. He starts from the theory of deprivation as a source of religious sects which formed the basis of H. Richard Niebuhr's[8] explanation. The concept of deprivation used by Niebuhr is essentially a concept of economic deprivation, and while this provides an explanation for those sects which arose among and recruits mainly from the economically under-privileged, it does not explain the existence of those sects and denominations which are primarily middle class or upper class in origin and membership or those which attract a cross section of the population.

The theory of the role of deprivation has been expanded by Glock by postulating the existence of other forms of deprivation as the source of such religious movements. In addition to economic deprivation, Glock suggests the individual may feel himself to be suffering from either social deprivation, organismic deprivation, ethical deprivation or psychic deprivation, and he goes on to suggest that 'a situation of felt deprivation [is] a necessary pre-condition for the rise of an organized social movement, whether it be religious or secular'.

In what respect were the founders of Spiritualism deprived and in what respect are those who join or form new Spiritualist groups deprived?

The membership of the Spiritualist movement has always been socially mixed in class terms, though the majority appear to be members of the lower middle and artisan classes. Some members

[6] E. E. P. Tisdale, *Queen Victoria's Private Life*, 1961.

[7] C. Y. Glock, 'The Role of Deprivation in the Origin and Evolution of Religious Groups' in R. Lee and M. M. Marty, *Religion and Social Conflict*, pp. 24–36, New York, 1964.

[8] C. Y. Glock and R. Stark, *Religion and Society in Tenson*, Ch. 13, Chicago, 1965.

of Spiritualist groups are economically deprived, others suffer from social deprivation, but many would appear to feel one of the other forms of deprivation.

The healing element within Spiritualism clearly arises from a felt organismic deprivation, and attracts persons who suffer from ill health and who do not feel that orthodox methods of healing are adequate in their cases; such persons are found in all social classes.

The majority of the members of the movement are attracted for reasons which Glock defines as ethical or psychic deprivation. By ethical deprivation Glock means that certain individuals no longer find the value system of their society meaningful as a guide to the organization of their way of life. They feel deprived of a set of ethical values and seek in a new religious movement a more satisfactory set of values. The Spiritualist movement offers a set of ethical values which are sanctioned by its teaching on the nature of the after life.

While Spiritualism provides a solution for those suffering ethical deprivation, its main appeal is to those suffering from psychic deprivation. Glock's definition is by no means clear. He says that in psychic deprivation 'there is a concern with philosophical meaning but in this case philosophy is sought for its own sake rather than as a source of ethical prescriptions as to how one is to behave in relation to others'.[9] We may clarify this concept by suggesting that psychic deprivation be used to describe a condition in which an individual feels that life and the universe has no meaning (not only in an ethical sense). He seeks for mental and psychic security and frequently finds this in the formation of new religious groups.

Glock believed that psychic deprivation is 'primarily a consequence of severe and unresolved social deprivation'.[10] In the case of Spiritualists, it appears that the social deprivation is in a high proportion of cases of one particular type. It is the deprivation that arises from the death of a close relative, or more rarely, of a friend.

The loss of a close personal associate (through death) is probably the most common stimulus to membership of the Spiritualist movement, but the problem of death as an abstract concept may

9 C. Y. Glock, op. cit., p. 28.
10 C. Y. Glock, op. cit., p. 29.

also stimulate an interest in the study and investigation of psychic phenomena, and lead to membership in the Spiritualist movement.

These factors account for the observed high proportion of widows, widowers and elderly people in the Spiritualist movement. [11]

The problems of death either in the concrete or abstract, the problems of ill health and of the search for meaning in life are not exclusive to any one social class, and neither are they related very closely to other forms of deprivation. All men face these problems at some time in life; some men find the traditional religious answers adequate, others are able to accept purely secular or scientific answers. Spiritualism attracts those who have found the purely scientific and the purely religious answers inadequate and who consequently seek scientific proof for a religious belief.

There are few major sources of recruitment into the Spiritualist movement. Two of these we have already considered, namely the recruitment of those who are suffering from the deprivation by death of loved ones and intellectual and scientific curiosity; the third is the search for healing by the organismically deprived. Finally, there is another and more fundamental source, one which is basic to the existence of the movement and to the birth of all religions. This is the discovery by certain individuals that they have psychic powers or abilities that do not appear to be possessed by the majority of their fellow men. Such persons are spontaneous mediums, and a study of the lives of well known mediums reveals that their powers arose spontaneously; they frequently, as children, saw visions, heard voices and had other psychic experiences.

The great revival of Spiritualism that followed the First World War was partly stimulated by the conversion of several famous persons, but the fundamental causes were deeper than this. They are to be found in the need for comfort and reassurance felt by many bereaved persons at the end of what was the most costly war in terms of human life in British history. The war came at a time when many people had doubts about the claims of conventional Christianity and the churches were unable to offer the concrete assurance of survival that many people needed.

The late 'twenties and early 'thirties were years of depression and hardship for many, and it is not surprising that the increasing

---

[11] Based on participant observation. Statistics not available.

number of people who had become detached from conventional Christianity should seek consolation in the new religion of Spiritualism. The movement was temporarily disorganized by the Second World War. It made rapid recovery, and was highly successful during the post-war period of austerity, reaching a peak about 1954. Since then, as our society has become increasingly affluent, the Spiritualist movement has continued to decline.

Conclusions

Modern Spiritualism arises amongst groups alienated from the traditional patterns of life and of religious behaviour and belief. It arises as a by-product of the secularization that appears to be a consequence of industrial urbanization.

Shamanism, which may be seen as a primitive form of Spiritualism, exists in the simplest forms of society. A clear distinction may be drawn between Primitive and Modern Spiritualism in terms of Weber's distinction between magic and rational-ethical religion, that is to say in terms of increasing rationality. Modern Spiritualism can therefore be seen as a 'new religion', emerging from the essentially magical world view of Shamanism and witchcraft. A religion influenced by the teachings and practices of previous higher religions, but whose basic elements derive from an older and more traditional religion, which continued to underlie the veneer of Christianity, and emerged when the superficial layer of Christian influence was removed by the changing social conditions of mass migration and urbanism.

The breakthrough to a higher, 'more rationalized and systematized'[12] religion did not occur as the result of the charismatic leadership of any one prophet, as Weber suggests was the typical way in which most religions arose. Instead Spiritualism arose with the recognition of the charismatic leadership of a large number of 'mediumistic' prophets, by individuals whose attitudes to religion had been changed by the impact of a changed social environment.

Spiritualism did not appeal to whole social groups. Many groups and individuals alienated by social change sought a solution in other ways, in the development of millenarian movements, in the rise of rationalism, and in political action directed at the solution of social and individual problems.

[12] T. Parsons. Introduction to M. Weber, *Sociology of Religion*, p. XXXIII, 1965

At the risk of being accused of reductionism, we must conclude that the ultimate reason why one solution is preferred to another by individuals can only be discovered by the psychological analysis of the individual. This is not to say that individuals are not greatly influenced by their social environment, or that social groups largely sharing a common social environment do not tend to have a similar reaction to events, for clearly such influences are important.

Social influences affecting whole groups are clearly of importance in shaping the behaviour in the individual members of such groups, and in differentiating between members and non-members, when the pattern of life of a particular social group can be clearly distinguished from that of all other social groups. When social change is rapid and migrations, social mobility and urbanization are playing an increasing part in disrupting the structure of traditional social groups, then conditions of anomie are maximized. In such conditions the personality of individuals is shaped by a diversity of social forces and it becomes difficult to distinguish groups whose members have all been conditioned by the same common culture. In such circumstances the unique life experiences of the individual begin to play an important part in determining his behaviour, and individualism emerges as an important element to be considered in social analysis. The common life experiences of groups still play a part, but are modified by the increasing influence of unique experiences. This paradoxically creates a situation in which a common element of the cultural pattern of whole classes in society is their consciousness of themselves as individuals.

Spiritualism arises amongst classes and in societies in which individualism, in this sense of a consciousness of the self as a unique personality, has arisen and has played an important part in shaping the world view of members. This is reflected in the drive to find proof of individual survival of the personality after death, a drive which in some arose at the manifest level from intellectual curiosity, but which in all was probably based upon a latent desire for survival.[13] In many cases the desire to prove survival is

[13] In societies that do not place a belief in the uniqueness of the individual personality at the centre of their culture pattern a belief in and search for some form of impersonal survival arises. This is to be found in India where the Hindus and Buddhists are occupied with the attempt to extinguish the individual personality and to unite with 'ultimate reality'.

directly the result of conscious anxieties about the survival of the unique self or the survival of the personality of friends and relations, but however it manifests itself, it is a consequence of the heightened awareness of the self that results from individualism.

It is interesting to note that it is in Brazil that Spiritualism has grown most rapidly since 1940. In that year there were 463,000 Spiritualists in Brazil; by 1950 the number had risen to 824,553.[14] Brazil is rapidly being urbanized, and the anomie resulting from social and geographical mobility has detached many people from the tradition of the Roman Catholic church. There has consequently been a growth in extreme Protestant sects and in the Spiritualist movement.

De Comarge and Labbens also point out that in Brazil there is a tradition of mediumistic religion in the Afro-Brazilian magic cults, which have retained considerable influence among the poorer classes, and in fact have never been superseded but only overlaid by a thin veneer of Catholicism throughout Latin America. When the veneer of Catholicism is removed by changing social and cultural conditions there is a reversion to mediumistic religion, a revival which among the more educated sections of society takes the form of an ethical-rational modern Spiritualism.

The Brazilian case seems to conform to the model we have previously outlined and to emphasize the possibility of testing our hypothesis. Spiritualism should arise wherever the conditions we have stated obtain. Wherever a traditional and formal religious order is broken by the process of urbanization allied to the development of scientific scepticism, and the emphasis is placed on the importance of the individual, we may expect a rational investigation of psychic phenomena to take place, and to give rise to a religion basically similar to modern Spiritualism.[15]

[14] C. P. Ferreira de Camargo and J. Labbens, 'Aspects Socio-cultural du Spiritisme au Brézil', *Social Compass*, Vol. 7 (5/6) 1960.
[15] A further example which supports this hypothesis is that of the Upi Espiritistas of the Philippine Islands. *See* Stuart A. Schlegal 'The Upi Espiritistas: A Case Study in Cultural Adjustment', *The Journal for the Scientific Study of Religion*, pp. 198–212, Spring, 1965. Schlegal comments: 'Their environment on the one hand is an ancient world of powerful saints and proximate Spirits, of charms as well as chalices; on the other hand it is a changing world of increasing complexity and rapid modernization where the traditional is being confronted by the radically new.'

APPENDIX

STATISTICS OF BRITISH SPIRITUALISM

Socio-Demography

The Geographical Spread of the Movement.—Spiritualism was introduced into Britain in two main centres in 1852 in London and at Keighley in the West Riding of Yorkshire. During the eighteen fifties the movement spread from Keighley to Bingley, Bradford, Hinckley, Leigh and other places in the West Yorkshire and Lancashire area, and other circles were reported at Coventry, Nottingham, Belfast and London.

The slow spread continued throughout the 'sixties mainly from and around the areas in which the movement had first become established. In the north during this period groups existed at Newcastle; Richmond, Yorkshire; West Hartlepool; Sunderland; Darlington; Bradford, Huddersfield; Hexham; Carlisle; Brotherton, Yorkshire; Halifax; Manchester; Sheffield and Liverpool.

In the midlands societies had been formed in Wolverhampton, Birmingham, Leicester and Nottingham.

There were several societies in London by 1870, and a society had been formed in Glasgow, the first in Scotland.

The movement continued to grow during the eighteen seventies but again mainly in a small number of areas. These were in (i) Lancashire; (ii) West Riding of Yorkshire; (iii) the North-east centring on Newcastle; (iv) the West Midlands; and (v) London.

The statistics collected by J. Morse and presented to the Conference of Spiritualists held at Manchester support this view and give us the clearest available picture of the spread of the movement by 1880.

Eight years later the magazine *Two Worlds* completed a census of societies, which showed that little change had taken place in the distribution of society though these had increased in number.

TABLE 2A

Source: STATISTICAL RETURN SHEET OF SPIRITUALISM IN THE UNITED KINGDOM
GENERAL CONFERENCE OF BRITISH SPIRITUALISTS, MANCHESTER, OCTOBER 1880

	Place	Name of Society	Meetings	Average attendance	Number on roll	Library	School No. of scholars	Circles Public	Circles Private	Medium Public	Medium Private	Estimated number of Spiritualists	Hall and meeting places
1	Ashington	Spiritual Society	Sunday	30	40	No	34	1	6	1	10	60	Rented
11	Barrow in Furness	Spiritualists Society	Sunday	30	30	—	—	—	6	1	7	36	Rented
14	Bingley	Spiritualists Society	Sun, Wed.	30	20	No	—	—	10	—	30	30	Rented
23	Coventry	Coventry Home Circle	Tuesday	7	—	—	—	—	2	—	—	30	—
33	Falmouth		Thursday	9	—	Yes	—	—	1	—	—	—	—
34	Felling	Spiritualist Society	Sun, Tues., Thursday	12	14	—	—	2	11	1	5	20	Rented
36	Glasgow	Spiritual Assoc.	Sun, Mon.	60	100	Yes	15	3	24	—	20	250	Rented
38	Hayfield	New Mills and Hayfield	Sunday	35	30	Yes	—	—	10	—	6	300	Rented
39	Halifax	Halifax Sp. Inst.	Sunday	25	32	—	—	10	—	1	26	200	Rented
44	Keighley	Spiritual Brothd.	Sunday	100	160	Yes	Yes No. not given	—	4	4	6	400	Rented
45	Kirkcaldy	No Society	—	—	—	—	—	—	4	—	—	50	—

No.	Place	Society	Meetings											Tenure
31	Darlington	Public work suspended	—	—	—	—	—	—	—	—	—	—	—	—
40	Hunwick	No Society		—	—	—	—	—	—	—	—	5	—
49	Leicester	Spiritualist Society	Sun., Thurs.	40	22	—	—	—	6	—	3	150	Rented
52	Manchester	Manchester Assoc.	Sun., Wed.	50	37	Yes	—	1	5	2	20	—	Rented
53	Macclesfield	Macclesfield	Sunday	35	27	No	—	—	3	1	5	70	Rented
56	Morley	Morley	Sunday	80	18	—	—	1	1	—	4	50	Rented
57	Newcastle	Spiritual Evidence	Everyday	120	169	Yes	—	3	20	2	Many	300	Rented
59	New Shildon	Sth Durham Dist. Com.	Sunday	40	—	—	—	8	4	3	16	500*	—
63	Ouston	No Society		—	—	—	—	—	4	1	4	50	—
66	Reddish	No Society		—	—	—	—	—	—	—	—	6	—
67	Rochdale	Spiritual Society	Sunday	30	24	—	—	—	8	—	8	120	Rented
69	N. Shields	No Society		—	—	—	—	1	2	—	3	—	—
75	Stamford	No Society		—	—	—	—	—	2	—	—	—	—
78	Ulverston	No Society		—	—	—	—	—	2	—	—	12	—
79	Whitworth	No Society		—	—	—	—	—	6	—	—	40	—
81	West Polton	Spiritualists Society	Sunday	100	50	—	—	—	6	—	12	150	—
82	West Hartlepool	No Society	Sunday	10	—	—	—	1	1	—	3	20	—
83	Walsall	Spiritualists Society	Sun., Mon.	90	37	Yes	—	1	9	1	20	100	Rented
85	Yarmouth	Spiritualists Society	Sun., Tues., Thurs.	20	—	—	—	1	20	—	1	50	Rented

* In district

TABLE 2B

	Place	Name of Society	Meetings	Average attendance	Number on roll	Library	School No. of scholars	Circles Public	Circles Private	Medium Public	Medium Private	Estimated number of Spiritualists	Hall and meeting places
A	London	B.N.A.S.	Every day	20	250	Yes	—	—	—	—	—	—	—
86	London	Spiritual Institute		—	—	—	—	—	—	—	—	—	—
87	London	Dalston	Thurs.	20	33	Yes	—	—	—	—	—	—	Rented
88	London	Hackney Spiritual Evidence Society	Sun., Thurs., Sat.	—	—	No	—	—	13	—	—	—	Rented
89	London	Marylebone	Every evening	50	50	Yes	—	—	2	—	—	—	Rented
90	London	Sth. London Spiritualist Society	Sun., Wed.	12	17	—	—	—	—	—	—	—	—
92	Dalton		Sunday	15	12	—	—	—	2	1	3	19	Rented
93	Willington	No Society		—	—	—	—	—	—	—	—	8	—
94	Sunnybrow	No Society		—	—	—	—	—	—	—	—	14	—
95	Honden le Wear	No Society		—	—	—	—	—	—	—	—	—	—
96	High Grange	No Society		—	—	—	—	—	—	—	—	5	—
97	Eyers Green	No Society		—	—	—	—	—	—	—	—	5	—
98	Sowerby Bridge	Lyceum	Sunday	50	30	Yes	20	—	—	—	4	200	Owned
99	Bacup	No Society		—	—	—	—	—	—	—	8	50	—

TABLE 2c

Morse wrote to Spiritualists in all those places in which he was aware that Spiritualism existed, but from the following places he received no reply. Where possible we have attempted to compile information regarding these places from other sources.

	Places	Name of Society	Meetings	Average attendance	Number on roll	Library	School No. of scholars	Circles Public	Circles Private	Medium Public	Medium Private	Estimated number of Spiritualists	Hall and meeting places
2	Alton												
3	Auckland Park			—	—	—	—	—	—	—	—	—	—
4	Bishop Auckland			—	—	—	—	—	—	—	—	—	—
5	Buxton												
6	Bradford	Society at Harker Meeting Room	Sunday	—	—	—	—	—	—	—	—	—	—
7	Bradford	Spiritualist Church, Manchester Road	Sunday	—	—	—	—	—	—	—	—	—	Yes
8	Bradford												
9	Benfieldside			—	—	—	—	—	—	—	—	—	—

TABLE 2C

	Place	Name of Society	Meetings	Average attendance	Number on roll	Library	School No. of scholars	Circles Public	Circles Private	Medium Public	Medium Private	Estimated number of Spiritualists	Hall and meeting places
10	Blackhill	No Society*		—	—	—	—	—	—	—	—	—	—
12	Blackburn		Sunday Services	—	—	—	—	—	—	—	—	—	—
13	Birmingham				—	—	—	—	—	—	—	—	—
15	Batley Carr	Society of Spiritualists		—	—	—	—	—	—	—	—	—	—
16	Belper	Society		—	—	—	—	—	—	—	—	—	—
17	Burnley	No Society†		—	—	—	—	—	—	—	—	—	—
18	Bolton	Society		—	—	—	—	—	—	—	—	—	—
19	Blundellsands			—	—	—	—	—	—	—	—	—	—
20	Bristol			—	—	—	—	—	—	—	—	—	—
21	Choppington			—	—	—	—	—	—	—	—	—	—
22	Chard			—	—	—	—	—	—	—	—	—	—
24	Consett			—	—	—	—	—	—	—	—	—	—
25	Chorley			—	—	—	—	—	—	—	—	—	—
26	Cambridge	(a) Town Society (b) University Society for Psychological Investigation		—	—	—	—	—	—	—	—	—	—

No.	Place	Society										
27	Cardiff	(a) Free Library and Meeting Room (b) Spiritual Society	—	—	—	—	—	—	—	—	—	—
28	Dumfries		—	—	—	—	—	—	—	—	—	—
29	Devonport		—	—	—	—	—	—	—	—	—	—
30	Derby	Psychological Society	—	—	—	—	—	—	—	—	—	—
32	Edinburgh		—	—	—	—	—	—	—	—	—	—
35	Gateshead		—	—	—	—	—	—	—	—	—	—
37	Hyde		—	—	—	—	—	—	—	—	—	—
41	Hull	Hull & East Riding of Yorkshire Assoc. of Spiritualists	—	—	—	—	—	—	—	—	—	—
42	Isle of Man		—	—	—	—	—	—	—	—	—	—
43	Jersey		—	—	—	—	—	—	—	—	—	—
46	Liverpool	Psychological Society	—	—	—	—	—	—	—	—	—	—
47	Low Fell		—	—	—	—	—	—	—	—	—	—
48	Leeds		—	—	—	—	—	—	—	—	—	—
50	Loughborough	No Society*	—	—	—	—	—	—	—	—	—	—
51	Leamington		—	—	—	—	—	—	—	—	—	—
54	Millom	Society of Spiritualists 1879*	—	—	—	—	—	—	—	—	—	—
55	Merthyr		—	—	—	—	—	—	—	—	—	—

* **Private Circles.**   † Regular Circles, two mediums, Society reviving December 1879

TABLE 2D

Place	Name of Society	Meetings	Average attendance	Number on roll	Library	School No. of scholars	Circles Public	Circles Private	Medium Public	Medium Private	Estimated number of Spiritualists	Hall and meeting places
58 Nottingham	(a) Universal Church of Christ* (b) Assoc. of Spiritualists	Sunday	—	—	—	—	—	—	—	—	—	Two Halls
60 Ossett	Spiritual Institution		—	—	—	—	·	—	—	—	—	No Hall
61 Old Shildon			—	—	—	—	—	—	—	—	—	—
62 Oldham	Society of Spiritualists†		—	—	—	—	—	—	—	—	—	—
64 Preston	No Society‡		—	—	—	—	—	—	—	—	—	—
65 Plymouth			—	—	—	—	—	—	—	—	—	—
68 Rochester			—	—	—	—	—	—	—	—	—	—
70 South Shields			—	—	—	—	—	—	—	—	—	—
71 Sunderland			—	—	—	—	—	—	—	—	—	—
72 Seghill			—	—	—	—	—	—	—	—	—	—
73 Southampton			—	—	—	—	—	—	—	—	—	—
74 Shotley Bridge			—	—	—	—	—	—	—	—	—	—
76 Torquay			—	—	—	—	—	—	—	—	—	—
77 Taunton			—	—	—	—	—	—	—	—	—	—
80 Windy Nook			—	—	—	—	—	—	—	—	—	—
84 Walditch			—	—	—	—	—	—	—	—	—	—

* November 1879, Christian Spiritualists.   † Many Spiritualists divided among selves.   ‡ Home Circles.

These statistics show a heavy concentration of societies in the northern industrial towns: Lancashire 6; Yorkshire 12; Durham and Northumberland 1; Cheshire 1; Cumberland 1; making a total of 25. In the Midlands there were only seven societies, in London six

Two Worlds First Annual Census of Societies, December 28th, 1868

	No. of Members	Seating capacity of hall	Average attendance	Lyceum Membership	Average attendance	Mediums		No. of Circles
						Public	Private	
Bacup	40	160	100	66	5	—	—	6
Barrow in Furness (Victoria Hall)	45	220	200	130	to 400	4	5	5
Batley, Wellington Street	30	200	100	—	—	—	2	4
Beeston, Conservative Club	16	110	80	47	30	—	—	1
Belper, Jubilee Hall	60	250	120–170	72	56	—	Several	4
Birmingham, 92 Ashted Row	7	200	40	100	80	2	1	Many
Blackburn, Exchange Lecture Hall	150	400	330	—	—	Yes	—	—
Bradford, Birk Street	46	200	100	—	—	Yes	Yes	Yes
Bradford, Bowling Harker Street	2	100	40	—	—	—	Yes	Several
Bradford, Little Horton Spicer Street	—	200	150	—	—	—	3	1
Bradford, Milton Room	50	400	200	93	45	21	Many	Many
Bradford, Otley Road	25	120	100	—	—	—	2	1
Bradford, St James	24	350–400	130	70	35	Yes	Yes	—
Bradford, Walton Street (a new society)	40	300	200	40	30	—	—	—
Brighouse, Commercial Street	59	150	170	110	30	—	6	9
Burnley, Tanner Street	24	350	300	36	26	1	20	30
Cleckheaton, Odd Fellows Hall	12	350	200	134	100	1	—	3
Colne, Cloth Hall (Society fifteen months old)	112	200	150	—	—	—	4	Many
Cowms, Lepton, Nr. Huddersfield	30	300	100	—	—	—	—	2
Cromford on High Park	—	30	20	—	—	—	Several	Several
Darwin, Church Bank Street	70	250	150	53	25	2	13	—
Denholme, Blue Hill (new Society)	15	50	40	—	—	—	3	1
Dewsbury, Vulcan Road	26	170	100	—	—	1	8	5
Eccleshill, Stone Hall Road (three months old)	24	120	—	—	—	—	2	3
Exeter, Longbrook Street Chapel	30	200	50	20–30	20–30	—	2	8
Felling, Felling Park Road	45	85	Full	17	14	3	2	1
Foleshill, Edgewick, Coventry	37	50	40	—	—	—	3	4
Glasgow, Bannockburn Hall	83	300	100	50	40	—	Yes	10

	No. of Members	Seating capacity of hall	Average attendance	Lyceum Membership	Average attendance	Mediums Public	Mediums Private	No. of Circles
Halifax, Winding Road	60	280	240	112	80	11	30	20
Heckmondwike Assembly Room	58	500	400	50	40	2	1	1
Hetton le Hole	11		20			2	1	2
Heywood, Argyle Buildings	19	100	40			1	3	Yes
Huddersfield, Brook Street	31	300	200				3	Many
Huddersfield, Kaye's Buildings	60	140	100	80	50		Yes	3
Idle, Back Lane	24	65	40	38	26	5	3	20
Keighley, Assembly Rooms			160			1	20	
Keighley, East Parade	60	200	160	130	120		Yes	5
Lancaster, Athanaeum Lecture Hall	70	200	100	90	60	1	1	
Leeds, Cookridge Street	80	180	60–180				Many	Many
Leicester	80	180	120	25	20	6	Yes	Yes
Liverpool, Daulby Hall	100	500	250				6	3
London, Canning Town	12	60	38					Yes
London, Kings Cross	20	150	60				4	7
London, Notting Hill Gate	32	200	100					Many
London, Peckham	82	110	30–100	40	30	3	4	5
Macclesfield, Free Church	56	130	16	30	42	4	4	Yes
Manchester Assembly Room, Downing Street	110	400	300	40	36		Yes	2
Mexborough	40	80	70				4	12
Middlesborough, Spiritual Hall	40	500	30–200	60	50		6	
Monkwearmouth, Ravensworth Terrace		80	60			1	3	Several
Nelson, Public Hall, Leeds Road	42	1200	100–200	85	80	Yes		Many
Newcastle upon Tyne, Cordwainers Hall	100	250	180	20–100	85			2
North Shields Borough Road		80	50					Yes
North Shields, Camden Street	55	350	190	30	40		Yes	Several
Nottingham, Morby Hall	50	250	30–90–250	38	30	2	Several	Many
Oldham, Spiritual Temple	80	500	200–350	135	90–100	5	50	Yes
Openshaw, Mechanics' Institute	125	600	550–600	80	80		Yes	

Parkgate, Pear Tree Road	37	300	80	50	40	5	2	4
Pendleton, Co-op Hall	70	600	350	36	28	5	1	Several
Rawtenstall	40	100	60	—	—	5	2	7
Rochdale, Regent Hall	—	—	100	—	—		2	5
Scholes, Silver Street	12	50	43	—	—	3	2	—
Sheffield, Cent. Board Schools	50	200	150	—	—		Yes	Yes
Skelmanthorpe, Board School	18	170	100	—	—			3
Slaithwaite, Laith Lane	23	200	125	52	28	1		2
South Shields, Cambridge Street	48	350	120	60	37		5	4
Sowerby Bridge, Lyceum	80	250	100	70	—		8	6
Stonehouse, Corpus Christi Chapel	50	350	100	—	—	2	Several	4 Public 5 Priv.
Tyldesley, Elliot Street	20	100	30	58	25		2	Several
Walsall, Exchange Buildings	50	120	45	21	16	3	7	6
Westhoughton, Spiritual Hall	35	100	40	35	—	1	4	3
West Palton, Spiritual Association	8	300	40	—	—		2	1
Wibsey, Hardy Street	11	100	50	—	—			—
Wellington, Durham	15	500	50	—	—			5
Wisbech, Lecture Room Public Hall	40	300	250	—	—	3		7
York, Abbott Street	12	20	16	—	—		1	—

The following societies did not reply:

Ashington
Batley Carr
Bingley
Birmingham (Oozells Street)
Bishop Auckland
Bradford (Ripley Street and Rooley Street)
Burslem
Byker
Leeds (Psychological)
Leigh
London (Several)
Lowestoft
Manchester (Collyhurst Road)
Middlesbrough (Sidney Street)
Morley
Northampton
Plymouth
Portsmouth
Ramsbottom
Rochdale (Backwater Street and Michael Street)
Salford
Saltash
Sheffield (Pond Street)
Sunderland
Tunstall
West Vale
Whitworth

An examination of these statistics reveals a great concentration of societies in the industrial towns of south-east Lancashire (21) and the adjoining areas of west Yorkshire (32) and north Cheshire (1). There was a further concentration in the Durham/Northumberland/north Yorkshire area (14). Small groups around Nottingham/Derby (4) and in the west Midlands (4) and a further large group in London.

TABLE 4

It was a further twenty years before a new table of statistics was compiled. There was still little change in geographical distribution.

DISTRIBUTION OF SPIRITUALIST SOCIETIES 1908

	County	Affiliated to S.N.U.	Independent	Total
1	Berkshire	1	—	1
2	Cheshire	7	9	16
3	Cumberland	1	2	3
4	Cambs.	—	1	1
5	Durham	17	—	17
6	Derbyshire	3	4	7
7	Devonshire	—	4	4
8	Edinburgh	1	—	1
9	Essex	1	—	1
10	Forfarshire	—	2	2
11	Fifeshire	—	2	2
12	Glamorganshire	3	2	5
13	Hampshire	4	1	5
14	Lanarkshire	1	2	3
15	Lincolnshire	1	3	4
16	Leicestershire	2	1	3
17	Lancashire	43	45	88
18	London	11	16	27
19	Monmouthshire	1	—	1
20	Nottinghamshire	2	6	8
21	Northamptonshire	1	2	3
22	Northumberland	—	10	10
23	Norfolk	—	1	1
24	Renfrewshire	—	1	1
25	Staffordshire	2	2	4
26	Sussex	1	—	1
27	Stirlingshire	1	—	1
28	Warwickshire	—	8	8
29	Yorkshire	21	41	62

Note the concentration of societies in Lancashire, London, Yorkshire and Durham/Northumberland.

TABLE 5

Membership of Spiritualist National Federation

Year	Societies
1891	41
1892	45
1893	34
1894	44
1895	45 (estimated 150 societies in Britain)
1896	58
1897	66
1898	89
1902	79 (240 societies in Britain)

284

TABLE 6

MEMBERSHIP OF SPIRITUALIST SOCIETIES (S.N.U.)

	Affiliated to S.N.U.	Membership S.N.U.	Other National Bodies	Total
1908	125	—	—	390
1913	141	—	—	—
1915	145	—	—	320
1916	158	—	—	—
1919	309 (1)	—	—	—
1922	332	—	—	—
1923	346	—	—	—
1924	371	—	—	—
1925	396	—	—	—
1927	393	—	—	—
1928	419	15,678	—	—
1929	401 + 41 subs. not paid	—	G.W.C.S. League	—
1932	465	14,734	360 (8,000)	1,300? (1)
1933	480	14,058	478 (10,000)	1,000? (2)
1934	496	14,695	562 (14,000)	2,000? (3)
1935	501	—	580 (20,000)	—
1937	511	12,927	—	—
1938	530	13,617	—	—
1939	485	14,028	—	—
1940	361	12,460	—	—
1941	313	10,250	—	—
1942	353	11,250	—	—

TABLE 7

S.N.U. Affiliated Churches 1940

District Councils	Churches
London	53
East Midlands	19
West Midlands	22
North East	49
South West Lancashire	17
Manchester	29
North Lancashire	21
Scottish	38
Southern	30
South Wales	27
Yorkshire	56
	361

12,460 members

TABLE 8

S.N.U. Summary of Membership 1944–1964

Year	Churches	Church Members	Church Associated Members	Class B Members	Kindred Associated Bodies
1944	400	13,255	—	1,021	—
1945	460	14,924	—	1,428	—
1946	486	16,446	—	1,404	—
1947	473	18,690	—	1,431	—
1948	475	17,768	—	1,529	—
1949	478	18,328	—	1,553	—
1950	491	19,003	2,496	1,006	—
1951	485	17,725	2,330	1,671	6
1954	498	—	—	—	—
1955	498	—	—	—	—
1956	494	16,857	—	—	—
1957	491	17,001	2,333	1,494	13
1958	470	17,025	2,244	1,490	12
1959	449	15,712	1,511	1,472	8
1960	453	15,738	1,609	1,482	10
1961	441	15,672	1,509	1,453	11
1962	434	15,497	1,477	1,596	9
1963	429	14,968	1,127	1,644	7
1964	464*	14,622	1,272	1,875*	9

Although the movement has not received as much publicity since the war as it did in the 'thirties, the membership figures of the S.N.U. were never higher than in 1950. Since then there has been a constant decline in total membership of S.N.U. churches.

* Apparent increase in churches and Class B membership arises because churches and members are no longer excluded from statistics where they have *not yet* paid subscriptions.

TABLE 9

S.N.U. Summary of Membership 1951

District Councils	Churches	Church Members	Church Associated Members	Class B Members	Kindred Associated Bodies
London	74	4,015	797	514	1
East Midlands	26	827	43	82	—
West Midlands	29	1,229	155	160	—
Northern	66	1,665	83	65	1
Manchester	37	1,206	282	161	1
North Lancashire	29	995	104	62	—
South West Lancashire and Cheshire	24	863	164	75	—
Scottish	57	1,947	204	124	—
Southern	25	1,082	117	60	1
South Western	29	1,051	137	102	1
South Wales	43	949	93	123	1
Sheffield	26	801	77	46	—
Yorkshire	39	1,135	74	84	—
Overseas	—	—	—	14	—
	504	17,765	2,330	1,672	6

TABLE 10

S.N.U. Membership 1964

District Councils	Churches	Church Members	Church Associated Members	Class B Members	Kindred Associated Bodies	Estimate of G.W.C.S.L. Churches	Estimate of Independent Churches
London	94	4,366	528	498	2	92	112+
East Midlands	23	672	49	112	1	13	6+
West Midlands	39	1,370	93	198	—	21	10+
Northern	51	1,090	33	73	1	8	3+
Manchester	37	806	68	146	1	9	3+
North Lancashire	23	619	54	83	—	5	3+
S.W. Lancashire and Cheshire	21	590	80	108	—	4	1+
Scottish	34	1,294	76	149	3	8	2+
Southern	24	963	73	97	—	1	6+
South Western	29	827	46	119	—	19	6+
South Wales	35	668	33	119	—	17	—
Sheffield	23	618	54	49	—	6	1+
Yorkshire	31	804	84	97	—	16	4+
Overseas	—	35	—	27	1	—	—
	464	14,722	1,271	1,875	9	—	—

BIBLIOGRAPHY

History of Spiritualism in America and Britain
ANON, *The Centennial Book of Modern Spiritualism in America*, Chicago, 1948
BRITTEN, Mrs. E. HARDINGE, The National Spiritualist Association, *Modern American Spiritualism*, New York, 1870
CAPRON, E. W., *Modern Spiritualism*, Boston, Bela Marsh, 1885
CAPRON, E. W. and BARRON, *Explanation and History of the Mysterious Communion with the Spirits*, New York, Auburn, 1850
CARRINGTON, H., *The Story of Psychic Science*, London, Rider & Co., 1931
DAVENPORT, R. R., *The Death Blow to Spiritualism*, New York, 1888
DOYLE, Sir A. CONAN, *The History of Spiritualism*, London, Cassell, 1926
HILL, J. ARTHUR, *Spiritualism. Its History, Phenomena and Doctrine*, London, Cassell, 1918
HOWITT, W., *The History of the Supernatural*, London, Longmans Green, 1863
MCCABE, JOSEPH, *Spiritualism: A Popular History from 1847*, London, T. Fisher Unwin, 1920
PHILLIMORE, M., *Brief History of London Spiritualist Alliance Ltd.*, London, Spiritualist Alliance, 1944
PODMORE, F., *Modern Spiritualism*, London, Methuen, 1902
ROBERTS, C. E. BECHOFER, *The Truth about Spiritualism*, London, Eyre and Spottiswoode, 1932
SALTER, W. H., *The Society for Psychic Research*, London, S.P.R., 1948
SWAFFER, HANNEN, *My Greatest Story*, London, W. H. Allen, 1945
THOMPSON, E., 'Spiritualism in the Evolution of Philosophy and Religion', *History of Modern Spiritualism*, Manchester, 1948
UNDERHILL, Mrs, *The Missing Link in Modern Spiritualism*, New York, 1885
World's Yearbook of Spiritualism, 1928, Belgium, Bureau International du Spiritisme, 1928

Studies of Spiritualist Cults

ELLIOTT, A. J. A., *Chinese Spirit-Medium Cults in Singapore*, London, L.S.E., 1955

FERREIRA, DE COMARGO C. P. and LABBENS, J., 'Aspects socio-cultural du Spiritisme au Brazil, *Social Compass,* Vol VII, 5/6, 1960

MCGREGOR, P., *The Moon and Two Mountains*, London, Souvenir Press, 1966

SCHLEGAL, STUART A., "The Upi Espiritistas: A Case Study in Cultural Adaptation," *Journal for the Scientific Study of Religion*, Spring, 1965

Psychic Phenomena in Christian Churches and Cults

HATHAWAY, W. G., *Spiritual Gifts in the Church*, London, Elim Publishing Co., 1926

KELSEY, MORTON T., *Speaking with Tongues*, London, The Epworth Press, 1965

THURSTON, H., *Surprising Mystics*, London, Rider, No Date (c. 1945)

THURSTON, H., *The Physical Phenomena of Mysticism,* London, Burns & Oates, 1952

WARDWELL, W. I., 'Christian Science Healing', *Journal for the Scientific Study of Religion*, Vol 4, No. 2, April 1962

Psychic Phenomena and Religion in Pre-Industrial Societies

ADDISON, J. T., *Life Beyond Death in the Beliefs of Mankind*, London, Allen & Unwin, 1958

BELO, JANE, *Trance in Bali*, New York, Columbia University Press, 1960

BENEDICT, R., *Patterns of Culture*, London, Routledge and Kegan Paul, 1935

CAMPBELL, J., *The Masks of God: Primitive Mythology*, London, Secker and Warburg, 1960

CARRINGTON, H. and FODOR, N., *The Story of the Poltergeist down the Centuries*, London, Rider, 1953

CODRINGTON, R. H., *The Melanesians*, Oxford, 1891

DAVID-NEEL, A., *With Mystics and Magicians in Tibet,* Harmonds-worth, Penguin, 1937

DAVIDSON, H. R. ELLIS, *Gods and Myths of Northern Europe*, Harmondsworth, Penguin, 1964

DEREN, M., *Divine Horsemen: The Living Gods of Haiti*, London, Thames and Hudson, 1953

DINGWELL, E. J., *Ghosts and Spirits in the Ancient World*, London, 1930

DURKHEIM, E., *The Elementary Forms of the Religious Life*, Collier-Mac, 1961

EVANS-PRITCHARD, E., *Nuer Religion*, Oxford, Clarendon Press, 1956

EVANS-PRITCHARD, E., *Witchcraft Among the Azande*, Oxford, Clarendon Press, 1937

FIRTH, R., *Tikopia Ritual and Belief*, London, Allen and Unwin, 1967

FORTUNE, R. F., 'Manus Religion', *Proceedings of the American Philosophical Society*, 1935

FORTUNE, R. F., *Sorcerers of Dobu*, London, Routledge and Kegan Paul, 1932

GOODE, W., *Religion Among the Primitives*, Glencoe, III Free Press, 1957

GUTHRIE, W. K. C., *The Greeks and Their Gods*, London, Methuen, 1950

HUGHES, P., *Witchcraft*, London, Longmans Green, 1952

HURSTON, Z., *Voodoo Gods*, London, Dent, 1939

JAMES, E. O., *Prehistoric Religion*, London, Thames and Hudson, 1957

JAMES, E. O., *The Ancient Gods*, London, Weidenfield and Nicolson

JAMES, E. O., *The Beginnings of Religion*, London, Arrow Books, 1958

JENSEN, A. E., *Myth and Cult Among Primitive Peoples*, Chicago, 1963

KITTERIDGE, G. L., *Witchcraft in Old and New England*, Cambridge Mass., Harvard University Press, 1929

LANTERNARI, V., *The Religions of the Oppressed*, New York, Mentor Books, 1965

METRAUX, A., *Voodoo*, London, Andre Deutsch, 1959

MARATT, R. R., *The Threshold of Religion*, London, Methuen, 1914

MURRAY, M. A., *The Witch Cult in Western Europe*, London, Oxford University Press, 1962

MICHELET, J., *Satanism and Witchcraft*, London, Tandem Books, 1965

NILSSON, M. P., *Greek Piety*, Oxford University Press, 1948

Bibliography

NORBECK, E., *Religion in Primitive Society*, New York, Harper, 1961

RADIN, P., *The World of Primitive Man*, New York, Shuman, 1953

READ, CARVETH, *Man and His Superstitions*, Cambridge University Press, 1920

ROSE, R., *Living Magic*, London, Chatto and Windus, 1957

TYLOR, Sir E., *Primitive Culture*, London, J. Murray, 1873

VESME, DE, C., *A History of Experimental Spiritualism*, Trans. S. De Brath, 2 Vols., London, Rider, 1931

VULLIAMY, C. E., *Immortal Man*, London, Methuen, 1926

WORSLEY, P., *The Trumpet Shall Sound. A Study of Cargo Cults in Melanesia*, London, MacGibbon and Kee, 1951

Mesmerism

BELL, DR, *Principles of Animal Electricity and Magnetism*, London, 1792

BILLOT, *Recherches Psychologiques – ou Correspondance sur le Magnetisme. Vital Entre un Solitaire et M. Deleuze*, Paris, 1839

CAHAGNET, A., *Arcanes de la vie Future Devoiles*, Paris, 1848

CROWE, Mrs., *Seeress of Prevorst*, London, 1845

GOLDSMITH, M., *Mesmer: The History of An Ideal*, London, Arthur Barker, 1935

MEIER, DR, *Hochst Merkwurdige Geschichte De Magnetism Hellsehenden Auguste Muller*, Stuttgart, 1818

MESMER, F. A., *Memorie Sur La Decouverte De Magnetisme Animal*, Trans. by V. R. Myers, London, Macdonald, 1948

ROMER, VON C., *Ausfuhrliche Historisch Darstellung Einer Hochst Merkwurdigen Somnambule*, Stuttgart, 1821

WYDENBRUCK, N., *Doctor Mesmer*, London, John Whitehouse, 1947

The Beliefs and Practices of Spiritualism

The literature devoted to Spiritualist beliefs and practices is voluminous and no attempt has been made to compile a comprehensive bibliography. The books included in this list are those which the author has found useful.

ANON, *Education Handbook*, London, Spiritualist National Union, 1953

ANON (Mrs De Morgan), *From Matter to Spirit: The Result of Ten Years Experience in Spirit Manifestations*, London, 1863

ANON, *Private Dowding*, London, Watkins, 1917

BARBANELL, MAURICE, *This is Spiritualism*, London, Herbert Jenkins, 1959

BARRETT, Sir WILLIAM, *On the Threshold of the Unseen*, London, Kegan Paul, 1917

BLATCHFORD, R., *More Things in Heaven and Earth*, London, Methuen, 1925

BLUNSDON, E., *Dictionary of Spiritualism*, London, Arco Publications, 1961

BRATH, S. DE, *The Physical Phenomena of Spiritualism*, London Spiritualist Alliance, 1947

BRITTEN, E. HARDINGE, KITSON, A. and KERSEY, H. A., *The Lyceum Officer's Manual*, 6th Edition, Manchester, S.L.U., 1957

CUMMINS, G., *Beyond Human Personality*, London, Nicholson and Watson, 1935

DOWDING, Lord, *The Dark Star*, London, Museum Press, 1951

DOWDING, Lord, *Many Mansions*, London, Rider, No Date (c. 1946)

DOYLE, Sir A. CONAN, *The New Revelation*, London, Hodder and Stoughton, 1918

EVANS, W. H., *Twelve Lectures on the Harmonial Philosophy*, Manchester Spiritual National Union, 1924

FINDLEY, J. ARTHUR, *On the Edge of the Etheric*, London, Rider, 1931

FINDLEY, J. ARTHUR, *The Rock of Truth*, London, Rider, 1933

FINDLEY, J. ARTHUR, *The Unfolding Truth*, London, Rider, 1935

FLAMMARION, C., *Mysterious Psychic Forces*, London, Fisher Unwin, 1907

FODOR, N., *Encyclopaedia of Psychic Science*, London, Arthurs Press, 1933

HAZARD, T. R., *Mediums and Mediumship*, London, J. Burns, No Date (c. 1873)

LEONARD, J. C., *The Higher Spiritualism*, London, Spiritualist Press, 1956

LODGE, Sir OLIVER, *Raymond*, London, Methuen, 1916

MYERS, F. W. H., *Human Personality and Its Survival of Bodily Death*, London, Longmans Green, 1903

OWEN, R. DALE, *Footfalls on the Boundary of Another World*, London, Trench, Trubner & Co., 1860

OWEN, VALE, *Life Beyond the Veil*, London, Thornton Butterworth, 1920–21

PRATT, J. GATHER, *Parapsychology*, London, W. H. Allen, 1964

V

PRICE, H., *Fifty Years of Psychical Research*, London, Longmans Green and Co., 1939

THOULESS, R. H., *Experimental Psychic Research*, Harmondsworth, Penguin, 1963

TWEEDALE, C. L., *News from the Next World*, London, Psychic Book Club, 1947

TYRRELL, G. N. M., *The Personality of Man*, Harmondsworth, Penguin, 1946

WEST, D. J., *Psychical Research Today*, Harmondsworth, Penguin, 1962

Spiritualism and Religion
BUTTERWORTH, G. W., *Spiritualism and Religion*, London, Society for Promoting Christian Knowledge, 1944

'F.C.B.F.', *Spiritualism Forbidden of God*, London, W. B. Horner, No Date (c. 1880)

HARDINGE, Mrs E., *The Creed of the Spirits*, London, J. Burns, 1871

JONES, W., *Is Spiritualism a Religion*, Manchester, Two Worlds Publishing Co., No Date (c. 1920)

RUSSELL, L. W., *'Thou Shalt Not'*, London Spiritualist Press, 1954

Biographies of Spiritualists
BEAUMONT, DE, *Emanuel Swedenborg*, London, Jack and Nelson, 1919

BURTON, J., *Heyday of a Wizard*, London, Harrap, 1948

CHASE, WARREN, *Forty Years on the Spiritual Rostrum*, Boston, Colby and Rich, 1888

DAVIS, A. J., *The Magic Staff*, Roston, Colby and Rich, 1857

EDWARDS, H., *The Mediumship of Jack Weber*, London, Psychic Book Club, 1940

KITSON, A., *Autobiography*, Batley, Author, No Date (c. 1920)

POND, MIRIAM B., *The Unwilling Martyrs*, London, Psychic Press

ROBERTS, ESTELLE, *Forty Years a Medium*, London, Jenkins, 1959

Spiritualist Periodicals
The historical section of this study is based largely on information obtained from contemporary Spiritualist periodicals. I list here

only those publications which have been consulted in the process
of compiling the history of the movement. While it is not ex-
haustive it includes all the major publications in this field produced in Britain.

Yorkshire Spiritual Telegraph		1855–57
British Spiritualist Telegraph		1857–59
The Spiritual Magazine		1859–77
Daybreak		1868–69
Medium and Daybreak		1870–95
Human Nature		1867–77
The Spiritualist		1869–82
Light	From	1881
Two Worlds	From	1887
Psychic News	From	1932
Borderland		1893–97
Spiritual Times		1864–66
Spirit World		1896
Spiritual Truth		1922–34
Psyche		1882
Psychic Journal		1946–49
Psychic Truth		1946–47
Psychic World		1946–51
Spiritual Quarterly		1902
The Occult Review		1905–48
Riders Review		1948–50
Spiritual Notes		1878–80
Greater World	From	1928
The Spiritual Healer	From	1953

Pamphlets and Occasional Publications

Spiritualist National Union
The Spiritualist Banner (formerly *Lyceum Banner*) Monthly from 1890
News Letter, Quarterly from 1963
S.N.U. 'Articles of Association'
      'Memorandum of Association'
      'Bye-laws'
      'Building Fund Pool. Trust Deed and Regulations'
      '(Model) Rules and Constitution (of churches)'

Bibliography

Greater World Christian Spiritualist League
'The League's Origin, Its Constitution, Aims and Objects'
'Tell the People'
How I became a Medium by Winifred Moyes
'Belief and Pledge of the G.W.C.S. League'
'Free Night Shelter and Home for Destitute Women'
'Notes regarding the Enrolment of Churches'
The Responsibilities of Church Officers and The Work of a Church Committee by F. Alloway
How a Home Circle grew into a World-wide Mission by W. Moyes
'An Order of Service for Spiritual Healing'
'The Greater World Sunday School Guide'

The Spiritualist Association of Great Britain
'Particulars of Membership and Activities'
Service (Bi-monthly)
The Spiritualist (Quarterly)

White Eagle Lodge
Stella Polaris (Bi-monthly)

Union of Spiritualist Mediums
The Medium (Quarterly since 1956)
'This Mediums Union – What is it?'

Science Rationalism and Religion
DAMPIER, Sir WILLIAM, *A History of Science and Its Relations with Philosophy and Religion*, Cambridge University Press, 1948
DRAPER, J. M., *History of the Conflict between Religion and Science*, (First Pub. 1873) London, Kegan Paul, 1927
LECKEY, W. E. H., *History of the Rise and Influence of the Spirit of Rationalism in Europe*, London, 1865
MC CABE, J., *The Religion of Sir Oliver Lodge*, London, Watts and Co., 1914
MERTON, R. K., *Social Theory and Social Structure*, Glencoe Ill., Free Press, 1949
METRAUX, G. S. and CROUZET, F., *The Evolution of Science*, New York, Mentor Books, 1963

296

Bibliography

ROBERTSON, J. M., *The Dynamics of Religion* (1897), London, Watts and Co. (2nd ed.), 1926

ROGERS, D. P., 'Some Religious Beliefs of Scientists', *Review of Religious Research*, Vol 7, No. 2, Winter 1966

WESTFALL, R. S., *Science and Religion in 17th century England*, New Haven, Yale University Press, 1958

WHITE, A. D., *A History of the Warfare of Science with Theology in Christendom*, New York, George Braziller, 1955 (1st ed. 1895)

WHITE, E. A., *Science and Religion in American Thought*, Stanford California, Stanford University Press, 1952

Social and Religious Conditions in nineteenth-century America

ANDREWS, E. D., *The People Called Shakers*, New York, Oxford University Press, 1953

BACON, LEONARD W., *A History of American Christianity*, London, J. Clarke, 1899

BROAD, CHARLES and MARY, *The Rise of American Civilization*, New York, Macmillan, 1930

BROAD, CHARLES and MARY, *The American Spirit*, New York, Macmillan, 1948

BRADEN, C. (Ed.), *Varieties of American Religion*, Chicago, Willett Clark and Co., 1936

CROSS, WHITNEY R., *The Burned over District: The Social and Intellectual History of Enthusiastic Religion in Western New York 1800–1850*, Ithaca, New York, 1950

DEVONPORT, F. M., *Primitive Traits in Religious Revivals*, New York, Macmillan, 1905

GISH, N. P., *Secret Societies: A Cultural Study of Fraternalism in the United States*, University of Missouri, 1940

HALL, T. C., *The Religious Background of American Culture*, Boston, Little Brown & Co., 1930

LUDHAM, D., *Social Ferment in Vermont 1791–1850*, New York, Columbia University Press, 1939

NORDHOFF, C., *The Communist Societies of the United States*, Harper Brothers, New York, 1875

O'DEA, T., *The Mormons*, Chicago, University of Chicago Press, 1957

PAXSON, F., *History of the American Frontier 1763–1893*, Boston, Houghton Mifflin, 1924

Bibliography

ROWE, H. K., *The History of Religion in the United States*, New York, Macmillan, 1924

SWEET, W. W., *The Story of Religions in America*, New York, Harper Bros., 1930

TURNER, F. S., *The United States 1830–50*, Gloucester, Mass., Smith, 1958

Social and Religious Conditions in Britain

BOOTH, Gen. W., *In Darkest England and the Way Out*, London, Salvation Army, 1890

CLARK, G. KITSON, *The Making of Victorian England*, London, Methuen, 1963

HALÉVY, E., *Victorian Years 1841–1895*, London, E. Benn, 1951

HAMMOND, J. L. and BARBARA, *The Town Labourer 1760–1382*, (1st ed. 1917) London, Longmans Green, 1949

INGLIS, K. S., *The Churches and the Working Classes in Victorian England*, London, Routledge and Kegan Paul, 1963

JESSOPP, A., *Arcady: For Better for Worse*, London, T. Fisher Unwin (c. 1886)

LATOURETTE, K. S., *Christianity in a Revolutionary Age*, London, Eyre and Spottiswoode, 1959–61

MASTERMAN, C. F. G., *The Condition of England*, (1st ed. 1909), London, Methuen, 1960

NEWBY, C. R., *The Story of Sunday Schools*, London, S.P.C.K., 1930

NORTHCOTT, C., *For Britain's Children*, London, National Sunday School Union, 1953

ROBERTSON, J. M., *The Dynamics of Religion* (First Pub. 1897), London, Watts and Co., 1926

SEVILLE, J., *Rural Deprivation in England and Wales*, London, Routledge and Kegan Paul, 1957

THOMPSON, E. P., *The Makings of the English Working Class*, London, Gollancz, 1963

VIDLER, ALEC R., *The Church in an Age of Revolution*, London, Hodder and Stoughton, 1962

WICKHAM, E. R., *Church and People in an Industrial City*, London, Lutterworth Press, 1957

WILLEY, BASIL, *The Seventeenth Century Background*, London, Chatto and Windus, 1934

Bibliography

WILLEY, BASIL, *The Eighteenth Century Background*, London, Chatto and Windus, 1940

WILLEY, BASIL, *Nineteenth Century Studies*, London, Chatto and Windus, 1956

Religion in Industrial Society

BLACKHAM, H. J., *Religion in a Modern Society*, London, Constable, 1966

CHARLTON, D. G., *Secular Religions in France 1815–1870*, London, Oxford University Press, 1963

COX, H., *The Secular City*, London, S.C.M. Press, 1966

HAPPOLD, F. C., *Religious Faith and 20th Century Man*, Harmondsworth, Penguin, 1966

KALLEN, H. M., 'Secularism as the Common Religion of a Free Society', *Journal for the Scientific Study of Religion*, Vol 4, No. 2, April 1965

Sociological Theory
General

DURKHEIM, E., *Suicide: A Study in Sociology*, London, Routledge and Kegan Paul, 1957

MERTON, R. K., *Social Theory and Social Structure*, Glencoe Ill., Free Press, 1949

PARSONS, T., *The Social System*, Glencoe Ill., Free Press, 1951

SEEMAN, M., 'On the Meaning of Alienation', *American Sociological Review*, Dec. 1959

WEBER, M., *The Theory of Social and Economic Organization*, New York, Oxford University Press, 1947

YINGER, J. MILTON, 'On Anomie', *Journal for the Scientific Study of Religion*, Spring 1964

Organization Theory

BLAU, P. H. and SCOTT, W. R., *Formal Organizations*, London, Routledge and Kegan Paul, 1962

ETZIONI, A., *Modern Organization*, Englewood Cliffs, New Jersey, Prentice-Hall, 1964

MERTON, R. K., GRAY, A. P., HOCKEY, B. and SELVIN, M. C., *Reader in Bureaucracy*, Glencoe, Ill., Free Press, 1952

MICHELS, R., *Political Parties*, London, Hutchinson, 1915

Sociology of Religion
1. General Works

CARRIER, H., *The Sociology of Religious Belonging*, London, Darton, Longman and Todd, 1965

FESTINGER, L., RIECKEY, H. W. and SCHACHTER, -. -., *When Prophecy Fails*, Minneapolis, University of Minnesota Press, 1958

GLOCK, C. Y. and STARK, R., *Religion and Society in Tension*, Chicago, Rand McNally & Co., 1965

LESSA, W. A. and VOGT, E. Z., *Reader in Comparative Religion*, New York, Harper and Row (2nd Ed.), 1965

NOTTINGHAM, E., *Religion and Society*, New York, Random House, 1954

O'DEA, T. F., *The Sociology of Religion*, Englewood Cliffs, New Jersey, Prentice Hall, 1966

VERNON, G. M., *Sociology of Religion*, New York, McGraw Hill, 1962

VETTER, G., *Magic and Religion*, New York, Philosophical Library, 1958

WACH, J., *The Sociology of Religion*, Chicago, University of Chicago Press, 1944

WEBER, M., *The Sociology of Religion*, London, Methuen, 1965

YINGER, J. MILTON, *Religion, Society and the Individual*, New York, Macmillan, 1957

2. Church-Sect Cult Typology

CLARK, E. T., *The Small Sects in America*, New York, Abingdon, Cokesbury Press, 1949

DYNES, R. RUSSELL, 'Church–Sect Typology and Socio-Economic Status', *American Sociological Review*, Oct. 1955

GLOCK, C. Y., 'The Role of Deprivation in the Origin and Evolution of Religious Groups', in Lee, R. and Marty M., *Religion and Social Conflict*, New York, Oxford University Press, 1964

HOWARD, BECKER, *Systematic Sociology on the Basis of the Beziehungslehre and Gebildelehre of Leopold von Wiese*, New York, Wiley, 1932

JOHNSON, B., 'Church and Sect', *American Sociological Review*, Aug. 1963

MARTIN, D., *Pacifism*, London, Routledge and Kegan Paul, 1965

MARTIN, D., 'The Denomination', *British Journal of Sociology*, March 1962

MUELDER, W., 'From Sect to Church', *Christendom*, Autumn 1945

NIEBUHR, H. RICHARD, *The Social Sources of Denominationalism*, New York, H. Holt, 1929

POBLETE, R., 'Sociological Approach to the Sects', *Social Compass*, VII, 5/6, 1960

POPE, LISTON, *Preachers and Millhands*, New Haven, Yale University Press, 1942

TROELTSCH, E., *The Social Teaching of the Christian Churches*, Trans. Olive Wyon, London, Allen & Unwin, 1931

WILSON, B. R., 'An Analysis of Sect Development', *American Sociological Review*, Jan. 1953

WILSON, B. R., *Sects and Society*, London, Heinemann, 1961

WILSON, B. R., *Religion in Secular Society*, London, 1966

3. Typology of Authority and Leadership

ELIADE, M., *Shamanism*, London, Routledge and Kegan Paul, 1964

JAMES, E. O., *The Nature and Function of Priesthood*, Thames and Hudson, 1956

THORNER, ISIDOR, 'Prophetic and Mystic Experience', *Journal for the Scientific Study of Religion*, Fall, 1965

WEBER, M., *Bureaucracy. The Sociology of Charismatic Authority and The Social Psychology of the World Religions*, in Gerth H. H. and Mills, C. Wright. *From Max Weber*, London, Kegan Paul, Trench, Trubner & Co., 1947

Studies of Particular Cults

BUCKNER, H. T., 'Flying Saucerians Linger On', *New Society*, September 9, 1965

JACKSON, J. A., 'Two Contemporary Cults', *The Advancement of Science*, June, 1966

The Psychology of Religion

BARTLETT, F. C., 'Religion as Experience, Belief, Action', *Riddell Memorial Lecture*, London, Oxford University Press, 1950

Bibliography

BAUDOUIN, C., *Suggestion and Auto Suggestion*, London, Allen and Unwin, 1920

BROAD, C. D., *Religion, Philosophy and Psychic Research*, London, Routledge and Kegan Paul, 1953

FROMM, E., *Psychoanalysis and Religion*, New Haven, Yale University Press, 1964

HUXLEY, A., *The Doors of Perception and Heaven and Hell*, Harmondsworth, Penguin, 1959

JAMES, W., *The Varieties of Religious Experience*, New York, Collier Books, 1961

OTTO, R., *The Idea of the Holy*, Harmondsworth, Penguin, 1959

PHILP, H. L., *Freud and Religious Belief*, London, Rockliff, 1956

INDEX

Index

Urbanism, 260–4, 269, 271

Victoria, Queen, 89, 265–6
Voluntarism, 66
Von Wiese, L., 218
Voodoo, 45

Wales, South, 190
War, effects on Spiritualism, 156–7, 162–8
War, Spiritualists attitude to, 153–5
Weber, Max, 47, 217, 230, 239–40, 251, 269

West Midlands, Spiritualism in, 164, 190, 261–2, 273
White Eagle Lodge, 201–3, 233
Wisbech, Cambs., 190–1
Witchcraft, 54–55, 234, 252, 254, 269
Wolverhampton, 101
Worsley, Peter, 76

Yinger, Milton, 219–20, 232
Yorkshire District Organizations, 111, 113, 115–16

Zodiac Mission, 149–50

307

The International Library of
Sociology
and Social Reconstruction

Edited by W. J. H. SPROTT
Founded by KARL MANNHEIM

ROUTLEDGE & KEGAN PAUL
BROADWAY HOUSE, CARTER LANE, LONDON, E.C.4

CONTENTS

PRINTED IN GREAT BRITAIN BY HEADLEY BROTHERS LTD
109 KINGSWAY LONDON WC2 AND ASHFORD KENT

GENERAL SOCIOLOGY

Brown, Robert. Explanation in Social Science. *208 pp. 1963. (2nd Impression 1964.) 25s.*

Gibson, Quentin. The Logic of Social Enquiry. *240 pp. 1960. (3rd Impression 1968.) 24s.*

Homans, George C. Sentiments and Activities: Essays in Social Science. *336 pp. 1962. 32s.*

Isajiw, Wsevelod W. Causation and Functionalism in Sociology. *165 pp. 1968. 25s.*

Johnson, Harry M. Sociology: a Systematic Introduction. *Foreword by Robert K. Merton. 710 pp. 1961. (5th Impression 1968.) 42s.*

Mannheim, Karl. Essays on Sociology and Social Psychology. *Edited by Paul Keckskemeti. With Editorial Note by Adolph Lowe. 344 pp. 1953. (2nd Impression 1966.) 32s.*

Systematic Sociology: An Introduction to the Study of Society. *Edited by J. S. Erös and Professor W. A. C. Stewart. 220 pp. 1957. (3rd Impression 1967.) 24s.*

Martindale, Don. The Nature and Types of Sociological Theory. *292 pp. 1961. (3rd Impression 1967.) 35s.*

Maus, Heinz. A Short History of Sociology. *234 pp. 1962. (2nd Impression 1965.) 28s.*

Myrdal, Gunnar. Value in Social Theory: A Collection of Essays on Methodology. *Edited by Paul Streeten. 332 pp. 1958. (3rd Impression 1968.) 35s.*

Ogburn, William F., and **Nimkoff, Meyer F.** A Handbook of Sociology. *Preface by Karl Mannheim. 656 pp. 46 figures. 35 tables. 5th edition (revised) 1964. 45s.*

Parsons, Talcott, and **Smelser, Neil J.** Economy and Society: A Study in the Integration of Economic and Social Theory. *362 pp. 1956. (4th Impression 1967.) 35s.*

Rex, John. Key Problems of Sociological Theory. *220 pp. 1961. (4th Impression 1968.) 25s.*

Stark, Werner. The Fundamental Forms of Social Thought. *280 pp. 1962. 32s.*

FOREIGN CLASSICS OF SOCIOLOGY

Durkheim, Emile. Suicide. A Study in Sociology. *Edited and with an Introduction by George Simpson. 404 pp. 1952. (4th Impression 1968.) 35s.*

Professional Ethics and Civic Morals. *Translated by Cornelia Brookfield. 288 pp. 1957. 30s.*

Gerth, H. H., and **Mills, C. Wright.** From Max Weber: Essays in Sociology. *502 pp. 1948. (6th Impression 1967.) 35s.*

Tönnies, Ferdinand. Community and Association. *(Gemeinschaft und Gesellschaft.) Translated and Supplemented by Charles P. Loomis. Foreword by Pitirim A. Sorokin. 334 pp. 1955. 28s.*

3

SOCIAL STRUCTURE

Andreski, Stanislav. Military Organization and Society. *Foreword by Professor A. R. Radcliffe-Brown. 226 pp. 1 folder. 1954. Revised Edition 1968. 35s.*

Cole, G. D. H. Studies in Class Structure. *220 pp. 1955. (3rd Impression 1964.) 21s. Paper 10s. 6d.*

Coontz, Sydney H. Population Theories and the Economic Interpretation. *202 pp. 1957. (3rd Impression 1968.) 28s.*

Coser, Lewis. The Functions of Social Conflict. *204 pp. 1956. (3rd Impression 1968.) 25s.*

Dickie-Clark, H. F. Marginal Situation: A Sociological Study of a Coloured Group. *240 pp. 11 tables. 1966. 40s.*

Glass, D. V. (Ed.). Social Mobility in Britain. *Contributions by J. Berent, T. Bottomore, R. C. Chambers, J. Floud, D. V. Glass, J. R. Hall, H. T. Himmelweit, R. K. Kelsall, F. M. Martin, C. A. Moser, R. Mukherjee, and W. Ziegel. 420 pp. 1954. (4th Impression 1967.) 45s.*

Jones, Garth N. Planned Organizational Change: An Exploratory Study Using an Empirical Approach. *About 268 pp. 1969. 40s.*

Kelsall, R. K. Higher Civil Servants in Britain: From 1870 to the Present Day. *268 pp. 31 tables. 1955. (2nd Impression 1966.) 25s.*

König, René. The Community. *232 pp. Illustrated. 1968. 35s.*

Lawton, Denis. Social Class, Language and Education. *192 pp. 1968. (2nd Impression 1968.) 25s.*

McLeish, John. The Theory of Social Change: Four Views Considered. *About 128 pp. 1969. 21s.*

Marsh, David C. The Changing Social Structure in England and Wales, 1871-1961. *1958. 272 pp. 2nd edition (revised) 1966. (2nd Impression 1967.) 35s.*

Mouzelis, Nicos. Organization and Bureaucracy. An Analysis of Modern Theories. *240 pp. 1967. (2nd Impression 1968.) 28s.*

Ossowski, Stanislaw. Class Structure in the Social Consciousness. *210 pp. 1963. (2nd Impression 1967.) 25s.*

SOCIOLOGY AND POLITICS

Barbu, Zevedei. Democracy and Dictatorship: Their Psychology and Patterns of Life. *300 pp. 1956. 28s.*

Crick, Bernard. The American Science of Politics: Its Origins and Conditions. *284 pp. 1959. 32s.*

Hertz, Frederick. Nationality in History and Politics: A Psychology and Sociology of National Sentiment and Nationalism. *432 pp. 1944. (5th Impression 1966.) 42s.*

Kornhauser, William. The Politics of Mass Society. *272 pp. 20 tables. 1960. (3rd Impression 1968.) 28s.*

Laidler, Harry W. History of Socialism. Social-Economic Movements: An Historical and Comparative Survey of Socialism, Communism, Co-operation, Utopianism; and other Systems of Reform and Reconstruction. *New edition. 992 pp. 1968. 90s.*

Lasswell, Harold D. Analysis of Political Behaviour. An Empirical Approach. *324 pp. 1947. (4th Impression 1966.) 35s.*

Mannheim, Karl. Freedom, Power and Democratic Planning. *Edited by Hans Gerth and Ernest K. Bramstedt. 424 pp. 1951. (3rd Impression 1968.) 42s.*

Mansur, Fatma. Process of Independence. *Foreword by A. H. Hanson. 208 pp. 1962. 25s.*

Martin, David A. Pacificism: an Historical and Sociological Study. *262 pp. 1965. 30s.*

Myrdal, Gunnar. The Political Element in the Development of Economic Theory. *Translated from the German by Paul Streeten. 282 pp. 1953. (4th Impression 1965.) 25s.*

Polanyi, Michael. F.R.S. The Logic of Liberty: Reflections and Rejoinders. *228 pp. 1951. 18s.*

Verney, Douglas V. The Analysis of Political Systems. *264 pp. 1959. (3rd Impression 1966.) 28s.*

Wootton, Graham. The Politics of Influence: British Ex-Servicemen, Cabinet Decisions and Cultural Changes, 1917 to 1957. *316 pp. 1963. 30s.*
Workers, Unions and the State. *188 pp. 1966. (2nd Impression 1967.) 25s.*

FOREIGN AFFAIRS: THEIR SOCIAL, POLITICAL AND ECONOMIC FOUNDATIONS

Baer, Gabriel. Population and Society in the Arab East. *Translated by Hanna Szöke. 288 pp. 10 maps. 1964. 40s.*

Bonné, Alfred. State and Economics in the Middle East: A Society in Transition. *482 pp. 2nd (revised) edition 1955. (2nd Impression 1960.) 40s.*
Studies in Economic Development: with special reference to Conditions in the Under-developed Areas of Western Asia and India. *322 pp. 84 tables. 2nd edition 1960. 32s.*

Mayer, J. P. Political Thought in France from the Revolution to the Fifth Republic. *164 pp. 3rd edition (revised) 1961. 16s.*

CRIMINOLOGY

Ancel, Marc. Social Defence: A Modern Approach to Criminal Problems. *Foreword by Leon Radzinowicz. 240 pp. 1965. 32s.*

Cloward, Richard A., and Ohlin, Lloyd E. Delinquency and Opportunity: A Theory of Delinquent Gangs. *248 pp. 1961. 25s.*

Downes, David M. The Delinquent Solution. A Study in Subcultural Theory. *296 pp. 1966. 42s.*

Dunlop, A. B., and **McCabe, S.** Young Men in Detention Centres. *192 pp. 1965. 28s.*

Friedländer, Kate. The Psycho-Analytical Approach to Juvenile Delinquency: Theory, Case Studies, Treatment. *320 pp. 1947. (6th Impression 1967). 40s.*

Glueck, Sheldon and **Eleanor.** Family Environment and Delinquency. *With the statistical assistance of Rose W. Kneznek. 340 pp. 1962. (2nd Impression 1966.) 40s.*

Mannheim, Hermann. Comparative Criminology: a Text Book. *Two volumes. 442 pp. and 380 pp. 1965. (2nd Impression with corrections 1966.) 42s. a volume.*

Morris, Terence. The Criminal Area: A Study in Social Ecology. *Foreword by Hermann Mannheim. 232 pp. 25 tables. 4 maps. 1957. (2nd Impression 1966.) 28s.*

Morris, Terence and **Pauline,** assisted by **Barbara Barer.** Pentonville: A Sociological Study of an English Prison. *416 pp. 16 plates. 1963. 50s.*

Spencer, John C. Crime and the Services. *Foreword by Hermann Mannheim. 336 pp. 1954. 28s.*

Trasler, Gordon. The Explanation of Criminality. *144 pp. 1962. (2nd Impression 1967.) 20s.*

SOCIAL PSYCHOLOGY

Barbu, Zevedei. Problems of Historical Psychology. *248 pp. 1960. 25s.*

Blackburn, Julian. Psychology and the Social Pattern. *184 pp. 1945. (7th Impression 1964.) 16s.*

Fleming, C. M. Adolescence: Its Social Psychology: With an Introduction to recent findings from the fields of Anthropology, Physiology, Medicine, Psychometrics and Sociometry. *288 pp. 2nd edition (revised) 1963. (3rd Impression 1967.) 25s. Paper 12s. 6d.*
The Social Psychology of Education: An Introduction and Guide to Its Study. *136 pp. 2nd edition (revised) 1959. (4th Impression 1967.) 14s. Paper 7s. 6d.*

Homans, George C. The Human Group. *Foreword by Bernard DeVoto. Introduction by Robert K. Merton. 526 pp. 1951. (7th Impression 1968.) 35s.*
Social Behaviour: its Elementary Forms. *416 pp. 1961. (3rd Impression 1968.) 35s.*

Klein, Josephine. The Study of Groups. *226 pp. 31 figures. 5 tables. 1956. (5th Impression 1967.) 21s. Paper 9s. 6d.*

Linton, Ralph. The Cultural Background of Personality. *132 pp. 1947. (7th Impression 1968.) 18s.*

Mayo, Elton. The Social Problems of an Industrial Civilization. With an appendix on the Political Problem. *180 pp. 1949. (5th Impression 1966.) 25s.*

Ottaway, A. K. C. Learning Through Group Experience. *176 pp. 1966. (2nd Impression 1968.) 25s.*

Ridder, J. C. de. The Personality of the Urban African in South Africa. A Thematic Apperception Test Study. *196 pp. 12 plates. 1961. 25s.*

Rose, Arnold M. (Ed.). Human Behaviour and Social Processes: an Interactionist Approach. *Contributions by Arnold M. Rose, Ralph H. Turner, Anselm Strauss, Everett C. Hughes, E. Franklin Frazier, Howard S. Becker, et al. 696 pp. 1962. (2nd Impression 1968.) 70s.*

Smelser, Neil J. Theory of Collective Behaviour. *448 pp. 1962. (2nd Impression 1967.) 45s.*

Stephenson, Geoffrey M. The Development of Conscience. *128 pp. 1966. 25s.*

Young, Kimball. Handbook of Social Psychology. *658 pp. 16 figures. 10 tables. 2nd edition (revised) 1957. (3rd Impression 1963.) 40s.*

SOCIOLOGY OF THE FAMILY

Banks, J. A. Prosperity and Parenthood: A study of Family Planning among The Victorian Middle Classes. *262 pp. 1954. (3rd Impression 1968.) 28s.*

Bell, Colin R. Middle Class Families: Social and Geographical Mobility. *224 pp. 1969. 35s.*

Burton, Lindy. Vulnerable Children. *272 pp. 1968. 35s.*

Gavron, Hannah. The Captive Wife: Conflicts of Housebound Mothers. *190 pp. 1966. (2nd Impression 1966.) 25s.*

Klein, Josephine. Samples from English Cultures. *1965. (2nd Impression 1967.)*
1. Three Preliminary Studies and Aspects of Adult Life in England. *447 pp. 50s.*
2. Child-Rearing Practices and Index. *247 pp. 35s.*

Klein, Viola. Britain's Married Women Workers. *180 pp. 1965. (2nd Impression 1968.) 28s.*

McWhinnie, Alexina M. Adopted Children. How They Grow Up. *304 pp. 1967. (2nd Impression 1968.) 42s.*

Myrdal, Alva and **Klein, Viola.** Women's Two Roles: Home and Work. *238 pp. 27 tables. 1956. Revised Edition 1967. 30s. Paper 15s.*

Parsons, Talcott and **Bales, Robert F.** Family: Socialization and Interaction Process. *In collaboration with James Olds, Morris Zelditch and Philip E. Slater. 456 pp. 50 figures and tables. 1956. (3rd Impression 1968.) 45s.*

Schücking, L. L. The Puritan Family. *Translated from the German by Brian Battershaw. 212 pp. 1969. About 42s.*

THE SOCIAL SERVICES

Forder, R. A. (Ed.). Penelope Hall's Social Services of Modern England. *288 pp. 1969. 35s.*

George, Victor. Social Security: Beveridge and After. *258 pp. 1968. 35s.*

Goetschius, George W. Working with Community Groups. *256 pp. 1969. 35s.*

Goetschius, George W. and **Tash, Joan.** Working with Unattached Youth. *416 pp. 1967. (2nd Impression 1968.) 40s.*

Hall, M. P., and **Howes, I. V.** The Church in Social Work. A Study of Moral Welfare Work undertaken by the Church of England. *320 pp. 1965. 35s.*

Heywood, Jean S. Children in Care: the Development of the Service for the Deprived Child. *264 pp. 2nd edition (revised) 1965. (2nd Impression 1966.) 32s.*

An Introduction to Teaching Casework Skills. *190 pp. 1964. 28s.*

Jones, Kathleen. Lunacy, Law and Conscience, 1744-1845: the Social History of the Care of the Insane. *268 pp. 1955. 25s.*

Mental Health and Social Policy, 1845-1959. *264 pp. 1960. (2nd Impression 1967.) 32s.*

Jones, Kathleen and **Sidebotham, Roy.** Mental Hospitals at Work. *220 pp. 1962. 30s.*

Kastell, Jean. Casework in Child Care. *Foreword by M. Brooke Willis. 320 pp. 1962. 35s.*

Morris, Pauline. Put Away: A Sociological Study of Institutions for the Mentally Retarded. *Approx. 288 pp. 1969. About 50s.*

Nokes, P. L. The Professional Task in Welfare Practice. *152 pp. 1967. 28s.*

Rooff, Madeline. Voluntary Societies and Social Policy. *350 pp. 15 tables. 1957. 35s.*

Timms, Noel. Psychiatric Social Work in Great Britain (1939-1962). *280 pp. 1964. 32s.*

Social Casework: Principles and Practice. *256 pp. 1964. (2nd Impression 1966.) 25s. Paper 15s.*

Trasler, Gordon. In Place of Parents: A Study in Foster Care. *272 pp. 1960. (2nd Impression 1966.) 30s.*

Young, A. F., and **Ashton, E. T.** British Social Work in the Nineteenth Century. *288 pp. 1956. (2nd Impression 1963.) 28s.*

Young, A. F. Social Services in British Industry. *272 pp. 1968. 40s.*

SOCIOLOGY OF EDUCATION

Banks, Olive. Parity and Prestige in English Secondary Education: a Study in Educational Sociology. *272 pp. 1955. (2nd Impression 1963.) 32s.*

Bentwich, Joseph. Education in Israel. *224 pp. 8 pp. plates. 1965. 24s.*

Blyth, W. A. L. English Primary Education. A Sociological Description. *1965. Revised edition 1967.*
1. Schools. *232 pp. 30s. Paper 12s. 6d.*
2. Background. *168 pp. 25s. Paper 10s. 6d.*

8

Collier, K. G. The Social Purposes of Education: Personal and Social Values in Education. *268 pp. 1959. (3rd Impression 1965.) 21s.*

Dale, R. R., and **Griffith, S.** Down Stream: Failure in the Grammar School. *108 pp. 1965. 20s.*

Dore, R. P. Education in Tokugawa Japan. *356 pp. 9 pp. plates. 1965. 35s.*

Edmonds, E. L. The School Inspector. *Foreword by Sir William Alexander. 214 pp. 1962. 28s.*

Evans, K. M. Sociometry and Education. *158 pp. 1962. (2nd Impression 1966.) 18s.*

Foster, P. J. Education and Social Change in Ghana. *336 pp. 3 maps. 1965. (2nd Impression 1967.) 36s.*

Fraser, W. R. Education and Society in Modern France. *150 pp. 1963. (2nd Impression 1968.) 25s.*

Hans, Nicholas. New Trends in Education in the Eighteenth Century. *278 pp. 19 tables. 1951. (2nd Impression 1966.) 30s.*
Comparative Education: A Study of Educational Factors and Traditions. *360 pp. 3rd (revised) edition 1958. (4th Impression 1967.) 25s. Paper 12s. 6d.*

Hargreaves, David. Social Relations in a Secondary School. *240 pp. 1967. (2nd Impression 1968.) 32s.*

Holmes, Brian. Problems in Education. A Comparative Approach. *336 pp. 1965. (2nd Impression 1967.) 32s.*

Mannheim, Karl and **Stewart, W. A. C.** An Introduction to the Sociology of Education. *206 pp. 1962. (2nd Impression 1965.) 21s.*

Morris, Raymond N. The Sixth Form and College Entrance. *231 pp. 1969. 40s.*

Musgrove, F. Youth and the Social Order. *176 pp. 1964. (2nd Impression 1968.) 25s. Paper 12s.*

Ortega y Gasset, José. Mission of the University. *Translated with an Introduction by Howard Lee Nostrand. 86 pp. 1946. (3rd Impression 1963.) 15s.*

Ottaway, A. K. C. Education and Society: An Introduction to the Sociology of Education. *With an Introduction by W. O. Lester Smith. 212 pp. Second edition (revised). 1962. (5th Impression 1968.) 18s. Paper 10s. 6d.*

Peers, Robert. Adult Education: A Comparative Study. *398 pp. 2nd edition 1959. (2nd Impression 1966.) 42s.*

Pritchard, D. G. Education and the Handicapped: 1760 to 1960. *258 pp. 1963. (2nd Impression 1966.) 35s.*

Richardson, Helen. Adolescent Girls in Approved Schools. *Approx. 360 pp. 1969. About 42s.*

Simon, Brian and **Joan** (Eds.). Educational Psychology in the U.S.S.R. *Introduction by Brian and Joan Simon. Translation by Joan Simon. Papers by D. N. Bogoiavlenski and N. A. Menchinskaia, D. B. Elkonin, E. A. Fleshner, Z. I. Kalmykova, G. S. Kostiuk, V. A. Krutetski, A. N. Leontiev, A. R. Luria, E. A. Milerian, R. G. Natadze, B. M. Teplov, L. S. Vygotski, L. V. Zankov. 296 pp. 1963. 40s.*

9

SOCIOLOGY OF CULTURE

Eppel, E. M., and M. Adolescents and Morality: A Study of some Moral Values and Dilemmas of Working Adolescents in the Context of a changing Climate of Opinion. *Foreword by W. J. H. Sprott. 268 pp. 39 tables. 1966. 30s.*

Fromm, Erich. The Fear of Freedom. *286 pp. 1942. (8th Impression 1960.) 25s. Paper 10s.*
The Sane Society. *400 pp. 1956. (4th Impression 1968.) 28s. Paper 14s.*

Mannheim, Karl. Diagnosis of Our Time: Wartime Essays of a Sociologist. *208 pp. 1943. (8th Impression 1966.) 21s.*
Essays on the Sociology of Culture. *Edited by Ernst Mannheim in co-operation with Paul Kecskemeti. Editorial Note by Adolph Lowe. 280 pp. 1956. (3rd Impression 1967.) 28s.*

Weber, Alfred. Farewell to European History: or The Conquest of Nihilism. *Translated from the German by R. F. C. Hull. 224 pp. 1947. 18s.*

SOCIOLOGY OF RELIGION

Argyle, Michael. Religious Behaviour. *224 pp. 8 figures. 41 tables. 1958. (4th Impression 1968.) 25s.*

Nelson, G. K. Spiritualism and Society. *313 pp. 1969. 42s.*

Stark, Werner. The Sociology of Religion. A Study of Christendom.
Volume I. Established Religion. *248 pp. 1966. 35s.*
Volume II. Sectarian Religion. *368 pp. 1967. 40s.*
Volume III. The Universal Church. *464 pp. 1967. 45s.*

Watt, W. Montgomery. Islam and the Integration of Society. *320 pp. 1961. (3rd Impression 1966.) 35s.*

SOCIOLOGY OF ART AND LITERATURE

Beljame, Alexandre. Men of Letters and the English Public in the Eighteenth Century: 1660-1744, Dryden, Addison. Pope. *Edited with an Introduction and Notes by Bonamy Dobrée. Translated by E. O. Lorimer. 532 pp. 1948. 32s.*

Misch, Georg. A History of Autobiography in Antiquity. *Translated by E. W. Dickes. 2 Volumes. Vol. 1, 364 pp., Vol. 2, 372 pp. 1950. 45s. the set.*

Schücking, L. L. The Sociology of Literary Taste. *112 pp. 2nd (revised) edition 1966. 18s.*

Silbermann, Alphons. The Sociology of Music. *Translated from the German by Corbet Stewart. 222 pp. 1963. 32s.*

SOCIOLOGY OF KNOWLEDGE

Mannheim, Karl. Essays on the Sociology of Knowledge. *Edited by Paul Kecskemeti. Editorial note by Adolph Lowe. 352 pp. 1952. (4th Impression 1967.) 35s.*

Stark, W. America: Ideal and Reality. The United States of 1776 in Contemporary Philosophy. *136 pp. 1947. 12s.*

The Sociology of Knowledge: An Essay in Aid of a Deeper Understanding of the History of Ideas. *384 pp. 1958. (3rd Impression 1967.) 36s.*

Montesquieu: Pioneer of the Sociology of Knowledge. *244 pp. 1960. 25s.*

URBAN SOCIOLOGY

Anderson, Nels. The Urban Community: A World Perspective. *532 pp. 1960. 35s.*

Ashworth, William. The Genesis of Modern British Town Planning: A Study in Economic and Social History of the Nineteenth and Twentieth Centuries. *288 pp. 1954. (3rd Impression 1968.) 32s.*

Bracey, Howard. Neighbours: On New Estates and Subdivisions in England and U.S.A. *220 pp. 1964. 28s.*

Cullingworth, J. B. Housing Needs and Planning Policy: A Restatement of the Problems of Housing Need and "Overspill" in England and Wales. *232 pp. 44 tables. 8 maps. 1960. (2nd Impression 1966.) 28s.*

Dickinson, Robert E. City and Region: A Geographical Interpretation. *608 pp. 125 figures. 1964. (5th Impression 1967.) 60s.*

The West European City: A Geographical Interpretation. *600 pp. 129 maps. 29 plates. 2nd edition 1962. (3rd Impression 1968.) 55s.*

The City Region in Western Europe. *320 pp. Maps. 1967. 30s. Paper 14s.*

Jackson, Brian. Working Class Community: Some General Notions raised by a Series of Studies in Northern England. *192 pp. 1968. (2nd Impression 1968.) 25s.*

Jennings, Hilda. Societies in the Making: a Study of Development and Redevelopment within a County Borough. *Foreword by D. A. Clark. 286 pp. 1962. (2nd Impression 1967.) 32s.*

Kerr, Madeline. The People of Ship Street. *240 pp. 1958. 28s.*

Mann, P. H. An Approach to Urban Sociology. *240 pp. 1965. (2nd Impression 1968.) 30s.*

Morris, R. N., and Mogey, J. The Sociology of Housing. Studies at Berinsfield. *232 pp. 4 pp. plates. 1965. 42s.*

Rosser, C., and Harris, C. The Family and Social Change. A Study of Family and Kinship in a South Wales Town. *352 pp. 8 maps. 1965. (2nd Impression 1968.) 45s.*

RURAL SOCIOLOGY

Chambers, R. J. H. Settlement Schemes in Africa: A Selective Study. *Approx. 268 pp. 1969. About 50s.*

Haswell, M. R. The Economics of Development in Village India. *120 pp. 1967. 21s.*

11

Littlejohn, James. Westrigg: the Sociology of a Cheviot Parish. *172 pp. 5 figures. 1963. 25s.*

Williams, W. M. The Country Craftsman: A Study of Some Rural Crafts and the Rural Industries Organization in England. *248 pp. 9 figures. 1958. 25s. (Dartington Hall Studies in Rural Sociology.)*
    The Sociology of an English Village: Gosforth. *272 pp. 12 figures. 13 tables. 1956. (3rd Impression 1964.) 25s.*

SOCIOLOGY OF MIGRATION

Humphreys, Alexander J. New Dubliners: Urbanization and the Irish Family. *Foreword by George C. Homans. 304 pp. 1966. 40s.*

SOCIOLOGY OF INDUSTRY AND DISTRIBUTION

Anderson, Nels. Work and Leisure. *280 pp. 1961. 28s.*

Blau, Peter M., and **Scott, W. Richard.** Formal Organizations: a Comparative approach. *Introduction and Additional Bibliography by J. H. Smith. 326 pp. 1963. (4th Impression 1969.) 35s. Paper 15s.*

Eldridge, J. E. T. Industrial Disputes. Essays in the Sociology of Industrial Relations. *288 pp. 1968. 40s.*

Hollowell, Peter G. The Lorry Driver. *272 pp. 1968. 42s.*

Jefferys, Margot, with the assistance of Winifred Moss. Mobility in the Labour Market: Employment Changes in Battersea and Dagenham. *Preface by Barbara Wootton. 186 pp. 51 tables. 1954. 15s.*

Levy, A. B. Private Corporations and Their Control. *Two Volumes. Vol. 1, 464 pp., Vol. 2, 432 pp. 1950. 80s. the set.*

Liepmann, Kate. Apprenticeship: An Enquiry into its Adequacy under Modern Conditions. *Foreword by H. D. Dickinson. 232 pp. 6 tables. 1960. (2nd Impression 1960.) 23s.*

Millerson, Geoffrey. The Qualifying Associations: a Study in Professionalization. *320 pp. 1964. 42s.*

Smelser, Neil J. Social Change in the Industrial Revolution: An Application of Theory to the Lancashire Cotton Industry, 1770-1840. *468 pp. 12 figures. 14 tables. 1959. (2nd Impression 1960.) 50s.*

Williams, Gertrude. Recruitment to Skilled Trades. *240 pp. 1957. 23s.*

Young, A. F. Industrial Injuries Insurance: an Examination of British Policy. *192 pp. 1964. 30s.*

ANTHROPOLOGY

Ammar, Hamed. Growing up in an Egyptian Village: Silwa, Province of Aswan. *336 pp. 1954. (2nd Impression 1966.) 35s.*

Crook, David and **Isabel.** Revolution in a Chinese Village: Ten Mile Inn. *230 pp. 8 plates. 1 map. 1959. (2nd Impression 1968.) 21s.*
    The First Years of Yangyi Commune. *302 pp. 12 plates. 1966. 42s.*

Dickie-Clark, H. F. The Marginal Situation. A Sociological Study of a Coloured Group. *236 pp. 1966. 40s.*

Dube, S. C. Indian Village. *Foreword by Morris Edward Opler. 276 pp. 4 plates. 1955. (5th Impression 1965.) 25s.*
India's Changing Villages: Human Factors in Community Development. *260 pp. 8 plates. 1 map. 1958. (3rd Impression 1963.) 25s.*

Firth, Raymond. Malay Fishermen. Their Peasant Economy. *420 pp. 17 pp. plates. 2nd edition revised and enlarged 1966. (2nd Impression 1968.) 55s.*

Gulliver, P. H. The Family Herds. A Study of two Pastoral Tribes in East Africa, The Jie and Turkana. *304 pp. 4 plates. 19 figures. 1955. (2nd Impression with new preface and bibliography 1966.) 35s.*
Social Control in an African Society: a Study of the Arusha, Agricultural Masai of Northern Tanganyika. *320 pp. 8 plates. 10 figures. 1963. (2nd Impression 1968.) 42s.*

Ishwaran, K. Shivapur. A South Indian Village. *216 pp. 1968. 35s.*
Tradition and Economy in Village India: An Interactionist Approach. *Foreword by Conrad Arensburg. 176 pp. 1966. (2nd Impression 1968.) 25s.*

Jarvie, Ian C. The Revolution in Anthropology. *268 pp. 1964. (2nd Impression 1967.) 40s.*

Jarvie, Ian C. and Agassi, Joseph. Hong Kong. A Society in Transition. *396 pp. Illustrated with plates and maps. 1968. 56s.*

Little, Kenneth L. Mende of Sierra Leone. *308 pp. and folder. 1951. Revised edition 1967. 63s.*

Lowie, Professor Robert H. Social Organization. *494 pp. 1950. (4th Impression 1966.) 50s.*

Mayer, Adrian C. Caste and Kinship in Central India: A Village and its Region. *328 pp. 16 plates. 15 figures. 16 tables. 1960. (2nd Impression 1965.) 35s.*
Peasants in the Pacific: A Study of Fiji Indian Rural Society. *232 pp. 16 plates. 10 figures. 14 tables. 1961. 35s.*

Smith, Raymond T. The Negro Family in British Guiana: Family Structure and Social Status in the Villages. *With a Foreword by Meyer Fortes. 314 pp. 8 plates. 1 figure. 4 maps. 1956. (2nd Impression 1965.) 35s.*

DOCUMENTARY

Meek, Dorothea L. (Ed.). Soviet Youth: Some Achievements and Problems. *Excerpts from the Soviet Press, translated by the editor. 280 pp. 1957. 28s.*

Schlesinger, Rudolf (Ed.). Changing Attitudes in Soviet Russia.
2. The Nationalities Problem and Soviet Administration. Selected Readings on the Development of Soviet Nationalities Policies. *Introduced by the editor. Translated by W. W. Gottlieb. 324 pp. 1956. 30s.*

Reports of the Institute
of Community Studies

(Demy 8vo.)

Cartwright, Ann. Human Relations and Hospital Care. *272 pp. 1964. 30s.*

Patients and their Doctors. A Study of General Practice. *304 pp. 1967. 40s.*

Jackson, Brian. Streaming: an Education System in Miniature. *168 pp. 1964. (2nd Impression 1966.) 21s. Paper 10s.*

Jackson, Brian and **Marsden, Dennis.** Education and the Working Class: Some General Themes raised by a Study of 88 Working-class Children in a Northern Industrial City. *268 pp. 2 folders. 1962. (4th Impression 1968.) 32s.*

Marris, Peter. Widows and their Families. *Foreword by Dr. John Bowlby. 184 pp. 18 tables. Statistical Summary. 1958. 18s.*
Family and Social Change in an African City. A Study of Rehousing in Lagos. *196 pp. 1 map. 4 plates. 53 tables. 1961. (2nd Impression 1966.) 30s.*
The Experience of Higher Education. *232 pp. 27 tables. 1964. 25s.*

Marris, Peter and **Rein, Martin.** Dilemmas of Social Reform. Poverty and Community Action in the United States. *256 pp. 1967. 35s.*

Mills, Enid. Living with Mental Illness: a Study in East London. *Foreword by Morris Carstairs. 196 pp. 1962. 28s.*

Runciman, W. G. Relative Deprivation and Social Justice. A Study of Attitudes to Social Inequality in Twentieth Century England. *352 pp. 1966. (2nd Impression 1967.) 40s.*

Townsend, Peter. The Family Life of Old People: An Inquiry in East London. *Foreword by J. H. Sheldon. 300 pp. 3 figures. 63 tables. 1957. (3rd Impression 1967.) 30s.*

Willmott, Peter. Adolescent Boys in East London. *230 pp. 1966. 30s.*
The Evolution of a Community: a study of Dagenham after forty years. *168 pp. 2 maps. 1963. 21s.*

Willmott, Peter and **Young, Michael.** Family and Class in a London Suburb. *202 pp. 47 tables. 1960. (4th Impression 1968.) 25s.*

Young, Michael. Innovation and Research in Education. *192 pp. 1965. 25s. Paper 12s. 6d.*

Young, Michael and **McGeeney, Patrick.** Learning Begins at Home. A Study of a Junior School and its Parents. *About 128 pp. 1968. 21s. Paper 14s.*

Young, Michael and **Willmott, Peter.** Family and Kinship in East London. *Foreword by Richard M. Titmuss. 252 pp. 39 tables. 1957. (3rd Impression 1965.) 28s.*

The British Journal of Sociology. *Edited by Terence P. Morris. Vol. 1, No. 1, March 1950 and Quarterly. Roy. 8vo., £3 annually, 15s. a number, post free. (Vols. 1-18, £8 each. Individual parts £2 10s.*

All prices are net and subject to alteration without notice

1268 H.B.